The Good Shepherd

Jesus Christ in Islam

A collection of his sayings and interfaith reflections

Bilal Muhammad

D1713610

"God did not raise a prophet until he made him a shepherd of sheep. Through that, He would teach him how to shepherd the people."

Table of Contents

3

Introduction

In the name of God, the Beneficent, the Merciful. All praise belongs to God, the Lord of the Worlds.

Growing up in Canada, attending Catholic school, I was always fascinated with Jesus. I heard his name mentioned in the tantalizing preaching of televangelists, in Christmas songs and Easter carols, in partisan political talks, and yes, in the Quran.

When the Muslims first fled persecution in Mecca, they went to the African kingdom of Abyssinia. The Muslims were told by their Prophet that Abyssinia was ruled by a righteous Christian king, Negus, who would treat them justly. When the Muslims made their plea to Negus, they recited the Quranic verses that pertain to Jesus and Mary. Negus wept. He affirmed to the Muslims that he would never give them up to their oppressors in Mecca.

Jesus serves as a bridge between the two greatest world religions. However, each religion's respective teaching about Jesus also serves as a point of contention. The Bible became a battleground for each party, sect, and denomination to prove that only they represent the *real* Jesus. Although differences in doctrine are of vital importance, ego often comes in the way when a debate becomes heated.

Meanwhile, the two great religions are becoming further and further eclipsed by a growing number of people who feel that organized religion doesn't quite resonate with them. When asked what religion they belong to, many young people simply answer "none." Some may be atheist, others agnostic, but an overwhelming number of them just fail to see the relevance of religion in their life. After all, they see technology, markets, and movements rising and falling, while the religious are in a constant state of stagnation and regression.

Frankly, what has happened is that many of us became pharisees. We used the scripture as a bludgeon to defend our honour, strike out the naysayers, and fight out every difference of opinion. We put all our attention into our appearance, our identity, our wealth, our assets, our competitive games, and our mental gymnastics. So many of us are simply a product of our upbringings and surroundings, yet we dismiss and even *hate* the other with little consideration. In a word, many of us are hypocrites.

Jesus of Nazareth came at a time when his people were occupied by the Romans. The Jews, a bookish and scholastic people, were overrun by pantheonic pagans that were controlled by "bread and circus." On top of that, the Romans installed their own puppet leaders to keep the Jews subdued. These puppets would step on the necks of their brethren, but eat kosher. They would persecute their own, but keep the Sabbath. Put yourself in their shoes – what choice do you have? If you want to keep your family safe, keep a stable job, and justify to yourself that *you are not your enemy*, you may do the same.

Others thought differently. The zealots wanted the Romans out, by hook or by crook. Religion, too, was their bludgeon and their source of pride. It fed their nationalism and their egoism. Of course, they bent the scripture in their favour – crowning this person or that person as the Messiah, regardless of his characteristics, just to satisfy their quench for power.

Where was Jesus amidst all of this? Jesus hated the corruption and the hypocrisy of the establishment – just look at what he did to the moneychangers! He used the strongest language possible against the sophistry of the pharisees. At the same time, he did not have a political blueprint that was particular to first century Judea. His kingdom was "not of this world."

Jesus was abiding by a well-known principle in Islam: "God does not change the condition of a people until they change what is in themselves." (Quran 13:11) He exemplified a deep, sacrificial commitment to God. He emphasized the *spirit* of the Law in a time when many were concerned only with the letter. He showed us that personal reform – starting with that mustard seed – must precede societal reform. He was not paving a road to Rome or Jerusalem – he was reminding us of our duty toward the Creator, the poor, the needy, the weak, the ill, the dispossessed, and our very souls – he paved the straight path to God.

We, today, live in a similar time. The flag of organized religion has become old. Preachers work for governments, political parties, or simply their pocket. We are *obsessed* with materialism, trampling over one another to get the latest i-something. We have our own "bread and circus" in the 24-hour entertainment machines that never take a break. We are neglecting our kids in favour of our jobs. We have forgotten textual authority and sacred personalities. We are trading God for vibes, feels, manifesting, and memes.

Remind yourself of the old adage, "What Would Jesus Do?" Would he be flying all over the world just to take selfies for his friends on Instagram? Would he be yelling at the television when his team is losing? Would he be dancing all night to the sound of his airpods? Would he be waiting in line for a week to get the latest gadget? Would he be mocking his "boomer" elders? Would he be denying you health care, locking you up in for-profit prisons, taking your kids to war, or selling his body for money? You already know the answer.

Jesus was a radical who rocked the boat in his day. Were he here today, we may even try to crucify him again.

Much of the Muslim world finds itself caring more about where its hands and feet are in prayer than where its heart is. We are proud that *some* of our men wear a beard like Jesus and that *some* of our women wear a gown like Mary. That is wonderful. But have you ever practiced silence? Have you ever given away your most prized possessions in the name of God? Have you fasted outside of necessity? Have you visited the prisons, the retirement homes, the homeless shelters, and the women's shelters to care for the disadvantaged and the incarcerated? Have we apologized to that person that we cut off or blocked? Have we admitted that we were wrong? Have we changed?

Even today, Jesus has much to teach us on the value of wisdom, on spirituality, on good manners, on asceticism and minimalism, and on the cures of common spiritual illnesses. He is not just a bridge between Christians and Muslims. He is the missing bridge between many of us and God. So, for that reason, I decided that I needed to rediscover him and reintroduce him to myself. Maybe that is what we need to turn the tide. Maybe that is what we need to forge ahead.

We live in a world of shepherds, lambs, and wolves. The shepherds are the prophets and *awliyā'*, the lambs are the learners and followers, and the wolves are the transgressors. The shepherd's job is to guide and protect his flock. A good shepherd works tirelessly to tend to his flock and gather those that wander off into harm's way. A lamb can only sojourn on its own for so long before it is lost, confused, and subject to danger. Wolves prey on the flock, hunting the lost sheep and sneaking into the flock in sheep's clothing. As we sojourn in this world, will we choose to follow the line of Good Shepherds that God has appointed over us, or will we fail to take heed?

METHODS

I have collected a treasure trove of sayings and stories of Jesus Christ from the Islamic tradition. Most of these aphorisms were penned between the 8th and 10th century AD. Some evidently came from the Bible and Christian apocrypha, but many of these accounts are unique to the Islamic tradition, and they have never been translated before.

After carefully translating each excerpt from Arabic to English, I wrote a commentary to give further explanations, I provided cross-references to the Bible and the Quran, and I shared the spiritual lessons that I gleaned.

I relied on a number of sources, including Ibn Kathīr's *al-Bidāya wa al-Nihāya*, Abu Nuʿaym's *Ḥilyat al-Awliyāʾ*, Kulaynī's *al-Kāfī*, Ṣadūq's *al-Amālī*, Malik's *Muwaṭṭaʾ* and many other Sunni and Shiʿa compilations of *ḥadīth*.

While the authors of these compilations were diligent, not every report should be treated as religiously-binding (*ḥujja*) or *ṣaḥīḥ*. These reports are part of a greater folklore and communal consciousness of Jesus and his message. They are goodly exhortations (*muwaʿith*) designed to improve your character and your connection with God and invigorate your faith.

Some of the sayings and stories come directly from the Prophet Muhammad and the *awliyā'*. Others come from the earliest generations (*tabi'in*). After Christ's ascension, many communities inherited his sayings and his traditions. The New Testament reflects a particular tradition, while others – including the Gnostics, the Ebionites, the Nazarenes, the Nestorians, and others – had their own genealogy to Jesus and his apostles. I believe, in large part, the Islamic world inherited much of these latter traditions in the cross-pollination that took place after the 7th century. For that reason, I feel that this book is important for those who are trying to understand the historical Jesus and the breadth of the Judaeo-Christian tradition.

Part Two of this book consists of an anthology on topics pertaining to Jesus Christ and Islam. I decided to include the perspectives of a confessional Catholic, Christian converts to Islam, Jews, and others. The topics of these chapters range from Mary the Mother of Jesus, to the Early Church, to the End Times, to the relevance of Jesus in modern politics, to materialism, to much more.

The process of writing this book has improved my spiritual life in unfathomable ways. I hope that reading it will have the same affect.

ABOUT THE AUTHOR

Bilal Muhammad is a teacher and educator based in Toronto, Canada. He is a Senior Fellow at the Berkeley Institute for Islamic Studies and the Regional Manager of Active Aql Inc in

Toronto. He holds a B.Ed. from the Ontario Institute for Studies in Education at the University of Toronto. He also holds an Honours B.A. in Political Science, History, and the History of Religions from the University of Toronto. He is a former research assistant to Dr. Shafique Virani at the University of Toronto Department of Historical Studies. He has translated the *Amālī* of Ṣadūq, many of the *Majālis* of Mu'ayyad al-Dīn al-Shīrāzī, and other works from Arabic to English.

Bilal Muhammad has written other books, including *All the Perfumes of Arabia* and *The Muhammadan Cure: The Modern Science of Prophetic Medicine*

Part 1: Sayings of Jesus Christ

Jesus' Birth and Childhood

And mention in the scripture ⸢O Prophet, the story of⸣ Mary when she withdrew from her family to a place in the east, Screening herself off from them. We sent to her Our Spirit, appearing before her as a well-made man.

She appealed, "Surely, I seek refuge in the Most Merciful from you! ⸢So leave me alone⸣ if you fear God."

He responded, "I am only a messenger from your Lord, ⸢sent⸣ to bless you with a pure son."

She wondered, "How can I have a son when no man has ever touched me, nor am I unchaste?"

He replied, "So will it be! Your Lord says, 'It is easy for Me. We will make him a sign for humanity and a mercy from Us.' It is a matter ⸢already⸣ decreed."

So, she conceived him and withdrew with him to a remote place.

Then the pains of labour drove her to the trunk of a palm tree. She cried, "Alas! I wish I had died before this, and was a thing long forgotten!"

Then a voice reassured her from beneath her, "Do not grieve! Your Lord has provided a stream at your feet.

Shake the trunk of this palm tree towards you, and it will drop fresh, ripe dates over you.

So, eat and drink, and put your heart at ease. But if you see any of the people, say, 'I have made a vow of silence for the Most Merciful, so I am not talking to anyone today.'"

Then, she returned to her people, carrying him. They said ˹in shock˺, "O Mary! You have certainly done a horrible thing! O sister of Aaron! Your father was not an indecent man, nor was your mother unchaste."

So, she pointed to the baby. They exclaimed, "How can we talk to someone who is an infant in the cradle?"

Jesus declared, "Surely, I am a Servant of God. He has given me the scripture and He has made me a prophet. He has made me blessed wherever I go. He has commissioned me to pray and give charity as long as I live and to be kind to my mother. He has not made me arrogant or defiant. Peace be unto me the day I was born, the day I die, and the day I will be raised back to life!"

That is Jesus, son of Mary. ˹And this is˺ a word of truth, about which they dispute. (Quran 19:16-34)

لما ولد عيسى بن مريم (عليه السلام) كان ابن يوم كأنه ابن شهرين فلما كان ابن سبعة أشهر أخذت والدته بيده، وجاءت به إلى الكتاب وأقعدته بين يدي المؤدب، فقال له المؤدب: قل بسم الله الرحمن الرحيم. فقال عيسى (عليه السلام): بسم الله الرحمن الرحيم. فقال له المؤدب: قل أبجد. فرفع عيسى (عليه السلام) رأسه فقال: وهل تدري ما أبجد؟ فعلاه بالدرة ليضربه، فقال: يا مؤدب، لا تضربني إن كنت تدري وإلا فسلني حتى أفسر لك. فقال: فسر لي. فقال عيسى (عليه السلام): الالف آلاء الله، والباء بهجة الله، والجيم جمال الله والدال دين الله، هوز الهاء هول جهنم، والواو ويل لاهل النار، والزاي زفير جهنم، حطي حطت الخطايا عن المستغفرين، كلمن كلام الله لا مبدل لكلماته، سعفص صاع بصاع والجزاء بالجزاء، قرشت قرشهم فحشرهم. فقال المؤدب: أيتها المرأة، خذي بيد ابنك، فقد علم ولا حاجة له في المؤدب

When Jesus the son of Mary was born, he was one day old, but it was as though he was two months old. When he was seven months old, his mother took him by the hand to the scribes and sat him in front of the teacher.

So, the teacher said, "Say: In the name of God, the Beneficent, the Merciful."

So, Jesus, peace be unto him, said, "In the name of God, the Beneficent, the Merciful."

So, the teacher said, "Say the alphabet."

So, Jesus, peace be unto him, raised his head and said, "Do you know what the alphabet is?"

Then, the teacher took a stick to discipline him, but Jesus said, "O teacher! Do not discipline me. If you do not know, then ask me so that I may explain it to you."

He said, "Explain it to me."

So, Jesus, peace be unto him, said,

"A" is the signs (alā') of God,
"B" is the delight (bahjā) of God,
"J" is the beauty (jamāl) of God,
"D" is the religion (dīn) of God.
"H" is the horror (hawl) of Hell,
"W" is the woe (wayl) of the people of the Fire,
"Z" is the roar (zafīr) of Hellfire.
"Ḥ" is the falling (ḥaṭṭat) of sins from those who repent.
"K" is the words (kalām) of God, for which there is no substitute.
"Ṣaʿfas" is a measure (ṣaʿ) for a measure, and a reward for a reward.

16

"Qarshat" means that He gathers them (*qarashahum*) and resurrects them."

So, the teacher said, "O woman! Take your son by the hand, for he is learned, and he has no need for a teacher."[1]

Commentary:

A homunculus, fully-grown baby Jesus is a motif in Christian and Muslim traditions. In both the Quran and the Syriac Infancy Gospel, Jesus speaks from the cradle. While this can be seen as a momentary miracle, a high Christology would allow for the possibility of a mature and wise baby that acts as the vicegerent of God on Earth.

This report echoes a similar story told in the Infancy Gospel of Thomas, where a teacher named Zacchaeus writes the alphabet down for the infant Jesus. As Zacchaeus teaches, Jesus remains silent, until an irritated Zacchaeus strikes Jesus on the head. Jesus then says that he knows the alphabet better than his teacher and proves it by narrating the alphabet and speaking on the nature of its first letter "alpha". Jesus stupefies Zacchaeus until Zacchaeus is convinced that Jesus is indeed special and otherworldly.

While the authorship of the Infancy Gospel of Thomas is unknown, it is referred to in ~180 AD by Irenaeus as

---

[1] Saduq, *al-Amali*, pp. 394.

apocrypha.[2] The earliest extant version of the Infancy Gospel of Thomas is an abridged Syriac manuscript.[3] The *ḥadīth*, too, appears to mostly correspond with the Syriac alphabet, which is different than the Arabic alphabet and closer to the Aramaic alphabet. This may hint at the common origin of both the *ḥadīth* and the Syriac version of the Infancy Gospel of Thomas.

The report has Jesus explaining the esoteric meaning behind part of the alphabet. There are similar reports in the Islamic tradition that are attributed to ʿAlī b. Abī Ṭālib. The words of God in the Islamic tradition are either uncreated (as per the Ashʿarī opinion) or created (as per the Muʿtazilī and Shīʿī opinions). Either way, the alphabet, like anything else, is a sign of God; but perhaps a more special sign, because it is the basis of revelation, scripture, and sacred knowledge.

قالت امرأة لعيسى عليه السلام :طوبى لحجر حملك ولثدي أرضعك. فقال :طوبى لمن قرأ كتاب الله واتبعه

---

[2] J.R.C. Cousland, *Holy Terror: Jesus in the Infancy Gospel of Thomas*, pp. 3

[3] Tony Burke, *The Childhood of the Saviour (Infancy Gospel of Thomas): A New Translation*, https://www.tonyburke.ca/infancy-gospel-of-thomas/the-childhood-of-the-saviour-infancy-gospel-of-thomas-a-new-translation/

A woman said to Jesus, peace be unto him, "Blessed is the lap that carried you and the breast that suckled you!"

So, he said, "Blessed is he who recites the Book of God and follows it."[4]

Commentary:

The measure for righteousness is not primarily familial, but ethical. Christ and his mother were certainly special, not because of the lap that they came from, but due to their devotion to God's revelation.

Sacred personalities are only completed by their loyalty to textual authority. Every civilization is built upon a book or a collection of books. Without textual authority, the people will follow their whims, and civilization will unravel.

It is not enough to recite and memorize scripture like prattle, but one must work to understand and follow it. In Ezekiel 3:3, God instructs Ezekiel to "eat" the scripture. This consumption is the act of becoming one with the text, digesting its meaning, and actualizing its principles. This is why the Prophet Muhammad ﷺ is called the Walking Quran.

---

[4] Abu Nu`aym, *Hilyat al-Awliya'*, Volume 4, pp. 119.

قَالَ رَسُولُ اللهِ صَلَّى اللهُ عَلَيْهِ وَسَلَّمَ: «أَحَبُّ شَيْءٍ إِلَى اللهِ تَعَالَى الْغُرَبَاءُ» , قِيلَ: وَمَنِ الْغُرَبَاءُ؟ قَالَ: «الْفَرَّارُونَ بِدِينِهِمْ , يَبْعَثُهُمُ اللهُ يَوْمَ الْقِيَامَةِ مَعَ عِيسَى ابْنِ مَرْيَمَ عَلَيْهِمَا السَّلَامُ»

The Messenger of God (Muhammad), blessings be unto him, said, "The most beloved of things to God are the strangers."

It was said, "Who are the strangers?"

He said, "Those who flee with their religion. On the Day of Judgment, God will raise them with Jesus the son of Mary, peace be unto them."[5]

Commentary:

According to the Gospel of Matthew, Herod I – the Roman puppet king put over Palestine – initiated the Massacre of the Innocents when he heard the Magi speak of a newborn "king of the Jews". Mary fled to Egypt, taking Jesus with her, where they sought refuge from Herod until his death sometime between 4 and 1 BC. For this reason, Jesus is sometimes contemporarily referred to as a "Syrian refugee", because he fled the Levant due to the threat on his life.

---

[5] Ibid, Volume 1, pp. 25.

Since one of the meanings of *masīḥ* may be Jesus' flight with his religion from place to place (*mashahul arḍ*), this report presents Jesus as an archetypal refugee. This may further be reinforced with the idea that Jesus escaped crucifixion.

The Prophet Muhammad ﷺ said, "Islam began as a stranger, and it will return to being a stranger as it began, so blessed are the strangers."[6] [7] The exact meaning of this tradition is uncertain, but it may be saying that the Muslim nation started off as something small, private, and obscure (consisting of Muhammad, his family, and a few companions), and that the misguidance of the End Times would cause it to return to this condition. The Imāmī Shīʿa tradition marks this time with a period of "occultation", where the Mahdi is obscured during a time of sectarian confusion and perplexity, until he returns with the Islam of the Prophet Muhammad ﷺ.

---

[6] Jamiʿ al-Tirmidhi, Book 40, Hadith 24.
https://sunnah.com/tirmidhi:2629
[7] Saduq, *Kamal al-Din*, Volume 1, Page 94.

Jesus and John the Baptist

كَانَ عِيسَى ابْنُ مَرْيَمَ وَيَحْيَى بْنُ زَكَرِيَّا عَلَيْهِمَا السَّلَامُ ابْنَيْ خَالَةٍ،

وَكَانَ عِيسَى عَلَيْهِ السَّلَامُ يَلْبَسُ الصُّوفَ، وَكَانَ يَحْيَى عَلَيْهِ السَّلَامُ

يَلْبَسُ الْوَبَرَ، وَلَمْ يَكُنْ لِوَاحِدٍ مِنْهُمَا دِينَارٌ وَلَا دِرْهَمٌ، وَلَا عَبْدٌ وَلَا أَمَةٌ،

وَلَا مَا يَأْوِيَانِ إِلَيْهِ، أَيْنَمَا جَنَّهُمَا اللَّيْلُ أَوَيَا، فَلَمَّا أَرَادَا أَنْ يَتَفَرَّقَا قَالَ لَهُ

يَحْيَى: أَوْصِنِي. قَالَ: لَا تَغْضَبْ. قَالَ: لَا أَسْتَطِيعُ إِلَّا أَنْ أَغْضَبَ.

قَالَ: فَلَا تَقْتَنِ مَالًا. قَالَ: أَمَّا هَذِهِ فَعَسَى

Jesus the son of Mary and John the son of Zechariah, peace be unto them both, were maternal cousins. Jesus would wear wool and John would wear lint. Neither of them had a gold or silver coin, nor did they have a slave or a concubine. They did not reside anywhere – they would reside wherever the night would befall them.

When they wanted to part, John said, "Advise me."

Jesus said, "Do not get angry."

John said, "I cannot help but get angry."

Jesus said, "Then, do not acquire wealth."

John said, "This is something I could perhaps do."[8]

Commentary:

Due to the angel's statement in Luke 1:13-15, it is presumed that John the Baptist had taken the Nazirite vow: a consecrated practice mentioned in Numbers 6. Nazirites abstained from wine, cutting their hair, and ritual impurity.

A man came to the Prophet Muhammad ﷺ and said, "Advise me!" The Prophet replied, "Do not get angry." The man asked the same question again and again, and in each case, the Prophet replied, "Do not get angry."[9] Anger causes one to behave irresponsibly and regrettably. Anger often comes from a bruised ego, serving little utility and offering no spiritual upliftment.

---

[8] Abu Nuʿaym, *Hilyat al-Awliya'*, Volume 4, pp. 117.
[9] Sahih al-Bukhari, Book 78, Hadith 143.

To reduce anger, the Prophet Muhammad ﷺ said, "When one of you becomes angry while standing, he should sit down. If the anger leaves him, well and good; otherwise, he should lie down."[10]

التقى يحيى وعيسى، فصافحه عيسى وهو يضحك فقال له يحيى يا ابن خالة مالي أراك ضاحكا كأنك قد أمنت؟ فقال له عيسى: مالي أراك عابسا كأنك قد يئست؟ فأوحى الله إليهما: إن أحبكما إلي أبشكما بصاحبه

John [the Baptist] met with Jesus, and Jesus smiled while he shook his hand.

So, John said to him, "O cousin! Why do I see you smiling, as though you are safeguarded?"

So, Jesus said to him, "Why do I see you frowning, as though you have despaired?"

Then, God revealed to them both, "Surely, the more beloved of you to Me is him who smiles more for his companion."[11]

---

10 Sunan Abi Dawud, Book 43, Hadith 10.
11 Ibn Kathir, *al-Bidaya wa al-Nihaya*, Volume 2, pp. 108.

Commentary:

In several reports, John the Baptist is depicted as more melancholy and more abstemious than Christ. This is echoed in Matthew 11:18-19, where Jesus says, "For John came neither eating nor drinking, and they say, He hath a devil. The Son of Man came eating and drinking, and they say, Behold a man gluttonous …"

Smiling in the face of fellow believers is itself a meritorious practice, as it acknowledges their presence and makes them feel welcomed. The Prophet Muhammad ﷺ was known to smile frequently at those whom he met.

كان يحيى بن زكريا يبكي ولا يضحك، وكان عيسى بن مريم (عليه
السلام) يضحك ويبكي وكان الذي يصنع عيسى (عليه السلام)
أفضل من الذي كان يصنع يحيى (عليه السلام)

John the son of Zechariah, peace be unto him, used to cry and not laugh, while Jesus the son of Mary, peace be unto him, used to cry and laugh. What Jesus did is better than what John did.[12]

قال عيسى بن مريم عليه السلام (ليحيى بن زكريا عليه السلام :إذا

قيل فيك ما فيك، فاعلم أنه ذنب ذكرته فاستغفر الله منه، وإن قيل

فيك ما ليس فيك، فاعلم أنه حسنة كتبت لك لم تتعب فيها

Jesus the son of Mary, peace be unto him, said to John the son
of Zechariah, peace be unto him, "If something true [of evil]
is said about you, then know that it is a sin, so ask for God's
forgiveness for it. If something false is said about you, then
know that a good deed will be recorded for you without
needing to toil for it."[13]

Commentary:

If one gossips falsely about you, you will receive some of the
good deeds of that person on the Day of Judgment.

---

[13] Saduq, *al-Amali*, pp. 603.

The Failed Temptation

إِنَّ إِبْلِيسَ قَالَ لِعِيسَى عَلَيْهِ السَّلَامُ حِينَ رَآهُ عَلَى جَبَلِ الْقُدْسِ:

زَعَمْتَ أَنَّكَ تُحْيِي الْمَوْتَى. قَالَ: كُنْتُ كَذَلِكَ. قَالَ: فَادْعُ اللهَ أَنْ

يَجْعَلَ هَذَا الْجَبَلَ خُبْزًا. فَقَالَ لَهُ عِيسَى عَلَيْهِ السَّلَامُ: أَوَ كُلُّ النَّاسِ

يَعِيشُونَ مِنَ الْخُبْزِ؟ فَقَالَ لَهُ إِبْلِيسُ: فَإِنْ كُنْتَ كَمَا تَقُولُ فَثِبْ مِنْ

هَذَا الْمَكَانِ فَإِنَّ الْمَلَائِكَةَ سَتَلْقَاكَ. قَالَ: إِنَّ رَبِّي أَمَرَنِي أَنْ لَا أُجَرِّبَ

نَفْسِي، فَلَا أَدْرِي هَلْ يُسَلِّمُنِي أَمْ لَا

27

Lucifer said to Jesus, peace be unto him, when he saw him on the Temple Mount, "You claim that you could bring the dead to life."

Jesus said, "It is as such."

He said, "Then pray to God that He makes this mountain into bread."

So, Jesus, peace be unto him, said to him, "Do all people live by bread?"

So, Lucifer said to him, "If it is as you say, then jump from this mount, for the angels will catch you."

He said, "Surely, my Lord commanded me to not try myself, for I do not know if He will deliver me or not."[14]

Commentary:

In Matthew 4, a famished Jesus is in the wilderness after forty days and forty nights of fasting. The devil appears to him and tells him to make stones into bread to feed himself. Jesus then quotes the Torah, saying, "Man shall not live on bread alone, but on every word that comes from the mouth of God." (Deuteronomy 8:3) People need more than material things to truly live. Simple necessities only satisfy the bottom of the pyramid of needs. It is the word of God – exemplified in Jesus – that brings order and meaning into the universe.

---

[14] Abu Nu`aym, *Hilyat al-Awliya'*, Volume 4, pp. 52.

Satan knew that Jesus was under the protection of God, as per Psalm 19:11-12, but nonetheless, a prophet should not test God's hedge just to satisfy the curiosity and wonder of others. As Jesus says, "It is written again, Thou shalt not tempt the Lord thy God." (Matthew 4:7)

إن إبليس قال: لعيسى بن مريم عليه السلام: أيقدر ربك على أن يدخل الارض بيضة لا يصغر الارض ولا يكبر البيضة ؟ فقال عيسى عليه السلام ويلك على أن الله لا يوصف بعجز، ومن أقدر ممن يلطف الارض ويعظم البيضة

Lucifer said to Jesus the son of Mary, peace be unto him, "Can your Lord fit the Earth in an egg without decreasing the size of the Earth or increasing the size of the egg?"

So, Jesus, peace be unto him, said, "Woe to you! God cannot be described with inability. Who would be more capable than Him in softening the Earth and magnifying the egg?"[15]

Commentary:

In a similar narration, someone asked Hishām b. al-Ḥakam, a companion of Jaʿfar al-Ṣādiq, if God can fit the Earth in an

---

[15] Saduq, *Kitab al-Tawhid*, Chapter 9, Hadith 5.

egg without decreasing the size of the Earth or increasing the size of the egg. Jaʿfar al-Ṣādiq replied that the pupil is smaller than the egg, yet God fit the Earth into our vision without increasing or decreasing the size of either.[16]

لقى ابليس عيسى بن مريم فقال: هل نالنى من حبائلك شئ ؟ قال:
جدتك التى قالت رب انى وضعتها انثى إلى الشيطان الرجيم

Lucifer met Jesus the son of Mary and [Jesus] said, "Have I been ensnared by any of your traps?"

He said, "[No,] it was your grandmother who said, 'O Lord! I have given birth to a female child ... and I ask refuge with You for her and for her offspring from the cursed Satan.'" (Quran 3:36)[17]

Commentary:

Who knows where we would be without the prayers of our mothers and grandmothers!

---

[16] Kulayni, *al-Kafi*, Volume 1, Page 79.
[17] Tafsir al-ʿAyashi, Volume 1, Page 171.

لما مضى لعيسى (عليه السلام) ثلاثون سنة، بعثه الله عز وجل إلى بني إسرائيل، فلقيه إبليس (لعنه الله) على عقبة بيت المقدس، وهي عقبة أفيق ، فقال الله يا عيسى أنت الذي بلغ من عظم ربوبيتك أن تكونت من غير أب؟ قال عيسى (عليه السلام): بل العظمة للذي كونني، وكذلك كون آدم وحواء. قال إبليس: يا عيسى، فأنت الذي بلغ من عظم ربوبيتك أنك تكلمت في المهد صبيا؟ قال عيسى (عليه السلام): يا إبليس. بل العظمة للذي أنطقني في صغري ولو شاء لأبكمني قال إبليس: فأنت الذي بلغ من عظم ربوبيتك أنك تخلق من الطين كهيئة الطير، فتنفخ فيه فيصير طيرا؟ قال عيسى (عليه السلام): بل العظمة للذي خلقني وخلق ما سخر لي. قال إبليس: فأنت الذي بلغ من عظم ربوبيتك أنك تشقي المرضى؟ قال عيسى (عليه السلام): بل العظمة للذي بإذنه أشفيهم، وإذا شاء أمرضني. قال إبليس: فأنت الذي بلغ من عظم ربوبيتك أنك تحيي الموتى؟ قال عيسى (عليه السلام): بل العظمة للذي بإذنه أحييهم، ولا بد من أن يميت ما أحييت، ويميتني. قال إبليس: يا عيسى فأنت الذي بلغ من عظم ربوبيتك أنك تعبر البحر فلا تبتل قدماك ولا ترسخ فيه؟ قال عيسى (عليه السلام): بل العظمة للذي ذلله لي

ولو شاء أغرقني. قال إبليس: يا عيسى، فأنت الذي بلغ من عظم

ربوبيتك أنه سيأتي عليك يوم تكون السماوات والارض ومن فيهن

دونك، وأنت فوق ذلك كله تدبر الامر وتقسم الارزاق؟ فأعظم

عيسى (عليه السلام) ذلك من قول إبليس الكافر اللعين، فقال

عيسى (عليه السلام): سبحان الله ملء سماواته وأرضيه، ومداد

كلماته، وزنة عرشه، ورضا نفسه. قال: فلما سمع إبليس (لعنه الله)

ذلك ذهب على وجهه لا يملك من نفسه شيئا حتى وقع في اللجة

الخضراء. قال ابن عباس، فخرجت امرأة من الجن تمشي على

شاطئ البحر، فإذا هي بإبليس ساجدا على صخرة صماء تسيل

دموعه على خدية، فقامت تنظر إليه تعجبا، ثم قالت له: ويحك يا

إبليس، ما ترجو بطول السجود؟ فقال لها: أيتها المرأة الصالحة، ابنة

الرجل الصالح، أرجو إذا أبر ربي عز وجل قسمه، وأدخلني نار

جهنم، أن يخرجني من النار برحمته

When Jesus reached thirty years of age, God sent him to the
Children of Israel.

Lucifer, the curse of God be unto him, came to him at a stop
of the Temple, which was the stop of Afek.

Then, Lucifer said, "O Jesus! Are you the one who – by the greatness of your lordship – was able to be created without a father?"

Jesus, peace be unto him, said, "Rather, the greatness belongs to the One who created me; that is how Adam and Eve were created [as well]."

Lucifer said, "O Jesus! Are you the one who – by the greatness of your lordship – was able to speak in the cradle as a child?"

Jesus, peace be unto him, said, "O Lucifer! Rather, the greatness belongs to the One who gave me speech in my childhood; and if He willed, He could have made me mute."

Lucifer said, "So, are you the one who – by the greatness of your lordship – was able to create the form of a bird out of clay, blow into it, and it was able to fly?"

Jesus, peace be unto him, said, "Rather, the greatness belongs to the One who created me and created what He subjected to me."

Lucifer said, "So, are you the one who – by the greatness of your lordship – cures the ill?"

Jesus, peace be unto him, said, "Rather, the greatness belongs to the One by whose permission I cured them; and if He willed, He could have made me ill."

Lucifer said, "So, are you the one who – by the greatness of your lordship – is able to resurrect the dead?"

Jesus, peace be unto him, said: "Rather, the greatness belongs to the One by whose permission I resurrected them; there is nothing stopping Him from causing those I resurrected to die and causing me to die."

Lucifer said, "O Jesus! Are you the one who – by the greatness of your lordship – is able to walk on the sea without wetting your feet and without sinking in it?"

Jesus, peace be unto him, said, "Rather, the greatness belongs to the One who overcame it for me; and if He willed, He could have drowned me."

Lucifer said, "O Jesus! Are you the one who – by the greatness of your lordship – will rule over the heavens and the Earth one day; and you will be above all that, running the affairs and distributing sustenance [to the world]?"

So, Jesus, peace be unto him, became astounded at the words of Lucifer, the accursed disbeliever, so Jesus, peace be unto him, said. "May God be glorified – His glory fills His heavens and His Earth, the extension of His words, the weight of His Throne, and His contentment."

So, when Lucifer heard that, he went on his face, not possessing anything, until he fell into the blue ocean.

A female Jinn walked on the shore of the ocean, seeing Lucifer prostrating upon a solid rock, with tears flowing on his cheeks.

She looked at him astonishingly, went to him and said to him, "Woe to you, Lucifer! What do you hope for in a long prostration?"

So, he said to her, "O righteous woman, daughter of a righteous man: I hope that, if I am good to my Lord, and He admits me to the Fire, that He takes me out of the Fire out of His mercy."[18]

وعن عيسى عليه السلام :إن الشيطان مع الدنيا ومكره مع المال

وتزيينه مع الهوى واستمكانه عند الشهوات

Jesus, peace be unto him, said, "Surely, Satan is with worldliness, his scheming is with wealth, his adorning is with whim, and his control is through desire."[19]

Commentary:

In the Quran, after Adam is selected as God's vicegerent, Satan vows to misguide his offspring. He says to God, "I will lie in wait for them in Your straight path. Then, I will surely come to them from before them and from behind them, and from their right and from their left. You will find that most of them

---

[18] Saduq, *al-Amali*, pp. 272.
[19] Abu Nu`aym, *Hilyat al-Awliya'*, Volume 5, pp. 251.

are ungrateful." (Quran 7:16-17) The test of this world is to focus on God and avert the machinations of Satan.

Satan awaits the believers on the pathway toward God. The believers are his primary target because the disbelievers have already been deluded by him or by themselves. He often cannot misguide a believer through spectacle, and so instead, he works slowly and subtly. He makes them value the Hereafter less, he commands them to gather wealth and keep it away from others, he corrupts their religion, and he makes them chase after pleasure. With these four tools, Satan can trap the believer, even whilst the believer thinks he is behaving correctly and rationally.

Jesus' Miracles

إن عيسى بن مريم كان من شرايعه السيح في البلاد ، فخرج في بعض سيحه ومعه رجل من أصحابه قصير وكان كثير اللزوم لعيسى (عليه السلام)، فلما انتهى عيسى إلى البحر قال: بسم الله، بصحة يقين منه فمشى على ظهر الماء فقال الرجل القصير حين نظر إلى عيسى (عليه السلام): جازه بسم الله بصحة يقين منه فمشى على الماء ولحق بعيسى (عليه السلام)، فدخله العجب بنفسه، فقال: هذا عيسى روح الله يمشي على الماء وأنا أمشي على الماء فما فضله علي، قال: فرمس في الماء فاستغاث بعيسى فتناوله من الماء فأخرجه ثم قال له: ما قلت يا قصير؟ قال: قلت: هذا روح الله يمشي على الماء وأنا أمشي على الماء فدخلني من ذلك عجب،

37

فقال له عيسى: لقد وضعت نفسك في غير الموضع الذي وضعك

الله فيه فمقتك الله على ما قلت فتب إلى الله عز وجل مما قلت،

قال: فتاب الرجل وعاد إلى مرتبته التي وضعه الله فيها، فاتقوا الله

ولا يحسدن بعضكم بعض

During one of the journeys of Jesus, one of his companions, who was of short height, accompanied him very often. When they reached the sea, Jesus with correct certainty said, "In the name of God," and began to walk over the water.

The short man, looking at Jesus walking over the water, also with correct certainty said, "In the name of God," walked over the water and reached Jesus. At this, he felt proud of himself and said, "This is Jesus, the Spirit of God who walks over the water, and I also walk over the water. Why then should he be more excellent than me?"

He then sunk in the water and cried for help from Jesus, who took him out of water and asked, "What did you say, O short man?"

He replied, "This is Jesus, the Spirit of God who walks over the water and I also walk over the water, and I sensed pride inside of me."

Jesus said to him, "You placed yourself in a position that God had not placed you in. God resented what you said. Repent and return to the Majestic God for what you have said."

The man repented and returned to his position that God had given him.[20]

Commentary:

This story corresponds to Matthew 14:22-33, where the disciples got on a boat, and saw a figure walking on the lake. To make sure that it was indeed Jesus, Peter decided to start walking on the water too. He succeeded in reaching Jesus, but when the wind frightened him, he began to sink.

The difference between the two accounts is that, in the *ḥadīth*, the reason for Peter's submersion was pride, while in the Gospel, the reason was fear. Both come from a deficiency in faith.

It is typically understood that Simon Peter was the deputy (*waṣī*) of Jesus Christ. While this *ḥadīth* does not actually mention the name of Peter, the two stories are so similar that one may question whether such a person could qualify as the vicar of Christ. It would not exactly be a contradiction, but it would imply a lower imamology than some Shiʿa are willing to accept.

---

[20] Kulayni, *al-Kafi*, Volume 2, Page 306.

.قِيلَ لِعِيسَى :بِأَيِّ شَيْءٍ تَمْشِي عَلَى الْمَاءِ ؟ قَالَ :بِالْإِيمَانِ وَالْيَقِينِ

قيل لعيسى بن مريم يا عيسى بأى شيء تمشى على الماء؟ قال:

بالإيمان واليقين. قالوا: فإنا آمنا كما آمنت، وأيقنا كما أيقنت.

قال: فامشوا إذا. قال فمشوا معه فى الموج فغرقوا. فقال لهم

عيسى: ما لكم؟ فقالوا: خفنا الموج. قال: ألا خفتم رب الموج؟

قال، فأخرجهم، ثم ضرب بيده إلى الأرض، فقبض بها ثم بسطها

:فإذا فى إحدى يديه ذهب، وفى الأخرى مدر أو حصى. فقال

أيهما أحلى فى قلوبكم؟ قالوا: هذا الذهب. قال: فإنهما عندى سواء

It was said to Jesus, "How is it that you walk on the water?"

He said, "With faith and certainty."

They said, "Surely, we believe just as you believe, and we have certainty just as you have certainty."

He said, "If that is the case, then walk."

So, they walked with him into a wave, and they sank under the water.

Jesus said to them, "What happened to you?"

So, they said, "We feared the wave."

40

He said, "Do you not fear the Lord of the wave?"

So, he took them out of the water. Then, he struck both his hands into the earth and grasped two fistfuls. He opened his hands, and there was gold in one, and dust or gravel in the other. Then, he said, "Which of these two is more beloved to your hearts?"

They said, "This gold."

He said, "To me, they are the same."[21]

أن عيسى بن مريم (عليه السلام) توجه في بعض حوائجه ومعه ثلاثة نفر من أصحابه، فمر بلبنات ثلاث من ذهب على ظهر الطريق فقال عيسى (عليه السلام) لاصحابه: إن هذا يقتل الناس. ثم مضى، فقال أحدهم: إن لي حاجة. قال: فانصرف، ثم قال آخر إن لي حاجة. فانصرف، ثم قال الآخر: لي حاجة. فانصرف، فوافوا عند الذهب ثلاثتهم، فقال اثنان لواحد: اشتر لنا طعاما. فذهب ليشتري لهما طعاما، فجعل فيه سما ليقتلهما كي لا يشاركاه في الذهب، وقال الاثنان: إذ جاء قتلناه كي لا يشاركنا. فلما جاء قاما

---

[21] Ibn Abi'l Dunya, *Kitab al-Yaqin*, pp. 52.

إليه فقتلاه، ثم تغذيا فماتا، فرجع إليهم عيسى (عليه السلام) وهم

موتى حوله، فأحياهم بإذن الله تعالى ذكره، ثم قال: ألم أقل لكم:

إن هذا يقتل الناس؟

Jesus, the son of Mary, went forth to fulfill a need of his, and he had three of his companions with him. He passed by three bars of gold on the road. So, Jesus said to his companions, "Surely, this kills people." Then, he continued walking.

Then, one of them said, "I have a need." So, he left.

Then, another one said, "I have a need." So, he left.

Then, the last one said, "I have a need." So, he left.

The three of them had gone to the gold. Two of them said to one of them, "Buy us food."

So, he went to buy food for the two of them. He put poison in it so that he may kill them and not share the gold with them.

The two said, "When he comes, let us kill him so that we do not have to share with him."

When he came, they went to him and killed him. Then, they ate, and they both died.

So, Jesus, peace be unto them, returned to it, and they were dead around it. So, he resurrected them by the permission of God; then said: "Did I not tell you that this kills people?"[22]

إنه كان له صديق مؤاخ له في الله، و كان عيسى يمر به فينزل عليه، و إن عيسى غاب عنه حينا ثم مر به ليسلم عليه، فخرجت إليه أمه لتسلم عليه، فسألها عنه، فقالت أمه: مات، يا رسول الله. فقال لها: أ تحبين أن تريه، قالت: نعم، قال لها: إذا كان غدا أتيتك حتى أحييه لك بإذن الله تعالى. فلما كان من الغد أتاها، فقال لها: انطلقي معي إلى قبره، فانطلقا حتى أتيا قبره، فوقف عيسى (عليه السلام) ثم دعا الله فانفرج القبر، و خرج ابنها حيا، فلما رأته امه و رآها بكيا فرحمهما عيسى (عليه السلام) فقال له: أ تحب أن تبقى مع أمك في الدنيا؟ قال: يا رسول الله، بأكل و برزق و مدة، أو بغير مدة و لا رزق و لا أكل؟ فقال له عيسى: بل برزق و أكل و مدة، تعمر عشرين سنة، و تزوج و يولد لك قال: فنعم إذن. فدفعه عيسى (عليه السلام) إلى أمه، فعاش عشرين سنة و ولد له

---

[22] Saduq, *al-Amali*, pp. 247.

Jesus had a friend who was as a brother to him in faith, and Jesus would pass by him and lodge with him.

Jesus had been absent from him for a time, then he passed by him to greet him, but his mother came out to him to greet him. So, he asked her about him, and his mother said, "He died, O Messenger of God."

So, he said to her, "Would you like to see him?"

She said, "Yes!"

He said to her, "When it is tomorrow, I will come to you that I might revive him for you by the permission of God."

So, when it was the next day, he came to her, and he said to her, "Set out with me to his grave."

Then, they set out until they came to his grave. Jesus, peace be unto him, stopped, then prayed to God and the grave opened, and her son came out alive.

When his mother saw him and he saw her, they cried and Jesus had mercy on them.

Then, he said to him, "Would you like to remain with your mother in the world?"

He said, "O Messenger of God, with eating, provision and a duration, or without a duration and not provision and no eating?"

So, Jesus said to him, "Rather, with provision and eating and a duration. You will live twenty years, marry, and a child will be born to you."

He said, "Then yes."

So, Jesus turned him over to his mother, and he lived twenty years and a child was born to him.[23]

Commentary:

This account is somewhat similar to the story of Lazarus, except it was Lazarus' sister that communicated with Jesus rather than his mother. According to St. Epiphanios of Cyprus (d. 403 AD), Lazarus remained alive for thirty years after his resurrection (rather than twenty). This could very well have been a different man that Jesus resurrected.

The emphasis on this man eating, marrying, and having children shows that the resurrected man was not a phantom, but a flesh-and-blood human being.

إن أصحاب عيسى (عليه السلام) سألوه أن يحيي لهم ميتا، قال: فأتى بهم إلى قبر سام بن نوح، فقال له: قم بإذن الله، يا سام بن

---

[23] Kulayni, *al-Kafi*, Volume 8, Page 337.

نوح. قال: فانشق القبر، ثم أعاد الكلام فتحرك، ثم أعاد الكلام

فخرج سام بن نوح، فقال له عيسى: أيهما أحب إليك تبقى أو

تعود؟ قال: فقال: يا روح الله، بل أعود، إني لأجد حرقة الموت- أو

قال: لذعة «1» الموت- في جوفي إلى يومي هذا

The companions of Jesus asked him to revive a deceased person for them. So, he brought them to the grave of Shem son of Noah.

He said to him, "Rise, by the permission of God, Shem son of Noah."

Then, the grave cracked open. He repeated himself, and it moved. He repeated himself again, and Shem son of Noah came out.

Then, Jesus said to him, "Which is more beloved to you, that you remain or that you return?"

So, he said, "O Spirit of God, rather that I return. Surely, I find the burning of death: – or he said the conflagration of death –: inside of me until now."[24]

Commentary:

---

[24] Tafsir al-`Ayashi, Volume 1, Page 174.

This is a unique account that is not found in the Bible or Christian texts. Shem ("Sam" in Arabic) was said to be the son of Noah and the forefather of all Jews and Arabs – his name is where the word "Semite" comes from.

بلغني أن عيسى كان إذا ذكر الموت يقطر جلده دما

When Jesus would mention death, his flesh would drip blood.[25]

Commentary:

Death is called certainty (*yaqīn*) in the Quran because it is the only certain thing in this world. Even life can end before it truly begins. Despite the certainty of death, most ordinary people avoid thinking about it, and try to change the topic when it comes up. The prophets would frequently remind their people of death. Those who understand the inner reality of death will not neglect it. ʿAlī b. Abī Ṭālib said, "By God, [I] am more familiar with death than an infant with the breast of its mother. I have hidden knowledge: were I to disclose it, you would tremble like ropes in deep wells."[26]

---

[25] Ibn al-Kathir, *al-Bidaya wa al-Nihaya*, Volume 2, Page 108.
[26] Nahjul Balagha, Part 1, Sermon 5.

وإن عيسى بن مريم عليه السلام قال: داويت المرضى فشفيتهم

بإذن الله، وأبرأت الأكمه والأبرص بإذن الله، وعالجت الموتى

فأحييتهم بإذن الله، وعالجت الأحمق فلم أقدر على إصلاحه.

فقيل: يا روح الله، وما الأحمق؟ قال: المعجب برأيه ونفسه، الذي

يرى الفضل كله له لا عليه، ويوجب الحق كله لنفسه ولا يوجب

عليها حقا، فذاك الأحمق الذي لا حيلة في مداواته

Jesus the son of Mary, peace be unto him, said, "I have treated the ill and cured them by God's permission. I have healed the born-blind and the lepers by God's permission. I have treated the dead and resurrected them by God's permission. Yet, when I treated the fool, I could not rectify him."

It was said, "O Spirit of God! What is a fool?"

He said, "He who is enamored by his opinion and his own self. He thinks that his blessings are his, rather than a test against him. He demands all rights for himself, without giving himself any responsibilities. That is the fool in whom there is no hope for treatment."[27]

---

[27] Al-Mufid, *al-Ikhtisas*, pp. 221.

Worldliness
and
Materialism

وَإِنْ شِئْتَ ثَنَّيْتُ بِصَاحِبِ الرُّوحِ وَالْكَلِمَةِ عِيسَى ابْنِ مَرْيَمَ كَانَ يَقُولُ:
إِدَامِي الْجُوعُ، وَشِعَارِي الْخَوْفُ، وَلِبَاسِي الصُّوفُ، وَصَلَاتِي فِي
الشِّتَاءِ مَشَارِقُ الشَّمْسِ، وَسِرَاجِي الْقَمَرُ، وَدَابَّتِي رِجْلَايَ وَطَعَامِي
وَفَاكِهَتِي مَا أَنْبَتَتِ الْأَرْضُ، أَبِيتُ وَلَيْسَ عِنْدِي شَيْءٌ، وَأُصْبِحُ وَلَيْسَ
عِنْدِي شَيْءٌ، وَمَا عَلَى الْأَرْضِ أَغْنَى مِنِّي

The Master of the Spirit and the Word, Jesus the son of Mary,
would say, "My condiment is hunger. My emblem is fear. My

49

apparel is wool. My warmth in winter is the sunrise. My lamp is the moon. My feet are my transportation. My food and my fruit are what grows from the Earth. I sleep with nothing, and I awake with nothing; and there is none upon the Earth that is richer than me."[28]

Commentary:

Jesus said in the beatitudes, "Blessed are the poor in spirit: for theirs is the kingdom of heaven ... Blessed are the meek: for they shall inherit the earth. Blessed are they which do hunger and thirst after righteousness: for they shall be filled." (Matthew 5:3-6) This saying also has some allusions to Genesis 28, where Jacob takes a stone and uses it as a pillow.

Jesus is a patron and an emblem for the downtrodden. He wanted nothing from the frills of this life – neither its delicious food, nor its soft cloth or smooth silk, nor its riding animals, nor its spacious houses. The more possessions one has, the more one's thoughts are dominated by the upkeep, competition, and enhancement of those possessions. In the case of Jesus, he was rich, not just due to his spiritual life, but his minimalistic lifestyle enabled him to be truly free from the nuisances of material life.

A similar report about Jesus is attributed to ʿAlī b. Abī Ṭālib, where he says, "If you desire, I will tell you about Jesus the son

---

[28] Abu Nuʿaym, *Hilyat al-Awliya'*, Volume 6, pp. 312.

of Mary. He used a stone for his pillow, put on coarse clothes and ate rough food. His condiment was hunger. His lamp at night was the moon. His shade during the winter was just the expanse of earth eastward and westward. His fruits and flowers were only what grows from the earth for the cattle. He had no wife to allure him, nor any son to give grief, nor wealth to deviate (his attention), nor greed to disgrace him. His two feet were his conveyance and his two hands his servant."[29]

قال عيسى بن مريم : لا يستقيم حب الدنيا وحب الآخرة في قلب
مؤمن كما لا يستقيم الماء والنار في إناء

Jesus the son of Mary said, "Love for worldliness and love for the Hereafter cannot coexist in the heart of the believer, just as water and fire cannot coexist in a vessel."[30]

Commentary:

God says in the Quran, "God does not put two hearts within one's breast." (Quran 33:4) Man cannot love a thing and love its opposite at the same time. He must choose between worldliness (*dunya*) and heaven. "Worldliness" here should not be mistaken for the Earth or the people of the world. The

---

[29] Nahj al-Balagha, Sermon 160.
[30] Ibn Kathir, *al-Bidaya wa al-Nihaya*, Volume 2, pp. 106.

Earth is a sign of God, and the people are a mix of good and evil. Rather, worldliness is a reference to the fleeting and capricious temptations of this world. Worldliness is the lower, appetitive aspect of this world that distracts us from God.

The Bible emphatically calls Satan "the god of this world" (2 Corinthians 4:4), which does not mean that Satan is in power, but that worldliness is his domain and tool during his time of respite. Jesus says in the Bible, "You are from beneath, and I am from above. You are of this world, and I am not of this world." (John 8:23)

قال عيسى :طالب الدنيا مثل شارب ماء البحر كلما ازداد شربا ازداد

عطشا حتى يقتله

Jesus said, "The seeker of this world is like one who drinks from the sea: the more he drinks, the thirstier he becomes, until it kills him."[31]

Commentary:

As a person consumes worldliness, worldliness consumes him. The bigger his appetite, the more perverse his taste. If the cycle of consumption is not broken, a person is inevitably destroyed.

---

[31] Ibid, Volume 2, pp. 106.

Addictions lead to overdoses. Material ambitions will not give a person lasting quiet of mind. "Surely, in the remembrance of God do hearts find rest." (Quran 13:28)

قال عيسى ابن مريم :يا معشر الحواريين ارضوا بدني الدنيا مع سلامة الدين كما رضي أهل الدنيا بدني الدين مع سلامة الدنيا

Jesus the son of Mary said, "O apostles! Be contented by the least of this world and securing your religion, just as the people of this world are contented by the least of their religion and securing this world."[32]

Commentary:

It is better to safeguard your religion by avoiding the frills of worldliness than to pursue materialism at the cost of your religion. Morality is all about making difficult decisions for the sake of goodness.

In this tradition, Jesus makes a distinction between those who are in the world and those who are of the world. Those who are of the world are satisfied with reaping the decadence and

---

[32] Ibid, Volume 2, pp. 106.

frivolity of a materialistic and hedonistic lifestyle. On the other hand, being a believer is difficult. The Prophet Muhammad ﷺ described this world as "the prison of the believer." The challenges of being moral in this life must be borne with the contentment of securing the next life.

قال عيسى :إن أكل الشعير مع الرماد والنوم على المزابل مع الكلاب لقليل في طلب الفردوس.

Jesus said, "Surely, eating barley with ash, and sleeping in the dumps with the dogs is little in the pursuit of Paradise."[33]

Commentary:

The spiritual illness of materialism was rampant at the time of Jesus Christ. His prescription for this illness was a high dose of asceticism. Poverty is the pride of the humble. However, it was not their poverty that made them righteous – it was their detachment from worldliness and their attachment to God. If we find ourselves dependant on the riches of this age, then periodic retreats into simpler places can help us wean off worldliness.

---

[33] Abu Nu`aym, *Hilyat al-Awliya'*, Volume 2, Page 369.

قال عيسى :اعملوا لله ولا تعملوا لبطونكم انظروا إلى هذا الطير

تغدو وتروح لا تحرث ولا تحصد والله يرزقها، فإن قلتم نحن أعظم

بطونا من الطير فانظروا إلى هذه الأباقر من الوحوش والحمر فإنها

تغدو وتروح لا تحرث ولا تحصد والله يرزقها]اتقوا فضول الدنيا فإن

فضول الدنيا عند الله رجز

Jesus said, "Work for God, and do not work for your
stomachs. Look to these birds – they come and go, and they
neither plow nor reap, for God provides for them. If you were
to say, 'we have greater stomachs than the bird', then look to
these cows and donkeys among the beasts. They come and go,
and they neither plow nor reap, for God provides for them.
Beware the excess of this world, for the excess of this world is
unclean to God."[34]

Commentary:

A similar passage can be found in Matthew 6:25-26. The
Islamic position on sustenance is that it has been divinely
apportioned by God for every person. Man must still work, as

---

[34] Ibn Kathir, *al-Bidaya wa al-Nihaya*, Volume 2, pp. 106.

that is a religious obligation; but richness is beyond our personal control and maneuverings. Even today, the market regularly dumbfounds our greatest economists, and the success of business ventures is difficult to predict. So long that you are alive, your provision for that day is written – the day your provision is exhausted is the day that you die.

Both poverty and wealth are a test. The wealthy is subject to more temptations, and he is accountable to more questioning on the Day of Judgment. The poor person must exercise a level of patience that may help his character in the long run.

مر عيسى عليه السلام على مدينة خربة، فأعجبه البنيان فقال :أي رب مر هذه المدينة أن تجييني؟ فأوحى الله إلى المدينة أيتها المدينة الخربة جاوبي عيسى .قال :فنادت المدينة عيسى حبيبي وما تريد مني قال :ما فعل أشجارك وما فعل أنهارك وما فعل قصورك وأين سكانك؟ قالت: حبيبي جاء وعد ربك الحق فيبست أشجاري ونشفت أنهاري وخربت قصوري ومات سكاني .قال :فأين أموالهم فقالت جمعوها من الحلال والحرام موضوعة في بطني .لله ميراث السماوات والأرض .قال فنادى عيسى عليه السلام :تعجبت)1(

من ثلاث أناس :طالب الدنيا والموت يطلبه، وباني القصور والقبر

منزله، ومن يضحك ملء فيه والنار أمامه !ابن آدم لا بالكثير تشبع

ولا بالقليل تقنع تجمع مالك لمن لا يحمدك وتقدم على رب لا

يعذرك إنما أنت عبد بطنك وشهوتك وإنما تملأ بطنك إذا دخلت

قبرك وأنت يا بن آدم ترى حشد مالك في ميزان غيرك .هذا حديث

غريب جدا وفيه موعظة حسنة فكتبناه لذلك

Jesus, peace be unto him, passed by a ruined city. He was astonished with the buildings, so he said, "O Lord! Will you allow this city to respond to me?"

So, God revealed to the city, "O ruined city! Respond to Jesus."

So, the city called out, "Jesus, my beloved, what do you want from me?"

He said, "What did your trees do? What did your rivers do? What did your palaces do? Where are your inhabitants?"

It said, "My beloved, the promise of your Lord came, so my trees shriveled, my rivers dried up, my palaces went to ruin, and my inhabitants died."

He said, "Where is their wealth?"

It said, "They gained it in both permitted and forbidden ways. It has been placed in my belly. The bequeathal of heaven and Earth is for God."

So, Jesus, peace be unto him, called out, "I am astonished at three types of people: one who seeks this world while death seeks him, one who builds palaces while the grave is his home, and one who is filled with laughter while Hellfire is before him! A child of Adam is neither satiated by much nor satisfied by little. You build wealth for those who do not praise you, and you proceed to a Lord that will not excuse you. Surely, you are but a slave to your stomach and your desires, but your stomach will only be filled [with dust] when you enter your grave. You, O child of Adam, will see the wealth that you gathered in the scale of someone else."[35]

Commentary:

One who makes it his goal to pursue wealth in this world, by hook or by crook, may neither secure this world nor the Hereafter. The chasing of wealth may lead one off a cliff. The place where we get to finally cash our check may be just passed our grave. Even if we achieve the wealth that we desire, some are so poor that all they have is money. Had we been created only for this world, then God would not have created death. The Prophet Muhammad ﷺ said, "If a child of Adam

---

were to have a valley of gold, he would want to have two valleys. He will not be filled with anything except dust."[36]

In the Islamic tradition, Jesus is depicted as a wanderer who finds and teaches moral lessons in the world. Several reports speak about this destroyed community or ones like it.

قال عيسى عليه السلام : يا معشر الحواريين اجعلوا كنوزكم في السماء فإن قلب الرجل حيث كنزه.

Jesus, peace be unto him, said, "O apostles! Make heaven the place of your treasure, for surely, the heart of man is where his treasure is."[37]

Commentary:

This report corresponds to Matthew 6:19-21, which further explains that worldly treasures are subject to rusting, becoming corrupted, or being stolen by thieves. The treasures of Paradise however, which include God's love and recognition, are everlasting. That is where our eyes and hearts are to be set upon, rather than the fleeting distractions of this world.

---

[36] Sahih al-Bukhari, Book 81, Hadith 28.
https://sunnah.com/bukhari:6439
[37] Ibn Kathir, *al-Bidaya wa al-Nihaya*, Volume 2, pp. 107.

كَانَ عِيسَى عَلَيْهِ السَّلَامُ لَا يَخْبَأُ غَدَاءً لِعِشَاءٍ , وَلَا عِشَاءً لِغَدَاءٍ ,
وَيَقُولُ: مَعَ كُلِّ يَوْمٍ وَلَيْلَةٍ رِزْقُهَا , لَيْسَ لَهُ بَيْتٌ يُخْرَبُ وَقِيلَ لَهُ: أَلَا
تَتَزَوَّجُ؟ قَالَ: أَتَزَوَّجُ امْرَأَةً تَمُوتُ؟ وَقِيلَ لَهُ: أَلَا تَبْنِي بَيْتًا؟ قَالَ: إِنِّي
عَلَى طَرِيقِ السَّبِيلِ

Jesus, peace be unto him, would not store something from the morning for the evening, nor would he store something in the evening for the morning. He would say, "With each day and night is its provision."

He did not have a house that would break down. It was said to him, "Will you not marry?"

He said, "Shall I marry a woman who will inevitably die?"

It was also said to him, "Will you not build a house?"

He said, "I am on a wayfaring path."[38]

بَيْنَمَا عِيسَى ابْنُ مَرْيَمَ عَلَيْهِمَا السَّلَامُ يَسِيحُ فِي بَعْضِ بِلَادِ الشَّامِ إِذِ
اشْتَدَّ بِهِ الْمَطَرُ وَالرَّعْدُ وَالْبَرْقُ فَجَعَلَ يَطْلُبُ شَيْئًا يَلْجَأُ إِلَيْهِ فَرُفِعَتْ لَهُ

---

38 Abu Nu`aym, *Hilyat al-Awliya'*, Volume 7, pp. 237.

خَيْمَةٌ مِنْ بَعِيدٍ فَأَتَاهَا فَإِذَا فِيهَا امْرَأَةٌ فَحَادَ عَنْهَا فَإِذَا هُوَ بِكَهْفٍ فِي

جَبَلٍ فَأَتَاهُ فَإِذَا فِي الْكَهْفِ أَسَدٌ فَوَضَعَ يَدَهُ عَلَيْهِ ثُمَّ قَالَ: إِلَهِي

جَعَلْتَ لِكُلِّ شَيْءٍ مَأْوًى وَلَمْ تَجْعَلْ لِي مَأْوًى، فَأَجَابَهُ الْجَلِيلُ جَلَّ

جَلَالُهُ: مَأْوَاكَ عِنْدِي فِي مُسْتَقَرٍّ مِنْ رَحْمَتِي لَأُزَوِّجَنَّكَ يَوْمَ الْقِيَامَةِ

مِائَةَ حَوْرَاءَ خَلَقْتُهُنَّ بِيَدِي وَلَأُطْعِمَنَّ فِي عُرْسِكَ أَرْبَعَةَ آلَافِ عَامٍ كُلُّ

يَوْمٍ مِنْهَا كَعُمْرِ الدُّنْيَا وَلَآمُرَنَّ مُنَادِيًا يُنَادِي: أَيْنَ الزُّهَّادُ فِي دَارِ الدُّنْيَا

زُورُوا عُرْسَ الزَّاهِدِ عِيسَى ابْنِ مَرْيَمَ

Jesus, the son of the Mary, peace be unto them, was wandering in one of the lands of the Levant when the rain, thunder, and lightning intensified. He hurried to find something to take refuge in. He saw a tent that was far away. When he went to it, he found a woman [alone] therein. He went away and found a cave in a mountain. When he went to it, he saw a lion therein.

He laid his hand on it and said, "My God! You have granted a safehouse to everyone, but You have not granted a safehouse to me."

So, the Glorious and Majestic God said, "Your safehouse is with Me, in the stable of My mercy. On the Day of Judgment, I will marry you to one hundred houris that I have created with My own two hands. At your wedding, I will feed [the guests] for four thousand years, each day of which is the equivalent to a lifetime in this world. I will command a caller to call: 'Where are the ascetics of the world? Go and visit the wedding of the [supreme] ascetic, Jesus the son of Mary.'"[39]

قَالَ الْحَوَارِيُّونَ: يَا عِيسَى مَنْ أَوْلِيَاءُ اللهِ الَّذِينَ لَا خَوْفٌ عَلَيْهِمْ وَلَا هُمْ يَحْزَنُونَ؟ قَالَ عِيسَى عَلَيْهِ السَّلَامُ: «الَّذِينَ نَظَرُوا إِلَى بَاطِنِ الدُّنْيَا حِينَ نَظَرَ النَّاسُ إِلَى ظَاهِرِهَا , وَالَّذِينَ نَظَرُوا إِلَى آجِلِ الدُّنْيَا حِينَ نَظَرَ النَّاسُ إِلَى عَاجِلِهَا , فَأَمَاتُوا مِنْهَا مَا يَخْشَوْنَ أَنْ يَشِينَهُمْ , وَتَرَكُوا مَا عَلِمُوا أَنْ سَيَتْرُكُهُمْ , فَصَارَ اسْتِكْثَارُهُمْ مِنْهَا اسْتِقْلَالًا , وَذِكْرُهُمْ إِيَّاهَا فَوَاتًا , وَفَرَحُهُمْ مِمَّا أَصَابُوا مِنْهَا حُزْنًا , فَمَا عَارَضَهُمْ مِنْ نَيْلِهَا رَفَضُوهُ , وَمَا عَارَضَهُمْ مِنْ رِفْعَتِهَا بِغَيْرِ الْحَقِّ وَضَعُوهُ , وَخَلِقَتِ الدُّنْيَا عِنْدَهُمْ فَلَيْسُوا يُجَدِّدُونَهَا , وَخَرِبَتْ بُيُوتُهُمْ فَلَيْسُوا يُعَمِّرُونَهَا , وَمَاتَتْ فِي صُدُورِهِمْ فَلَيْسُوا يُحْيُونَهَا بَعْدَ مَوْتِهَا , بَلْ يَهْدِمُونَهَا فَيَبْنُونَ بِهَا آخِرَتَهُمْ , وَيَبِيعُونَهَا فَيَشْتَرُونَ بِهَا مَا يَبْقَى لَهُمْ , وَرَفَضُوهَا فَكَانُوا فِيهَا هُمُ الْفَرِحِينَ , وَنَظَرُوا إِلَى أَهْلِهَا صَرْعَى قَدْ خَلَتْ بِهِمُ الْمُثَلَاتُ , وَأَحْيَوْا ذِكْرَ الْمَوْتِ , وَأَمَاتُوا ذِكْرَ الْحَيَاةِ , يُحِبُّونَ اللهَ عَزَّ وَجَلَّ وَيُحِبُّونَ ذِكْرَهُ

[39] Abu Nuʿaym, *Hilyat al-Awliya'*, Volume 10, pp. 136.

وَيَسْتَضِيئُونَ بِنُورِهِ وَيُضِيئُونَ بِهِ , لَهُمْ خَيْرٌ عَجِيبٌ , وَعِنْدَهُمُ الْخَبَرُ
الْعَجِيبُ , بِهِمْ قَامَ الْكِتَابُ وَبِهِ قَامُوا , وَبِهِمْ نَطَقَ الْكِتَابُ وَبِهِ نَطَقُوا
, وَبِهِمْ عُلِمَ الْكِتَابُ وَبِهِ عَمِلُوا , وَلَيْسُوا يَرَوْنَ نَائِلًا مَعَ مَا نَالُوا , وَلَا
أَمَانًا دُونَ مَا يَرْجُونَ , وَلَا خَوْفًا دُونَ مَا يَحْذَرُونَ» قَالَ الشَّيْخُ رَحِمَهُ
اللهُ تَعَالَى : وَهُمُ الْمَصُونُونَ عَنْ مُرَامَقَةِ حَقَارَةِ الدُّنْيَا بِعَيْنِ الِاغْتِرَارِ ,
الْمُبْصِرُونَ صُنْعَ مَحْبُوبِهِمْ بِالْفِكْرِ وَالِاعْتِبَارِ

The apostles said, "O Jesus! Who are the Friends of God who will neither fear nor grieve?"

Jesus, peace be unto him, said, "Those who look to the inner nature of this world whilst the people [only] look to its outer nature. They are those who look to the lasting aspects of this world whilst the people [only] look to its fleeting aspects. They have deserted the aspects of it that would bring them shame. They have abandoned that which they knew would [inevitably] abandon them. For them, taking much from the world became taking little. Thinking about it became disregarding it. Their glee over what they could take from it became grief. They rejected the suggestion to seize it. They denied its false exaltation. When their world becomes antiquated, they do not bother renewing it. When their homes break down, they do not bother rebuilding them. They do not bother reviving what has died in their heart [of this world] – rather, they destroy it so that they may build their

Hereafter; and they sell it so that they may purchase that which will last for them. They have rejected this world, so they are the ones who achieve happiness in it. They look to its people as though they are bygone proverbs of the past. They enliven the remembrance of death, and they deaden the remembrance of life. They love God and they love remembering Him. They are illuminated in His light, and they enlighten by it. For them is astounding goodness and astounding tidings. Through them, the scripture is established, and through it, they are established. Through them, the scripture speaks, and through it, they speak. Through them, the scripture is known, and through it, they work. They neither see the fruit of their labour nor a safeguard besides that which they hope for. They have no fear except in that which they have been admonished about."[40]

Commentary:

The Friends of God (*awliyā'ullāh*) are His allies and His near ones. They are the supreme believers whom God loves. They go above and beyond what is obligatory and attain God's nearness through worship and high morals. They may not even be messengers or prophets, but instead, they are akin to saints. Since the *awliyā'* have submitted themselves fully to God's will, harming the *awliyā'* is an act of war against God.

---

[40] Ibid, Volume 1, pp.9.

The Quran describes most people as knowing "what is apparent of this life" but being neglectful of the Hereafter. (Quran 30:7) The *awliyā'* however have renounced worldliness and put all their hope in God. For this, God gives them surreal insight and ability, He grants them all their prayers, and He becomes their refuge. God even hates to cause the *awliyā'* to die, because He hates letting them down in any way.[41] [42]

بَلَغَنِي أَنَّ عِيسَى عَلَيْهِ السَّلَامُ قَالَ لِأَصْحَابِهِ: أَجِيعُوا أَنْفُسَكُمْ

وَأَظْمِئُوهَا وَأَعْرُوهَا وَأَنْصِبُوهَا لَعَلَّ قُلُوبَكُمْ أَنْ تَعْرِفَ اللهَ عَزَّ وَجَلَّ

Jesus, peace be unto him, said to his companions, "Starve your ego, parch it, strip it, and straighten it, so that your hearts may know God."[43]

Commentary:

Jesus said, "Blessed are the pure in heart: for they shall see God." (Matthew 5:8)

Our ego is constantly sizing-up our wealth, beauty, nobility, intelligence, and fame. The ego only wants more, and it can

---

[41] Sahih al-Bukhari, Book 81, Hadith 91.
https://sunnah.com/bukhari:6502
[42] Kulayni, *al-Kafi*, Volume 2, Chapter 145, Hadith 8.
[43] Abu Nu`aym, *Hilyat al-Awliya'*, Volume 2, pp. 370.

never be fully satisfied. Our ego is constantly offended and ungrateful. It is afraid of losing control, rather than trusting the One in control of everything.

The believer should always question their own intention – does he act for God's glory or for his own? The believer should give others excuses rather than constantly giving himself excuses. It is only through self-observation and self-accountability (*murāqaba wa muḥāsaba*) that one can know God. Otherwise, the ego will blur one's vision; and he will only worship himself or a god of his own making.

كَانَ عِيسَى عَلَيْهِ السَّلَامُ يَلْبَسُ الشَّعْرَ، وَيَأْكُلُ الشَّجَرَ، وَيَبِيتُ حَيْثُ أَمْسَى، لَمْ يَكُنْ لَهُ وَلَدٌ يَمُوتُ، وَلَا بَيْتٌ يُخَرَّبُ وَلَا يُخَبِّئُ شَيْئًا لِغَدٍ

Jesus, peace be unto him, would wear hair, eat [from] trees, and sleep wherever the night would befall him. He did not have a child that could die, nor a house that could break down; nor would he store anything for tomorrow.[44]

Commentary:

If we have tomorrow, we will have sustenance for tomorrow. The day we die is the day that our sustenance runs dry. Jesus

---

[44] Ibid, Volume 3, pp. 273.

did not busy himself with the collection and upkeep of possessions – that was not his goal. His prescription for the spiritual illness of his people at his time was a high dose of asceticism. If one finds themselves consumed by worldliness, then perhaps minimalism will restore them too.

قَالَ عِيسَى عَلَيْهِ السَّلَامُ لِلْحَوَارِيِّينَ: بِحَقٍّ أَقُولُ لَكُمْ، إِنَّ أَشَدَّكُمْ جَزَعًا عَلَى الْمُصِيبَةِ أَشَدُّكُمْ حُبًّا لِلدُّنْيَا

Jesus, peace be unto him, said to the apostles, "In truth, I tell you: The most terrified of you from calamities is the most intense in his love for worldliness."[45]

Commentary:

Attachment to the world will inevitably lead one to suffer. One should only invest emotion into something if he is prepared to eventually lose it. We only take our deeds with us in the next world, not our possessions.

---

[45] Ibid, Volume 4, pp. 67.

قَالَ عِيسَى عَلَيْهِ السَّلَامُ لِرَجُلٍ مِنْ أَصْحَابِهِ، وَكَانَ غَنِيًّا: " تَصَدَّقَ

بِمَالِكَ. فَكَرِهَ ذَلِكَ، فَقَالَ عِيسَى عَلَيْهِ السَّلَامُ: مَا يُدْخِلُ الْغِنَى

الْجَنَّةَ

Jesus, peace be unto him, said to a wealthy man from among
his companions, "Give of your wealth in charity."

He disliked that, so Jesus, peace be unto him, said, "The rich
shall not enter Paradise."[46]

Commentary:

This exchange can be found in Matthew 19:21-24, where Jesus
says, "If thou wilt be perfect, go and sell that thou hast, and
give to the poor, and thou shalt have treasure in heaven: and
come and follow me ... a rich man shall hardly enter into the
kingdom of heaven. And again I say unto you, It is easier for a
camel to go through the eye of a needle, than for a rich man
to enter into the kingdom of God."

Concerned, the disciples asked, "Who then can be
saved?" Jesus looked at them and said, "With man this is
impossible, but with God all things are possible."

A similar analogy is made in the Quran: "Those that deny Our
signs and act arrogantly against them – the gates of heaven

---

[46] Ibid, Volume 4, Page 119.

shall not be opened to them, nor shall they enter Paradise until the camel passes through the eye of the needle. Thusly we recompense the criminals." (7:40)

Material wealth is apportioned by the Creator. Poverty is certainly a test of one's patience, but a poor man's reckoning in the Hereafter will not be like that of a rich man. The rich have much more to answer for – did they obtain their wealth ethically? Were they charitable with their wealth? Were they wasteful? Did they support an unjust cause? Did they give their workers and their clients their proper dues? Did they spend their money on sin? On top of this, the wealthy are often victims of envy and theft; and for these reasons among others, one should not desire to be rich, as they open themselves up to insurmountable danger.

By the same token, Islam as a religion still recognizes hierarchies. Even if we attempted to equalize man in wealth, beauty, intelligence, power, and status, we would fail, because God distributes these qualities based on His wisdom. These qualities are not always good for a person, nor are they always bad for a person. In the story of Joseph, Joseph had an inimitable beauty and lineage, and he was his father's favourite child. However, that only led to the envy of his brothers and the plotting of transgressing women.

The poor once came to the Prophet Muhammad ﷺ, and they complained that the rich were able to collect more good deeds than the poor, as the wealthy people of Medina were giving their money in charity and freeing slaves. The Prophet ﷺ instructed them to recite the *tasbīḥ Fāṭima* after every prayer.

69

This would uplift their status with God. Eventually, the rich became aware of this deed, and they began incorporating it into their practice as well. The poor returned to the Prophet, and the Prophet simply quoted the verse, "That is the blessing of God: He gives it to whomever He wills." (62:4).[47] [48]

أَنَّهُ لَيْسَ مِنْ كَلِمَةٍ كَانَتْ تُقَالُ لِعِيسَى عَلَيْهِ السَّلَامُ أَحَبُّ إِلَيْهِ مِنْ أَنْ يُقَالَ هَذَا الْمِسْكِينُ

وَبِإِسْنَادِهِ قَالَ عِيسَى عَلَيْهِ السَّلَامُ: لَيْسَ كَمَا أُرِيدُ وَلَكِنْ كَمَا تُرِيدُ، وَلَيْسَ كَمَا أَشَاءُ وَلَكِنْ كَمَا تَشَاءُ

There was not a title that Jesus would be called by that was more beloved to him than "this needy person (hadhal miskīn)."

Jesus, peace be unto him, said, "Not as I will, but as You will. Not as I want, but as You want."[49]

Commentary:

[47] Riyad al-Salihin, Hadith 572. https://sunnah.com/riyadussalihin:572
[48] Saduq, al-Amali, pp. 128.
[49] Abu Nu`aym, Hilyat al-Awliya', Volume 6, pp. 125.

One of God's 99 names is *al-Ghanī*. This is colloquially understood as "the Rich", but more accurately, it means "the Needless." God is self-sufficient and free of all needs, whilst the believer is in need of His sustenance and guidance. Just as the Bible speaks of "the Servant", such titles are honorific and noble, because no person is really a master, and no person is really self-sufficient. Remarkably, one of the Jewish Christian sects that carried the apostolic message was the Ebionites. In Hebrew, they were called *evyonīm*, which means "the poor ones."

When the Romans were coming to arrest Jesus, he fell on his face in prayer, saying, "Let this cup pass from me. Nevertheless, not as I will, but as thou wilt." (Matthew 26:39) Jesus did not desire crucifixion, and he beseeched God for His support. Nonetheless, Jesus was ready to accept God's will, whatever it may be. A Muslim, by definition, is "one who submits his will to God." Jesus' surrender to God's will is an act of *islām*. God is our all-knowing Patron, and the believer should put his full trust in God when he is tried.

قال عيسى بن مريم (عليه السلام): الدينار داء الدين ، والعالم
، طبيب الدين ، فإذا رأيتم الطبيب يجر الداء إلى نفسه فاتهموه
. واعلموا أنه غير ناصح لغيره

Jesus the son of Mary, peace be unto him, said, "Wealth is the disease of religion, and the scholar is the doctor of religion. So, if you see the doctor drawing the disease to himself, then suspect him, and know that he is not an adviser unto others."[50]

Commentary:

This is an interesting report in light of "render unto Caesar the things that are Caesar's, and unto God the things that are God's." (Mark 12:17) Of course, one cannot have politics without ethics; and much of religion is social and economic in nature. However, it is often said that "Power corrupts; absolute power corrupts absolutely." Jesus knew that wealth has its challenges and temptations, and that the true scholar should not have a proclivity toward wealth and power. The "scholars for dollars" made religion into a business, and business runs on cost and benefit, rather than on right and wrong. This dollar-scholar will only speak on topics that make him the most money, and he will not tell his audience that which they do not want to hear. Once the market and the whims run religion, then it becomes another idol in need of smashing.

Scholars should do their best to have monetizable skills and professions, so that their religion does not become their main

---

[50] Saduq, *al-Khisal*, Chapter 93, Hadith 91.

source of livelihood. The best work is done for free, seeking God's contentment.

There will always be a need for full-time scholars, and they should be taken care of by the community of believers, but their work is a service, not a commercial enterprise.

قام عيسى بن مريم (عليه السلام) خطيبا في بني إسرائيل فقال: يا بني إسرائيل لا تأكلوا حتى تجوعوا، وإذا جعتم فكلوا ولا - تشبعوا، فانكم إذا شبعتم غلظت رقابكم، وسمنت جنوبكم، ونسيتم ربكم

Jesus the son of Mary, peace be unto him, gave a sermon to the Children of Israel, so he said, "O Children of Israel! Do not eat until you are hungry. If you are hungry, then eat, but do not fill yourselves. If you fill yourselves, your necks will thicken, your sides will fatten, and your Lord will be forgotten."[51]

Commentary:

Prophet Muḥammad ﷺ encouraged us to only eat when we are hungry, and to stop eating before we are full. He encouraged us to only fill one third of our stomachs with food

---

[51] Al-Barqi, *Kitab al-Mahasin*, 447.

and one third with beverages. He encouraged voluntary fasting long before the experts declared that it was healthy. He encouraged us to share our meals with our families, neighbours, and community. He encouraged us to seek natural remedies in healthy foods for common illnesses.

Faith in God is often stronger in developing countries than it is in developed countries. The hungry feel the need for God in a way that the satiated do not. They feel gratitude in a different way as well. Sometimes, God puts us in a needy state to remind us that only He is the Needless.

قَالَ عِيسَى عَلَيْهِ السَّلَامُ: «حُبُّ الْفِرْدَوْسِ , وَخَشْيَةُ جَهَنَّمَ يُورِثَانِ الصَّبْرَ عَلَى الْمَشَقَّةِ وَيُبَاعِدَانِ الْعَبْدَ مِنْ رَاحَةِ الدُّنْيَا»

Jesus, peace be unto him, said, "The love of Paradise and the fear of Hell will produce patience in hardship, and divert a worshiper from finding peace in worldlines."[52]

Commentary:

A genuine belief in the Hereafter will produce uprightness in a person. Without a belief in Hell, if we are utilitarian, we will take whichever shortcut we can to get to pleasure. A truly

---

[52] Abu Nu`aym, *Hilyat al-Awliya'*, Volume 8, pp. 142.

moral person will take a loss if it means doing the right thing. Anyone that sticks to an ethic will inevitably face a situation where they must sacrifice time, wealth, reputation, or physical health. It is faith that gives a person patience in that hardship.

Faith is a little piece of heaven in your heart – in it, you find peace amidst tribulation; but when you sin, the light leaves your heart. Once it re-enters your heart, you feel the regret of the sin, and you rectify it with repentance.

كان عيسى بن مريم عليه السلام، يقول لاصحابه: يا بني آدم،

اهربوا من الدنيا إلى الله، وأخرجوا قلوبكم عنها، فإنكم لا تصلحون

لها ولا تصلح لكم، ولا تبقون فيها ولا تبقى لكم، هي الخداعة

الفجاعة، المغرور من اغتر بها، المغبون من اطمأن إليها، الهالك

من أحبها وأرادها، فتوبوا إلى بارئكم، واتقوا ربكم، واخشوا يوما لا

يجزي والد عن ولده، ولا مولود هو جاز عن والده شيئا. أين

آباؤكم، أين أمهاتكم، أين إخوتكم، أين أخواتكم، أين أولادكم؟

دعوا فأجابوا، واستودعوا الثرى، وجاوروا الموتى، وصاروا في الهلكى،

وخرجوا عن الدنيا، وفارقوا الاحبة، واحتاجوا إلى ما قدموا، واستغنوا

عما خلفوا، فكم توعظون، وكم ترجرون، وأنتم لاهون ساهون! مثلكم في الدنيا مثل البهائم، همتكم بطونكم وفروجكم، أما تستحيون ممن خلقكم؟! وقد وعد من عصاه النار ولستم ممن يقوى على النار، ووعد من أطاعه الجنة ومجاورته في الفردوس الاعلى، فتنافسوا فيه وكونوا من أهله، وأنصفوا من أنفسكم، وتعطفوا على ضعفائكم، وأهل الحاجة منكم، وتوبوا إلى الله توبة نصوحا، وكونوا عبيدا أبرارا ولا تكونوا ملوكا جبابرة ولا من العتاة الفراعنة المتمردين على من قهرهم بالموت، جبار الجبابرة رب السماوات ورب الارضين، وإله الاولين والآخرين، مالك يوم الدين، شديد العقاب، أليم العذاب، لا ينجو منه ظالم، ولا يفوته شئ، ولا يعزب عنه شئ، ولا يتوارى منه شئ أحصى كل شئ علمه، وأنزله منزلته في جنة أو نار. ابن آدم الضعيف، أين تهرب ممن يطلبك في سواد ليلك وبياض نهارك وفي كل حال من حالاتك، قد أبلغ من وعظ، وأفلح من اتعظ

Jesus the son of Mary, peace be unto him, would say to his companions:

"O children of Adam! Run from this world to God, and take your hearts out of it, for surely, you will not fix it, nor will it fix you; you will not remain in it, nor will it remain for you. It is deception and grief. Conceited is he who is deceived by it, dismayed is he who is contented by it, and destroyed is he who loves it and wants it. Repent to your Maker, be conscious of your Lord, and fear a Day in which a father will not be rewarded on behalf of his son, nor will a son be rewarded on behalf of his father.

Where are your fathers, where are your mothers, where are your brothers, where are your sisters, where are your children? They were called back [by your Lord] and were made to answer. They were placed in graves adjacent to the dead and joined the perished ones. They left this world and departed from their loved ones. They became in need of what was placed before them [in the Hereafter] and became needless of what they left behind [in this world]. So, how much exhortation and how much rebuke do you need while you are distracted and heedless?!

Your like in this world is like that of the beasts – your concern is over your stomachs and your privates. Are you not ashamed before Him that created you? He has promised the Fire to those who disobey Him, and you are not capable of overpowering the Fire. He has promised Paradise and living in the Highest Heaven to those who obey Him. So, compete for it and be of its people.

Be fair to yourselves. Be gracious to the weak and the needy among you. Repent sincerely to God. Be righteous servants, and do not be arrogant kings or haughty pharaohs who oppose Him who conquers them with death – He is the Mighty of the mighty, the Lord of the heavens and the Earths,

God of the former and the latter peoples, the Master of the Day of Requital, the stern in reprisal, and the harsh in torment. No oppressor will be delivered from Him, nor does He miss anything, nor is anything left out with Him, nor is anything hidden from Him – His knowledge accounts for all things, and He will place it in Paradise or in the Fire.

O weak child of Adam! Where will you run from Him who seeks you in the darkness of your night, and in the illumination of your day, and in every condition of yours? He who is exhorted becomes informed, and he who gives heed will succeed."[53]

أَنَّ عِيسَى ابْنَ مَرْيَمَ، كَانَ يَقُولُ يَا بَنِي إِسْرَائِيلَ عَلَيْكُمْ بِالْمَاءِ الْقَرَاحِ

وَالْبَقْلِ الْبَرِّيِّ وَخُبْزِ الشَّعِيرِ وَإِيَّاكُمْ وَخُبْزَ الْبُرِّ فَإِنَّكُمْ لَنْ تَقُومُوا

بِشُكْرِهِ

Jesus the son of Mary used to say, "O Children of Israel! Betake to pure water, vegetables of the land, and barley bread. Beware of wheat bread, for you will not be grateful enough for it."[54]

---

[53] Saduq, al-Amali, pp. 650.
[54] Malik, al-Muwatta', Book 49, Hadith 27.

قال عيسى بن مريم (عليه السلام) للحواريين: يا بني إسرائيل، لا تأسوا على ما فاتكم من دنياكم، إذا سلم دينكم، كما لا يأسى أهل الدنيا على ما فاتهم من دينهم إذا سلمت دنياهم

Jesus the son of Mary, peace be unto him, said to the apostles, "O Children of Israel! Do not regret what you miss from your world when your religion advances for you, just as the people of this world do not regret what they miss from their religion when their world advances for them."[55]

مَنْ شَرِبَ بِيَدِهِ وَهُوَ يَقْدِرُ عَلَى إِنَاءٍ يُرِيدُ التَّوَاضُعَ كَتَبَ اللَّهُ لَهُ بِعَدَدِ أَصَابِعِهِ حَسَنَاتٍ وَهُوَ إِنَاءُ عِيسَى ابْنِ مَرْيَمَ عَلَيْهِمَا السَّلَامُ إِذْ طَرَحَ الْقَدَحَ فَقَالَ أُفٍّ هَذَا مَعَ الدُّنْيَا

The Prophet Muhammad ﷺ said, "He who drinks out of his hand instead of a glass, wanting to be humble, God shall grant him good deeds equivalent to his fingers. [The hand] is the glass of Jesus the son of Mary, peace be unto them. He threw away the cup and said, "Ah, this is from this world."[56]

---

[55] Saduq, *al-Amali*, pp. 585.
[56] Sunan Ibn Maja, Book 30, Hadith 61.

The Value of Wisdom

قال عيسى بن مريم :من تعلم وعلم وعمل دعي عظيما في ملكوت
السماء

Jesus the son of Mary said, "He who learns, teaches, and works shall be called great in the kingdom of heaven."[57]

Commentary:

---

[57] Abu Nu`aym, *Hilyat al-Awliya'*, Volume 6, pp. 93.

In Matthew 5:19, Jesus says, "Whosoever therefore shall break one of these least commandments, and shall teach men so, he shall be called the least in the kingdom of heaven: but whosoever shall do and teach them, the same shall be called great in the kingdom of heaven."

One of the key points of divide between Christians and Muslims is on the role of divine law. Protestants especially emphasize that faith alone is the key to salvation in the Hereafter. Catholics and Orthodox Christians observe sacraments and fasts, but they are otherwise divorced from Mosaic law. Christians believe that Jesus Christ "fulfilled" the Law – that the object of the laws of Moses was to act as prophecies for the coming of Jesus. In this sense, Jesus manifests the Law in its entirety, and his death on the cross puts an end to the exacting expectations of the Law. This brings about a new, enlightened, messianic age where the people rise above the need for divine laws.

Matthew 5, when read in context, does not preach antinomianism. If anything, it preaches a more ambitious Law – the spirit of the Law. Jesus does not just prohibit adultery, but he prohibits thinking about adultery, because it is not enough to ritualistically tick the boxes of divine law. One must actualize it from within and from without, and let it cleanse their spirit along with their body, as Christ did. He did not tell the people not to pray, but to pray sincerely in private, so as to not draw attention to themselves in pride.

In the Epistle of James, James makes a robust case for faith *and* works being needed for salvation (James 2:14-26). The

Quran, similarly, repeats this mantra of faith and works over forty times. In Acts 15, some of the Christians believed that the laws of Moses were even binding on the gentiles; and Simon Peter and James ruled that gentiles were to follow certain dietary and sexual laws.

Faith still supersedes works, and grace still supersedes judgment – this is the case in both Christianity and Islam.

روي أن عيسى عليه السلام قال :لا خير في علم لا يعبر معك الوادي ويعبر بك النادي.

Jesus, peace be unto him, said, "There is no good in knowledge that takes you across the playground but does not take you across the valley."[58]

Commentary:

It is reported that the Prophet Muhammad ﷺ found a group of people standing around a man in the mosque. He said, "Who is this?" It was said, "An intellectual." He said, "What is an intellectual?" So, they said to him, "He is the most knowledgeable of people in the genealogy of the Arabs, the

---

[58] Ibn Kathir, *al-Bidaya wa al-Nihaya*, Volume 2, pp. 107.

days of Jahiliyya, and Arabic poetry." So, the Prophet Muhammad ﷺ said, "That is a knowledge that does not harm one who is unaware of it and does not benefit one who is aware of it." Then, the Prophet ﷺ said, "Surely, knowledge is of three types: a firm sign, a just obligation, and an established tradition. All else is superfluous."[59] [60] [61]

The three branches of knowledge that bring the most benefit to our life and our Hereafter are metaphysics, ethics, and praxis. In metaphysics, there is the knowledge of logic, mathematics, and science. In ethics, there is the knowledge of morality, rights, and responsibilities. In praxis, there is the running of families, institutions, and everyday tasks.

One can learn about a worldly matter, but that is not our purpose here. The "playground" in this report is the place of leisure, sport and play; whilst the valley is the gulf between us and our Lord.

أن عيسى قام في بني إسرائيل فقال: يا معشر الحواريين لا تحدثوا

بالحكم غير أهلها فتظلموها ولا تمنعوها أهلها فتظلموهم والأمور

[59] Sunan Abi Dawud, Book 19, Hadith 1.
https://sunnah.com/abudawud:2885
[60] Sunan al-Nasa'i, Book 10, Hadith 6. https://sunnah.com/nasai:782
[61] Al-Kafi, Volume 1, Page 32, Hadith 1.
https://web.archive.org/web/20181007024457/http://www.yasoob.c
om/books/htm1/m012/09/no0979.html

ثلاثة :أمر تبين رشده فاتبعوه، وأمر تبين غيه فاجتنبوه، وأمر اختلف

عليكم فيه فردوا علمه إلى الله عز وجل

Jesus stood among the Children of Israel and said, "O
apostles! Do not impart wisdom to other than its folk, or you
will have oppressed it; and do not prevent it from its folk, or
you will have oppressed them. There are three matters: a
matter whose guidance is evident, so follow it; a matter whose
error is evident, so avoid it; and a matter about which you
have differed, so cede its knowledge to the Glorious and
Majestic God."[62]

Commentary:

It is reported that the Prophet Muhammad ﷺ said, "We, the
prophets, were commanded to speak to the people at the level
of their intellect."[63] [64] The prophets had the complex task of
translating celestial knowledge into Earthly terms. They used
literary devices, including parables and analogies, to reach the
people where they were at.

Some higher forms of knowledge must be treated delicately. If
the nuclear codes were disseminated freely, destruction would

[62] Ibn Kathir, *al-Bidaya wa al-Nihaya*, Volume 2, pp. 107.
[63] Ghazali, Ihya' `Ulum al-Din, Volume 1, Page 144.
[64] Al-Kafi, Volume 1, Page 23, Hadith 15.

be guaranteed. Likewise, sensitive religious knowledge can be misused to manipulate others. It is easily misunderstood outside of its proper context, and so its bearers can be oppressed by those who misconstrue it.

The Prophet Muhammad ﷺ also said, "Wisdom is the lost belonging of the believer: wherever he finds it, it is rightfully his."[65] [66] It is mandatory for every believing man and woman to seek knowledge wherever it is. Thus, knowledge should not be kept away from believers, because that deprivation could harm them in this world and the Hereafter.

قال عيسى :لا تطرحوا اللؤلؤ إلى الخنزير فإن الخنزير لا يصنع باللؤلؤ

شيئا، ولا تعطوا الحكمة من لا يريدها فإن الحكمة خير من اللؤلؤ

ومن لا يريدها شر من الخنزير.

Jesus said, "Do not cast a pearl to the swine, for surely, the swine cannot do anything with a pearl. Do not give wisdom to one who does not want it, for surely, wisdom is better than a pearl, and one who does not want it is worse than swine."[67]

[65] Jami' al-Tirmidhi, Book 41, Hadith 43.
https://sunnah.com/tirmidhi:2687
[66] Kulayni, *al-Kafi*, Volume 8, Hadith 186.
[67] Ibn Kathir, *al-Bidaya wa al-Nihaya*, Volume 2, pp. 107.

Commentary:

This report is similar to Matthew 7:6, where Jesus says, "Give not that which is holy unto the dogs, neither cast ye your pearls before swine, lest they trample them under their feet, and turn again and rend you." Wisdom is being compared to pearls, as pearls were among the costliest of all jewels. However, wisdom, ultimately, is far superior to jewels.

It is reported that ʿAlī b. Abī Ṭālib said: "God has given angels intellect and no lust, and He has given animals lust and no intellect, and He has given the children of Adam both. So, whoever can overcome his lust with his intellect is better than the angels, and whoever lets his lust overcome his intellect is worse than the animals."[68]

قال لأصحابه: أنتم ملح الأرض فإذا فسدتم فلا دواء لكم، وإن فيكم خصلتين من الجهل: الضحك من غير عجب والصبحة من غير سهر

He said to his companions, "You are the salt of the Earth. If you become corrupted, then there is no remedy for you.

---

[68] ʿIlal al-Sharāʾiʿ, Volume 1, Chapter 6, Hadith 1.

Beware of two characteristics of ignorance: laughing at something that is not astonishing and awaking without keeping vigil [at night]."[69]

Commentary:

This report corresponds to Matthew 5:13, where Jesus says, "Ye are the salt of the earth: but if the salt have lost his savour, wherewith shall it be salted? It is thenceforth good for nothing, but to be cast out, and to be trodden under foot of men." This is part of Jesus' famous "Sermon on the Mount", where Jesus praises the meek. Today, the English expression "salt of the Earth" refers to good, honest people who persevere amidst demanding circumstances.

Salt was a valuable commodity due to its use as a preservative. It also provides energy and helps the body prevent illness. Salt is used in small quantities, and it is barely visible, yet it safeguards and transforms a meal. Similarly, the "salt of the Earth" may not be prominent, but they keep a community from collapsing.

It is reported that the Prophet Muhammad ﷺ said, "I am to the prophets as salt is to food."[70] This may be a reference to the practice of starting and ending each meal with salt, as Muhammad ﷺ was the first prophet to be created and the last

---

[69] Abu Nu`aym, *Hilyat al-Awliya'*, Volume 5, pp. 73.
[70] Tibb al-Nabi by al-Mustaghfiri.

to be sent. It may further be a reference to Muhammad
preserving the message of the prophets. Lastly, it may be a
reference to him being the "finishing touch" to the prophetic
tradition after it was gradually built from Adam onward.

مَنْ عَمِلَ بِمَا يَعْلَمُ وَرَّثَهُ اللَّهُ مَا لَمْ يَعْلَمْ

He said, "He who acts on what he knows, God will grant him
that which he does not know."[71]

Commentary:

The interpretation of this report can be found in a popular
saying attributed to Jaʿfar al-Ṣādiq, in which he says,
"Knowledge is not attained from an abundance of discursive
learning. Rather, it is not but a light that has been placed in
the heart of one whom God wishes to guide. If you want
knowledge, then first demand sincere worship from yourself,
then seek knowledge by applying it and asking God to help
you understand it."[72]

This genre of reports emphasizes that the key to sacred
knowledge is not just research, but sincerity and praxis. Sacred
knowledge is granted by God to the believer in proportion to

---

[71] Abu Nuʿaym, *Hilyat al-Awliya'*, Volume 10, pp. 15.
[72] Shahid al-Thani, *Munayat al-Murid*, pp. 167.

his nearness to Him. It is a form of knowledge that cannot be measured by IQ or any other compass, but by wisdom, insight, and clairvoyance. The Prophet Muhammad ﷺ said, "Beware the discernment of the believer, for surely, he sees by the light of God."[73] [74]

قَالَ عِيسَى عَلَيْهِ السَّلَامُ: إِنَّ لِلْحِكْمَةِ أَهْلًا , فَإِنْ وَضَعْتَهَا فِي غَيْرِ أَهْلِهَا ضُيِّعَتْ , وَإِنْ مَنَعْتَهَا مِنْ أَهْلِهَا ضُيِّعَتْ , كُنْ كَالطَّبِيبِ , يَضَعُ الدَّوَاءَ حَيْثُ يَنْبَغِي

Jesus, peace be unto him, said, "Wisdom has its folk. If it is given to other than its folk, it is wasted; and if it is prevented from its folk, it is wasted. Be like a doctor that places the medicine where it is needed."[75]

قَالَ عِيسَى عَلَيْهِ السَّلَامُ: «كُونُوا أَوْعِيَةَ الْكِتَابِ , وَيَنَابِيعَ الْعِلْمِ , وَسَلُوا اللهَ رِزْقَ يَوْمٍ بِيَوْمٍ , وَلَا يَضُرُّكُمْ أَنْ لَا يُكْثِرَ لَكُمْ»

---

[73] Al-Kafi, Volume 1, Page 218.
[74] Jami' al-Tirmidhi, Book 47, Hadith 179.
https://sunnah.com/tirmidhi:3127
[75] Abu Nu`aym, *Hilyat al-Awliya'*, Volume 7, pp. 273.

Jesus, peace be unto him, said, "Be vessels of the scripture and sources of knowledge. Ask God for sustenance day by day – even if it is not in abundance, this shall not harm you."[76]

وَقَالَ: إِنَّ الرِّزْقَ إِذَا نُقِبَ لَمْ يَصْلُحْ أَنْ يَكُونَ فِيهِ الْعَسَلُ وَإِنَّ قُلُوبَكُمْ
قَدْ نُقِبَتْ فَلَا تَصْلُحُ فِيهَا الْحِكْمَةُ

He said, "If there is a hole in a jar, it is not suitable to put honey in it. Surely, your hearts have been punctured, so they are not a suitable place for wisdom."[77]

Commentary:

Honey is sweet, nourishing, and valuable. It must be encased in a jar that is durable and whole. Likewise, a corrupted heart cannot properly hold wisdom. One cannot fill a cup that is already full. One cannot awaken one who pretends to be asleep. Hearts must be made humble, sincere, and sensitive before they can properly receive the light of faith.

---

[76] Ibid, Volume 7, pp. 274.
[77] Ibid, Volume 8, pp. 206.

Corrupt Scholars

قال: يا علماء السوء جعلتم الدنيا على رؤوسكم والآخرة تحت

أقدامكم قولكم شفاء وعملكم داء مثلكم مثل شجرة الدفلى تعجب

من رآها وتقتل من أكلها

Jesus said, "O evil scholars! You have put this world over your heads, and you have put the Hereafter beneath your feet. Your words are a remedy, but your works are a malady. You are like oleander, which astonishes those who see it and kills those who consume it."[78]

---

[78] Ibn Kathir, *al-Bidaya wa al-Nihaya*, Volume 2, pp. 108.

Commentary:

A genre of Jesus' reports in Islamic sources deals with corrupt scholars. These scholars talk the talk, but they fail to walk the walk. Hence, Jesus says, "That except your righteousness shall exceed the righteousness of the scribes and Pharisees, ye shall in no case enter into the kingdom of heaven." (Matthew 5:20)

Oleander is a shrub that grows in temperate climates. It grows beautiful clusters of bright pink flowers. However, oleander has toxic compounds, and its bitterness is unpalatable to humans and most animals. Likewise, evil preachers dazzle those who listen to them, but they do not practice what they preach. Jesus says, "O generation of vipers, how can ye, being evil, speak good things?" (Matthew 12:34)

وعنه أنه قيل له: من أشد الناس فتنة؟ قال زلة العالم فإن العالم إذا
زل يزل بزلته عالم كثير

It was said to him, "What is the greatest calamity for the people?"

He said, "The fall of a scholar, for if he falls, his fall causes many people to fall."[79]

---

[79] Ibid, Volume 2, pp. 108.

Commentary:

A righteous scholar is the pillar of his community. He is the emissary of divine knowledge, and he sets order in a society of chaotic forces. When God wishes to take knowledge away from a people, He removes its scholars.[80] When a scholar becomes corrupted, their corruption trickles down to the people who rely on them. This was the case, arguably, with the Pharisees and Sadducees.

قال عيسى: يا علماء السوء جلستم على أبواب الجنة فلا تدخلوها ولا تدعون المساكين يدخلونها، إن شر الناس عند الله عالم يطلب الدنيا بعلمه

Jesus said, "O evil scholars! You have sat at the gates of Paradise, but you do not enter it, nor do you call the poor to it. Surely, the evillest of people with God is a scholar who seeks this world with his knowledge."[81]

---

[80] Sahih Muslim, Book 47, Hadith 22.
[81] Ibn Kathir, *al-Bidaya wa al-Nihaya*, Volume 2, pp. 108.

Commentary:

This report corresponds to Matthew 23:13, where Jesus says, "But woe unto you, scribes and Pharisees, hypocrites! For ye shut up the kingdom of heaven against men: for ye neither go in yourselves, neither suffer ye them that are entering to go in."

Corrupt scholars focus their energy on the rich and powerful, and they neglect the poor. Till now, the homeless, the addicts, and the prisoners are ignored, even though they are the ones that need the most help from compassionate people.

فِي كَلَامِ عِيسَى ابْنِ مَرْيَمَ عَلَيْهِ السَّلَامُ: تَعْمَلُونَ لِلدُّنْيَا وَأَنْتُمْ تُرْزَقُونَ

فِيهَا بِغَيْرِ الْعَمَلِ وَلَا تَعْمَلُونَ لِلْآخِرَةِ وَأَنْتُمْ لَا تُرْزَقُونَ فِيهَا إِلَّا بِالْعَمَلِ،

وَيْلَكُمْ عُلَمَاءَ السُّوءِ الْأَجْرَ تَأْخُذُونَ وَالْعَمَلَ تُضَيِّعُونَ يُوشِكُ رَبُّ الْعَمَلِ

أَنْ يَطْلُبَ عَمَلَهُ وَتُوشِكُونَ أَنْ تَخْرُجُوا مِنَ الدُّنْيَا الْعَرِيضَةِ إِلَى ظُلْمَةِ

الْقَبْرِ وَضِيقِهِ، اللهُ يَنْهَاكُمْ عَنِ الْخَطَايَا كَمَا يَأْمُرُكُمْ بِالصَّلَاةِ وَالصِّيَامِ،

كَيْفَ يَكُونُ مِنْ أَهْلِ الْعِلْمِ مَنْ سَخِطَ رِزْقَهُ وَاحْتَقَرَ مَنْزِلَتَهُ وَقَدْ عَلِمَ أَنَّ

ذَلِكَ مِنْ عِلْمِ اللهِ وَقُدْرَتِهِ، كَيْفَ يَكُونُ مِنْ أَهْلِ الْعِلْمِ مَنِ اتَّهَمَ اللهَ

فِيمَا قَضَى لَهُ فَلَيْسَ يَرْضَى بِشَيْءٍ أَصَابَهُ، كَيْفَ يَكُونُ مِنْ أَهْلِ الْعِلْمِ

مَنْ دُنْيَاهُ عِنْدَهُ آثَرُ عِنْدَهُ مِنْ آخِرَتِهِ وَهُوَ فِي دُنْيَاهُ أَفْضَلُ رَغْبَةً، كَيْفَ

يَكُونُ مِنْ أَهْلِ الْعِلْمِ مَنْ مَسِيرُهُ إِلَى آخِرَتِهِ وَهُوَ مُقْبِلٌ عَلَى دُنْيَاهُ وَمَا

يَضُرُّهُ أَشْهَى إِلَيْهِ - أَوْ قَالَ: أَحَبُّ إِلَيْهِ - مِمَّا يَنْفَعُهُ

Jesus the son of Mary, peace be unto him, said, "You work for this world, even though you are given sustenance in it without work. Yet, you do not work for the Hereafter, even though you will only be given sustenance in it with your work. Be wary of evil scholars, who take rewards and lose deeds. The Lord of deeds will ask about their work, and you will go from this expansive world to the darkness and narrowness of your grave. God prohibits you from sins just as He commands you to pray and fast. How can one be a person of knowledge if he is discontented with his sustenance and despising of his status, whilst knowing that these are from the knowledge and power of God? How can one be a person of knowledge if he blames God for what He has decreed for him, and is dissatisfied with what befalls him? How can one be a person of knowledge if this world is more important to him than the Hereafter, and he is desirous in this world? How can one be a person of knowledge when he journeys to the Hereafter whilst relishing in this world and loving what is harmful to him more than what benefits him?"[82]

---

[82] Abu Nu`aym, *Hilyat al-Awliya'*, Volume 6, pp. 279.

قال عيسى ابن مريم على نبينا وآله وعليه السلام: ويل للعلماء السوء

!كيف تلظى عليهم النار؟.

Jesus the son of Mary, peace be unto him, as well as our
Prophet and his family, "Woe to bad scholars! How the Fire
will engulf them."[83]

Commentary:

Once, the Prophet Muhammad ﷺ said to Abu Dharr, "There
is something I fear more for my nation than the Antichrist."
Abu Dharr became afraid and asked, "O Messenger of God,
which thing is that?" The Prophet replied, "Misguided and
deviant scholars."[84]

---

[83] Kulayni, *al-Kafi*, Volume 1, pp. 47.
[84] Musnad Ahmad b. Hanbal, Hadith 21,334.

God's Revelations

كان فيما وعظ الله تبارك وتعالى به عيسى بن مريم (عليه السلام)

أن قال له: يا عيسى، أنا ربك ورب آبائك، اسمي واحد، وأنا الاحد

المتفرد بخلق كل شئ، وكل شئ من صنعي، وكل خلقي إلي

راجعون. يا عيسى، أنت المسيح بأمري، وأنت تخلق من الطين

كهيئة الطير باذني، وأنت تحيي الموتي بكلامي، فكن إلي راغبا،

ومني راهبا، فإنك لن تجد مني ملجأ إلا إلي. يا عيسى، اوصيك

وصية المتحنن عليك بالرحمة حين حقت لك مني الولاية بتحريك

مني المسرة فبوركت كبيرا، وبوركت صغيرا حيثما كنت، أشهد أنك

عبدي ابن أمتي. يا عيسى، أنزلني من نفسك كهمك، واجعل ذكري لمعادك، وتقرب إلي بالنوافل، وتوكل علي أكفك، ولا تول غيري فآخذ لك.

يا عيسى، اصبر على البلاء، وارض بالقضاء، وكن كمسرتي فيك فإن مسرتي أن أطاع فلا أعصى. يا عيسى، أحي ذكري بلسانك وليكن ودي في قلبك. يا عيسى، تيقظ في ساعات الغفلة، واحكم لي بلطيف الحكمة. يا عيسى، كن راغبا راهبا، وأمت قلبك بالخشية. يا عيسى، راع الليل لتحري مسرتي، واظمأ نهارك ليوم حاجتك عندي. يا عيسى، نافس في الخير جهدك، لتعرف بالخير حيثما توجهت. يا عيسى، احكم في عبادي بنصحي، وقم فيهم بعدلي، فقد أنزلت عليك شفاء لما في الصدور من مرض الشيطان. يا عيسى، لا تكن جليسا لكل مفتون. يا عيسى، حقا أقول: ما آمنت بي خليقة إلا خشعت لي، وما خشعت لي إلا رجت ثوابي، فأشهدك أنها آمنة من عقابي ما لم تغير أو تبدل سنتي. يا عيسى ابن البكر البتول، إبك على نفسك بكاء من قد ودع الاهل، وقلى الدنيا وتركها لاهلها، وصارت رغبته فيما عند الله. يا عيسى، كن مع ذلك تلين الكلام، وتفشي السلام، يقظان إذا نامت عيون

98

الابرار، حذارا للمعاد، والزلازل الشداد، وأهوال يوم القيامة، حيث لا ينفع أهل ولا ولد ولا مال. يا عيسى، اكحل عينيك بميل الحزن إذا ضحك البطالون. يا عيسى، كن خاشعا صابرا، فطوبى لك إن نالك ما وعد الصابرون. يا عيسى، رح من الدنيا يوما فيوما، وذق ما قد ذهب طعمه، فحقا أقول: ما أنت إلا بساعتك ويومك، فرح من الدنيا بالبلغة، وليكفك الخشن الجشب، فقد رأيت إلى ما تصير ومكتوب ما أخذت وكيف أتلفت. يا عيسى، إنك مسؤول، فارحم الضعيف كرحمتي إياك، ولا تقهر اليتيم. يا عيسى، إبك على نفسك في الصلاة، وانقل قدميك إلى مواضع الصلوات، وأسمعني لذاذة نطقك بذكري، فإن صنيعي إليك حسن. يا عيسى، كم من أمة قد أهلكتها بسالف ذنب قد عصمتك منه. يا عيسى، ارفق بالضعيف، وارفع طرفك الكليل إلى السماء، وادعني فإني منك قريب، ولا تدعني إلا متضرعا إلي وهمك هم واحد فإنك متى تدعني كذلك أجبك. يا عيسى، إن لم أرض بالدنيا ثوابا لمن كان قبلك، ولا عقابا لمن انتقمت منه. يا عيسى، إنك تفنى وأنا أبقى ومني رزقك، وعندي ميقات أجلك، وإلي إيابك، وعلي حسابك فسلني، ولا تسأل غيري، فيحسن منك الدعاء ومني الاجابة. يا

عيسى، ما أكثر البشر وأقل عدد من صبر! الاشجار كثيرة، وطيبها قليل، فلا يغرنك حسن شجرة حتى تذوق ثمرتها. يا عيسى، لا يغرنك المتمرد علي بالعصيان، يأكل رزقي، ويعبد غيري، ثم يدعوني عند الكرب فأجيبه، ثم يرجع إلى ما كان عليه، أفعلي يتمرد، أم لسخطي يتعرض؟ فبي حلفت لآخذنه أخذة ليس له منها منجى ولا دوني ملتجأ، أين يهرب من سمائي وأرضي؟ يا عيسى، قل لظلمة بني إسرائيل: لا تدعوني والسحت تحت أحضانكم والاصنام في بيوتكم، فإني وأيت أن أجيب من دعاني، وأن أجعل إجابتي إياهم لعنا عليهم حتى يتفرقوا. يا عيسى، كم أجمل النظر وأحسن الطلب، والقوم في غفلة لا يرجعون، تخرج الكلمة من أفواههم لا تعيها قلوبهم، يتعرضون لمقتي، ويتحببون بي إلى المؤمنين. يا عيسى، ليكن لسانك في السر والعلانية واحدا وكذلك فليكن قلبك وبصرك واطو قلبك ولسانك عن المحارم وغض طرفك عما لا خير فيه، فكم ناظر نظرة زرعت في قلبه شهوة ووردت به موارد الهلكة. يا عيسى، كن رحيما مترحما، وكن للعباد كما تشاء أن يكون العباد لك، وأكثر ذكر الموت ومفارقة الاهلين ولا تله فإن اللهو يفسد صاحبه، ولا تغفل فإن الغافل مني بعيد

100

واذكرني بالصالحات حتى اذكرك. يا عيسى، تب إلي بعد الذنب وذكر بي الاوابين، وآمن بي، وتقرب إلى المؤمنين، ومرهم يدعوني معك، وإياك ودعوة المظلوم، فإني وأيت على نفسي أن أفتح لها باب من السماء، وأن أجيبه ولو بعد حين. يا عيسى، اعلم أن صاحب السوء يغوي، وأن قرين السوء يردي، فاعلم من تقارن واختر لنفسك إخوانا من المؤمنين. يا عيسى، تب إلي فإنه لا يتعاظمني ذنب أن أغفره وأنا أرحم الراحمين. يا عيسى، اعمل لنفسك في مهلة من أجلك قبل أن لا يعمل لها غيرك، واعبدني ليوم كألف سنة مما تعدون، فإني أجزي بالحسنة أضعافها، وإن السيئة توبق صاحبها، فامهد لنفسك في مهلة، وتنافس في العمل الصالح، فكم من مجلس قد نهض أهله وهم مجارون من النار. يا عيسى، ازهد في الفاني المنقطع، وطأ رسوم منازل من كان قبلك، فادعهم وناجهم، هل تحس منهم من أحد، فخذ موعظتك منهم، واعلم أنك ستلحقهم في اللاحقين. يا عيسى، قل لمن تمرد بالعصيان وعمل بالادهان، ليتوقع عقوبتي، وينتظر إهلاكي إياه، سيصطلم مع الهالكين. طوبى لك يا بن مريم ثم طوبى لك أن أخذت بأدب إلهك الذي يتحنن عليك ترحما، وبدأك بالنعم منه تكرما، وكان لك

101

في الشدائد، لا تعصه - يا عيسى - فإنه لا يحل لك عصيانه، قد عهدت إليك كما عهدت إلى من كان قبلك، وأنا على ذلك من الشاهدين. يا عيسى، ما أكرمت خليقة بمثل ديني، ولا أنعمت عليها بمثل رحمتي. يا عيسى، اغسل بالماء منك ما ظهر، وداو بالحسنات ما بطن، فإنك إلي راجع. يا عيسى، شمر، فكل ما هو آت قريب، واقرأ كتابي وأنت طاهر، وأسمعني منك صوتا حزينا قال: وكان فيما وعظ الله عز وجل به عيسى بن مريم (عليه السلام) أيضا أن قال له: يا عيسى، لا تأمن إذا مكرت مكري، ولا تنس عند خلوتك بالذنب ذكري. يا عيسى، تيقظ ولا تيأس من روحي وسبحني مع من يسبحني، وبطيب الكلام فقدسني. يا عيسى، إن الدنيا سجن ضيق منتن الريح وحش، وفيها ما قد ترى مما قد ألح عليه الجبارون، فإياك والدنيا فكل نعيمها يزول، وما نعيمها إلا قليل. يا عيسى، إن الملك لي وبيدي وأنا الملك، فإن تطعني أدخلتك جنتي في جوار الصالحين. يا عيسى، ادعني دعاء الغريق الذي ليس له مغيث. يا عيسى، لا تحلف باسمي كاذبا فيهتز عرشي غضبا. يا عيسى، الدنيا قصيرة العمر، طويلة الأمل، وعندي دار خير مما يجمعون. يا عيسى، قل لظلمة بني إسرائيل، كيف أنتم

صانعون إذا أخرجت لكم كتابا ينطق بالحق، فتنكشف سرائر قد كتمتموها. يا عيسى، قل لظلمة بني إسرائيل غسلتم وجوهكم ودنستم قلوبكم، أبي تغترون. أم علي تجترئون، تتطيبون بالطيب لاهل الدنيا وأجوافكم عندي بمنزلة الجيف المنتنة، كأنكم أقوام ميتون، يا عيسى، قل لهم: قلموا أظفاركم من كسب الحرام وأصموا أسماعكم عن ذكر الخنا ، واقبلوا علي بقلوبكم فإني لست أريد صوركم. يا عيسى، افرح بالحسنة فإنها لي رضى، وابك على السيئة فإنها لي سخط، وما لا تحب أن يصنع بك فلا تصنعه بغيرك، وإن لطم خدك الايمن فاعط الايسر، وتقرب إلي بالمودة جهدك، وأعرض عن الجاهلين. يا عيسى، قل لظلمة بي إسرائيل، الحكمة تبكي فرقا مني، وأنتم بالضحك تهجرون ، أتتكم براءتي أم لديكم أمان من عذابي، أم تتعرضون لعقوبتي؟ فبي حلفت - لاتركنكم مثلا للغابرين. ثم إني اوصيك - يا بن مريم البكر البتول بسيد المرسلين وحبيبي منهم أحمد، صاحب الجمل الاحمر، والوجه الاقمر المشرق بالنور، الطاهر القلب، الشديد البأس، الحيي المتكرم، فإنه رحمة للعالمين، وسيد ولد آدم عندي، يوم يلقاني أكرم السابقين علي، وأقرب المرسلين مني، العربي الامي، الديان

بديني، الصابر في ذاتي، المجاهد للمشركين ببدنه عن ديني. يا
عيسى، آمرك أن تخبر به بني إسرائيل، وتأمرهم أن يصدقوا ويؤمنوا به
ويتبعوه وينصروه. قال عيسى: إلهي، من هو؟ قال: يا عيسى أرضه
فلك الرضا. قال: اللهم رضيت، فمن هو؟ قال: محمد رسول الله
إلى الناس كافة، أقربهم مني منزلة، وأوجبهم عندي شفاعة، طوباه
من نبي، وطوبى لأمته إن هم لقوني على سبيله، يحمده أهل
الارض، ويستغفر له أهل السماء، أمين ميمون مطيب، خير الماضين
والباقين عندي، يكون في آخر الزمان، إذا خرج أرخت السماء
عزاليها ، وأخرجت الارض زهرتها، وأبارك فيما وضع يده عليه، كثير
الازواج، قليل الاولاد، يسكن بكة موضع أساس إبراهيم. يا عيسى
دينه الحنيفية، وقبلته مكية، وهو من حزبي وأنا معه، فطوباه طوباه
له الكوثر والمقام الاكبر من جنات عدن، يعيش أكرم معاش
ويقبض شهيدا، له حوض أبعد من مكة إلى مطلع الشمس من
رحيق مختوم، فيه آنية مثل نجوم السماء، ماؤه عذب، فيه من كل
شراب، وطعم كل ثمار في الجنة، من شرب منه شربة لم يظمأ
بعدها أبدا، أبعثه على فترة بينك وبينه، يوافق سره علانيته، وقوله
فعله، لا يأمر الناس إلا بما يبدأهم به، دينه الجهاد في عسر ويسر

تنقاد له البلاء، ويخضع له صاحب الروم على دينه ودين أبيه إبراهيم، يسمي عند الطعام، ويفشي السلام، ويصلي والناس نيام، له كل يوم خمس صلوات متواليات، يفتتح بالتكبير، ويختتم بالتسليم ويصف قدميه في الصلاة كما تصف الملائكة أقدامها، ويخشع لي قلبه، النور في صدره، والحق في لسانه، وهو مع الحق حيثما كان تنام عيناه ولا ينام قلبه، له الشفاعة، وعلى أمته تقوم الساعة، ويدي فوق أيديهم إذا بايعوه، فمن نكث فإنما ينكث على نفسه، ومن أوفى وفيت له بالجنة، فمر ظلمة بني إسرائيل لا يدرسوا كتبه، ولا يحرفوا سنته، وأن يقرئوه السلام، فإن له في المقام شأنا من الشأن يا عيسى، كل ما يقربك مني، فقد دللتك عليه، وكل ما ياعدك مني قد نهيتك عنه، فارتد لنفسك. يا عيسى، إن الدنيا حلوة وإنما استعملك فيها لتطيعني، فجانب منها ما حذرتك، وخذ منها ما أعطيتك عفوا، انظر في عملك نظر العبد المذنب الخاطئ، ولا تنظر في عمل غيرك نظر الرب، وكن فيها زاهدا، ولا ترغب فيها فتعطب. يا عيسى، اعقل وتفكر، وانظر في نواحي الارض كيف كان عاقبة الظالمين. يا عيسى، كل وصيتي نصيحة لك، وكل قولي حق، وأنا الحق المبين، وحقا أقول لئن أنت عصيتني بعد أن أنبأتك

105

،مالك من دوني ولي ولا نصير. يا عيسى، ذلل قلبك بالخشية

وانظر إلى من هو أسفل منك، ولا تنظر إلى من هو فوقك، واعلم أن

رأس كل خطيئة وذنب حب الدنيا، فلا تحبها فإني لا أحبها. يا

عيسى، أطب بي قلبك ، وأكثر ذكري في الخلوات، واعلم أن

سروري أن تبصبص إلي، وكن في ذلك حيا ولا تكن ميتا. يا

،عيسى، لا تشرك بي شيئا، وكن مني على حذر، ولا تغتر بالصحة

،ولا تغبط نفسك، فإن الدنيا كفئ زائل، وما أقبل منها كما أدبر

فنافس في الصالحات جهدك، وكن مع الحق حيثما كان، وإن

قطعت وأحرقت بالنار فلا تكفر بي بعد المعرفة، ولا تكن مع

الجاهلين. يا عيسى، صب لي الدموع من عينيك، واخشع لي

بقلبك. يا عيسى، استغفرني في حالات الشدة، فإني أغيث

المكروبين، وأجيب المضطرين، وأنا أرحم الراحمين

From among that which God exhorted Jesus the son of Mary, peace be unto him, is that He said:

O Jesus! I am your Lord and the Lord of your forefathers. My name is One, and I am the Only, Alone, who created everything, and all things are made by My making, and all will return to Me.

106

O Jesus! You are the Messiah by My command, and you create from clay that which is in the form of a bird by My permission, and you revive the dead by My words. So, be attentive to Me, and devote yourself to Me, and you will not find a place of refuge except with Me.

O Jesus! I assign to you a compassionate bequest with mercy, until the order is ordained from Me and I am pleased. You are blessed as an adult, and you are blessed as an infant, so long that you testify that you are My servant, the son of my maidservant. Bring Me into your self, like your concerns, and make My remembrance your retreat, and come closer to Me with voluntary prayers, and rely on Me and I will suffice for you, and do not rely on other than Me or I will abandon you.

O Jesus! Be patient upon calamities and be pleased with destiny. Be like My felicity in you, for My felicity is in being obeyed and not disobeyed.

O Jesus! Give life to My remembrance with your tongue and bring My love into your heart.

O Jesus! Be vigilant in the hours of neglect and consider Me of gentle wisdom.

O Jesus! Be attentive, devoted, and set your heart upon fear [of Me].

O Jesus! Shepherd the night in search of My felicity, and glorify Me in your day for your needs from Me.

O Jesus! Strive to complete the good, and you will be known by the good wherever you may turn to.

O Jesus! Judge among My servants by My instructions, and stand among them by My justice, for I have descended a healing upon you for that which is in the chests from the illness of Satan.

O Jesus! Do not be seated with the infatuated.

O Jesus! Truly I say, no creature has believed in Me except that it gains humility towards Me, and it does not gain humility towards Me except that it hoped for My reward. Bear witness that it is safe from My punishment, and that I do not replace or change My way.

O Jesus, son of the chaste virgin, weep for your self with a weeping like one who bids farewell to his family and reject the world and leave it to its people and be like one who has taken interest in that which is with his God.

O Jesus! Be, with that, soft-spoken, and offer peaceful greetings, and be vigilant when the eyes of the righteous are asleep. Be cautious of the Return, the severe earthquakes, and the horrors of the Day of Resurrection when neither the family, nor the sons, nor wealth will be of any benefit.

O Jesus! Apply the kohl of grief to your eyes whilst the people of falsehood laugh.

O Jesus! Be humble and patient, for blessing is for you if you achieve what has been prepared for the patient.

O Jesus! Leave this world day by day, and taste that which has become tasteless. I truly say, you are with nothing but your hour and your day, so leave this world with provision. Rough [clothes] and plain food will suffice for you, for you have seen what becomes of it. What you take and how you consume it is written.

O Jesus! You are the caretaker, so be merciful to the weak just like My mercy towards you, and do not subdue the orphan.

O Jesus! Weep over yourself in private, and move your feet to the timings of prayer, and let Me hear your sweet [supplication in] remembrance of Me, for My actions to you are good.

O Jesus! How many communities have I destroyed before you for their sins, while I have protected you from that.

O Jesus! Be gentle to the weak and raise your tired eye towards the sky and supplicate to Me, for I am near you. Do not supplicate to Me unless you are beseeching Me, for your concern is one concern. If you supplicate to Me like that, I will answer you.

O Jesus! I was not pleased with presenting this world as a reward for those who came before you, nor as a punishment for those I wanted to seek vengeance from.

O Jesus! You shall be annihilated, and I shall remain. From Me is your sustenance, and with Me is the timing of your term. To Me is your return, and upon Me is your judgment, so ask from Me and do not ask from any other, for the best from you is the supplication, and from Me is its answering.

O Jesus! How numerous are the humans, yet how few in number are the patient! The trees are many, but the good ones are few, so do not be deceived by the beauty of the tree until you have tasted its fruit.

O Jesus! Do not be deceived by a rebellious one who disobeys Me, who eats from My sustenance yet worships something other than Me, who then calls on Me during calamities and I answer him, who then returns to what which he was upon, rebelling against Me or exposing himself to My anger. For I swear by Myself, I will take him with a taking that he will not find a saviour from and find no refuge except in Me. Where will he run to, from My skies and My earth?

O Jesus! Say to the unjust of the Children of Israel, 'Do not supplicate to Me whilst your illegal earnings are under your hearts and the idols are in your houses', for I have undertaken that I shall answer he who supplicates to Me, and that I shall make my response a curse upon those [who disobey] until they disperse.

O Jesus! How have I given them lengthy consideration, and goodly fulfillment, but the people are in neglect and they will not return. The words come out of their mouths, but their hearts are not congruent. They expose themselves to My abhorrence yet display their love for my nearness to the believers.

O Jesus! Make your tongue one, both in private and in public, and do the same with your heart and your sight. Turn your heart and your tongue away from that which I have prohibited and restrain your sight from that which has no good in it. How many glances of a looker have planted lust into his heart and returned him by it to the fountains of destruction.

O Jesus! Be merciful and compassionate and be as you would like the servants to be towards you. Increase your remembrance of death and the dispersal of families. Do not trifle, for trifling corrupts its doer. Do not neglect, for the neglectful is far from Me. Remember Me with righteous deeds so that I may remember you [in return].

O Jesus! Repent to Me after the sin, and remember Me by the penitence, and believe in Me, and come closer to the believers by Me, and urge them to supplicate to Me with you. Be weary of the supplication of the oppressed, for I have taken an oath upon Myself to open for it the doors of the heavens in acceptance and answer him even if after a while.

O Jesus! Know that the companion of evil infects, and the consort of evil destroys. Know the one whom you befriend and choose brothers for yourself from the believers.

O Jesus! Repent to Me, for there is not a grand sin that I do not forgive, and I am the Most Merciful of the merciful ones.

Work for yourself during your term before someone else works for it, and worship for a day [which will be counted] like a thousand years of your measurement, during which I will exponentially reward the good deeds, and the sins shall remain with their doers. Prepare yourself in this term, and complete the righteous deeds, for how many gatherings have dispersed and its people uprooted - and they are neighbours in the Fire.

O Jesus! Abstain from the fleeting, that which will be cut-off, and avoid the expenses of the houses of those who were before you. Call to them and whisper to them. Do [you think] any of them feel? Take up your protection from them and know that you will follow them [in fleeting].

O Jesus! Tell he who rebels against Me with arrogance and opposing deeds to expect My punishment and to await My destruction of him, so that he will be joined with those who are destroyed.

Blessing is for you, O son of Mary. Then, blessing is for you if you take the etiquette of your God, who is compassionate towards you and Merciful. He initiated you with favours from Him honourably, and He was for you amidst difficulties, and you did not disobey Him.

O Jesus! It is not lawful for you to disobey Him who has taken a covenant with you, just as He has taken a covenant to those who were before you. And I am one of witnesses over that.

O Jesus! I have not honoured any creature with the like of My religion, nor have I bestowed a favour unto it with the like of My mercy.

O Jesus! Wash what is apparent with the water with you, and heal what is hidden with your good deeds, for you will be returning to Me.

O Jesus! I have continually given to you that which I had favoured you with. I sought from you a loan for your self, so if you are stingy with it, you will be with the destroyed ones.

O Jesus! Adorn yourself with religion and the love of the poor, and walk upon the earth with humility, and pray upon its places, for it is all pure.

O Jesus! Wrap up [your affairs], for all that comes is close by. Read My Book whilst you are pure and make Me listen to your sorrowful voice.

O Jesus! There is no good in enjoyment that does not last. The life of the enjoyer is in decline.

O son of Mary! If you were to see what I have prepared for My righteous friends, your heart would melt, and your being would leave you in desire for it. There is no abode like the Abode of the Hereafter, in which the neighbours are the righteous, and the Angels of Proximity enter upon them, and they are those who will meet the Day of Resurrection safe from its horrors. An Abode in which there is no change in its bliss, nor are its people in any decline.

O son of Mary! Compete for it with the competitors, for it is the desire of the desirous, and it is of beautiful scenery. Blessing is for you, O son of Mary, if you are of the workers for it, along with your forefathers Adam and Abraham, in Paradise and Bliss, not seeking to exchange it or transfer from it. That is how I deal with the pious.

O Jesus! Flee to Me like those who flee from the flaming Fire; the Fire of chains and torture. No soul that enters it will ever be relieved from its grief. Its part is like the part of the dark night. He who is delivered from it is successful, and he who is not delivered from it will be of the destroyed. This is the Abode of the Tyrants, the hardened oppressors, and every harsh and rude one, and every arrogant boaster.

O Jesus! It is a calamitous abode for those who reside in it, and a calamitous dwelling for the unjust. I caution you so that you may be informed about it.

O Jesus! Be, wherever you are, an observer for Me, and bear witness that I have created you, and you are My servant, and I have formed you, and I have sent you down to the Earth.

O Jesus! Two tongues are not proper for one mouth, nor are two hearts proper for one chest, and same with the minds.

O Jesus! Do not wake up as a disobedient one, and do not indulge in vanities whilst awake, and turn yourself away from the tempting vices, and every desire that distances you from Me. So, migrate from it, and know that you are to Me at the position of a Trustworthy Messenger. So be cautious of Me and know that your world will deliver you to Me, and I will take you upon My knowledge. So, humble your self with My remembrance, and have a revering heart whenever you remember Me - conscious whilst the neglectful sleep.

O Jesus! This is My advice to you and My trust to you, so take it from Me. I am the Lord of the Worlds.

O Jesus! If My servant is patient beside Me, the reward for his deeds will be upon Me. It is upon him to supplicate to Me, and I am sufficient in taking revenge from those who disobey Me. Where will the unjust run to from Me?

O Jesus! Speak good words, and be, wherever you are, a sagacious sage.

O Jesus! Bestow the good deeds towards Me until it is mentioned in My presence, and betake to My bequest, for there is a healing for the hearts therein.

O Jesus! Do not hesitate when you plan My plan, and do not forget My remembrance in the privacy of this world.

O Jesus! Take account of yourself by returning to Me until I distribute the rewards for what the workers have worked towards. Those are the ones who will receive their reward, and I am the best of givers.

O Jesus! You were created by My Word, and Mary gave birth to you by My command, and the messenger I sent to her was My Spirit Gabriel the Trustworthy from the Angels, until you stood upon the Earth alive and walking. All of that had been encompassed by My knowledge.

O Jesus! Zechariah is at the status of your father and the guardian of your mother. When he entered her presence in the prayer-niche, he found [heavenly] sustenance there with her. Your counterpart John is from My creatures, and I gifted him to his mother after old age had set in and she had no strength in her. I wanted, by that, to display My authority to her, and to display My power in you. The most beloved of you to Me is he who is obedient to Me and most fearful of Me.

O Jesus! Be vigilant, and do not despair from My Spirit. Glorify Me with those who glorify Me and sanctify Me with good words.

O Jesus! How can the servants disbelieve in Me whilst their forelocks are in My grip, whilst they traverse My Earth, whilst they are ignorant of My favours, and whilst they align with My enemies? And like that, the disbelievers will be destroyed.

O Jesus! Verily, this world is a prison with a rotten smell. The bounty in it is in what you see the tyrants slaughter for. Be wary of this world, for every bounty in it will decline, and there is no bounty in it except for a little.

O Jesus! Reach for Me near your pillow, and you will find Me. Supplicate to Me, and you will be beloved to Me, for I am the most Hearing of the hearers. I answer the supplicant when he supplicates to Me.

O Jesus! Fear Me, and instill fear of Me in My servants so that the sinners may hold from what they are doing, so that no one would be destroyed except those who are aware of it.

O Jesus! Be in awe of Me as you are awed by the beasts and by the death you will encounter, for I created all of those things, so it is Me that they should be awed of.

O Jesus! The Kingdom is Mine and in My Hands, and I am the King, so if you obey Me, I shall enter you into My Paradise amidst righteous neighbours.

O Jesus! If I am angry at you, the happiness of those who are pleased with you will not avail you. If I am pleased with you, the anger of those who are angry will not harm you.

O Jesus! Remember Me in your self, and I will remember you in My Self. Speak of Me in [your] public, and I will speak of you in [My] public, which is better than man's public.

O Jesus! Supplicate to Me with the Supplication of the Drowning (du 'a' al-gharīq), the sorrowful one who has no helper.

O Jesus! Do not swear by Me falsely, for My throne shakes in anger. This world has a short life, but its hopes are protracted. With Me is an Abode that is better than that which you accumulate.

O Jesus! How will you be when I bring out a Book for you which speaks by the truth? You will testify to the secrets that you have concealed, and the deeds you have performed.

O Jesus! Say to the unjust of the Children of Israel, 'You have washed your faces, but left your hearts unclean. Are you trying to deceive Me, or are you being audacious against Me? You are applying fragrance for the people of this world, whilst your insides to Me are at the status of a rotten carcass. It is as if you are a dead people.'

O Jesus! Say to them, 'Cut your fingernails off from unlawful gains, and deafen your hearing from indecency, and turn towards Me with your hearts, for I am not after your appearances.'

O Jesus! Be happy with good deeds, for in them is My pleasure. Weep over sins, for they are a disgrace. Do not like to do for others what you do not like for them to do for you. If one slaps your right cheek, then give him your left. Come closer to Me with love and striving and keep away from the ignorant.

O Jesus! Be humble to the people of good deeds and participate with them in goodness. Be a witness upon them and say to the unjust of the Children of Israel, 'O companions of evil - who are seated upon it - if you do not desist, I will transfigure you into apes and swine.'

O Jesus! Say to the unjust of the Children of Israel, 'Wisdom weeps from its separation from Me, and you laugh whilst fleeing from Me. Has My disavowal come to you? Or have you found security from My punishment? Or are you exposing yourselves to My punishment? I swear by Myself that I will abandon you as an example for the coming generations.'

Then I inform you, O son of Mary the chaste virgin, of the [coming of] the Master of Messengers, My Beloved – he is Ahmad – the owner of the red camel, with a face illuminated with the light of the full moon, the pure heart, the stern in reprisal, the honourable and prestigious. Verily, he is the Mercy to the Worlds, the Master of the Children of Adam on the Day that he will meet Me. He is the most honourable to Me from those who came before, and the closest of the messengers to Me. The Arab, the Trustworthy, the trustee of My religion, the patient in that, the striving against the polytheists with his hands for the sake of My religion. Inform the Children of Israel of this, and order them to ratify him, believe in him, to obey him, and to support him.

Jesus said: My God, who is he, whom if I please it would please You?

God said: He is Muhammad, the Messenger of God to all the people. His status is nearest to Me, and He is the presenter of intercession. Blessing is for him from the prophets, and blessing is for his Nation who will meet Me upon his way. The people of the Earth praise him, and the people of the skies seek forgiveness through him. The trustworthy, the entrusted, the pleasant, the pleasing, the best of the remaining ones to Me, who will come in the End Times. When he appears, the sky will loosen its rainfall, and the Earth will bring out its blossoms, until they see the blessing. I will bless for them whatever he places his hand upon. He will have many wives and few children. He will live in Bacca, the place of the foundation of Ibrahim.

O Jesus! His religion is uprightness, and his direction is right. He is from My party, and I am with him. So, Blessing is for him, then blessing is for him [again]. Al-Kawthar is his, in the greatest position in the Gardens of Eden. His living is more honourable than any life, and he will pass away as a martyr. For him is a Pond that is larger than [the area between] Bacca and the Sunrise. Therein are springs of a Sealed Drink, similar in number to the stars of the sky, and cups similar in number to the grains of the Earth, sweetened therein from every drink and food of every fruit in Paradise. Whoever drinks from it will never thirst again, and that is from what I have apportioned for him and my favour for him upon the epoch between you and him. His private self will match his public self, his words are his actions, and he will not order [a thing to] the people except that he will do it first.

His religion is striving in hardship and in ease. The cities will surrender to him, and the emperor of Rome will yield to him. He will be upon the religion of Ibrahim. He will mention My name when eating, and he will express the greeting of peace. He will pray when the people are asleep. He will pray five prayers every day, calling out to the prayer in sequence, just as an army is called out to with a slogan. He will begin [prayers] with the takbir, and he will end [them] with a *taslīm*. He will line his feet up in prayer just as angels line their feet up. His heart will be humble before Me, as well as his head. The light will be in his chest, and the truth will be upon his tongue - and he will be upon the truth wherever he is.

His origin will be as an orphan, wandering for a time required from him. His eyes will sleep, but his heart will never sleep. Intercession is for him, and the Hour will rise upon his Nation. My Hand will be above their hands, so whoever breaks [My covenant] will have broken it upon himself, and whoever fulfills My covenant to him, I will fulfill him with Paradise. So, command the unjust of the Children of Israel to study his Books, and to not alter his Sunna, and to recite the greetings of peace to him, for his status is of great consequence.

O Jesus! All that brings you closer to Me, I have led you to it, and all that distances you from Me, I have prohibited you from it, so refer to it for your self.

O Jesus! Verily, this world is sweet, and I have utilized you in it, so leave aside that which I have cautioned you from and take that which I have given to you in allowance.

O Jesus! Look to your actions with the consideration of a servant who has sinned and erred. Do not look to the actions of others with the position of the Lord. Be ascetic therein, and do not be allured therein lest you become corrupted.

O Jesus! Think, contemplate, and look around the Earth; see how the unjust have vanished.

O Jesus! All that I have described to you is advice, and all that I have said to you is truth. I am the Manifest Truth, so truth is what I speak, and if you were to disobey Me after I have informed you, there will be no guardian nor a helper for you.

O Jesus! Humble your heart with humility, and look to the one who is below you, and do not look to the one who is above you. Know that the head of all error and sin is love of this world, so do not love it, for I do not love it.

O Jesus! Soften your heart for Me, remember Me very often in private, and know that My pleasure is in your humility before Me, so become alive in that, and do not be dead.

O Jesus! Do not associate partners with Me, and be cautious of Me. Do not be deceived by [good] health, and do not be envious, for this world is like a fleeting shadow. What approaches it is like what it leaves behind. So, compete in righteous deeds with your striving, and be with the truth wherever it may be, even if you are cut or burned with fire. Do not disbelieve in Me after knowing Me. Do not be of the ignorant, for a thing is with a [similar] thing.

O Jesus! Pour your tears out from your eyes for Me, and humble your heart for Me.

O Jesus! Cry out to Me during harsh conditions, for I help the broken, I answer the restless, and I am the Most Merciful of the merciful ones.[85]

---

[85] Saduq, *al-Amali*, pp. 606.

أَوْحَى اللهُ تَعَالَى إِلَى عِيسَى عَلَيْهِ السَّلَامُ يَا عِيسَى عِظْ نَفْسَكَ فَإِنِ

اتَّعَظْتَ فَعِظِ النَّاسَ وَإِلَّا فَاسْتَحْيِ مِنِّي

God revealed to Jesus, peace be unto him, "O Jesus! Exhort
yourself. If you exhort yourself, then exhort the people; and if
you do not, then feel shame before Me."[86]

Commentary:

To exhort is to give glad tidings and warnings, and to urge
one toward faith and righteousness. One should always begin
with themselves before they begin with others. God says in
the Quran, "God changes not what is in a people, until they
change what is in themselves." (13:11)

One can barely change themselves, let alone change society.
However, if a collective of people all work on themselves,
then a true paradigm shift will occur within society.

إِنَّ اللهَ عزوجل أوحى إلى عيسى بن مريم (عليه السلام): يا عيسى،

ما أكرمت خليقة بمثل ديني، ولا أنعمت عليها بمثل رحمتي،

---

[86] Abu Nu`aym, *Hilyat al-Awliya'*, Volume 2, pp. 382.

اغسل بالماء منك ما ظهر، وداو بالحسنات ما بطن، فإنك إلي

راجع، شمر فكل ما هو آت قريب، وأسمعني منك صوتا حزينا

God revealed to Jesus the son of Mary, peace be unto him, "O
Jesus! I have not honoured a creature with the like of My
religion, and I have not blessed it with the like of My grace.
Wash what is apparent with the water with you, and heal
what is hidden with your good deeds, for you will be
returning to Me. Gather [your affairs], for all that comes is
nearby. Let Me hear a sorrowful voice from you."[87]

قال الله تبارك وتعالى لعيسى ابن مريم (عليه السلام): يا عيسى

ليكن لسانك في السر و العلانية لسانا واحدا وكذلك قلبك، إني

احذرك نفسك وكفى بي خبيرا، لا يصلح لسانان في فم واحد ولا

سيفان في غمد واحد ولا قلبان في صدر واحد، وكذلك الاذهان

God said to Jesus the son of Mary, peace be unto him, "O
Jesus! You must have one tongue both in private and in
public -- same with your heart. I warn you of your own self,
and My cognizance is sufficient for you. Two tongues are not
proper for one mouth, nor are two swords proper for one

[87] Saduq, *al-Amali*, pp. 610.

sheath, nor are two hearts proper for one chest, and same with the minds."[88]

Commentary:

God says in the Quran, "God does not put two hearts within one's breast." (Quran 33:4). In this report, He gives further examples of this same principle. It is not proper for one to have a filthy, gossiping tongue in private whilst feigning uprightness in front of the people. One should not give promises in public, only to mock them in private.

Furthermore, one cannot love a thing and love its opposite at the same time. One cannot love his mother and her killer in the same way. Even God said that He loved Jacob and hated Esau. (Malachi 1:2-3) One cannot love God and fight for His enemy at the same time.

One cannot believe in paradoxical ideas either. A and A' cannot both be true at the same time. The law of non-contradiction is a basic logical principle that the universe is governed by.

---

[88] Kulayni, *al-Kafi*, Volume 2, pp. 343.

قال الله عز وجل لعيسى (عليه السلام): يا عيسى اذكرني في
نفسك أذكرك في نفسي واذكرني في ملائك أذكرك في ملاء خير
من ملاء الآدميين، يا عيسى ألن لي قلبك وأكثر ذكري في الخلوات
واعلم أن سروري أن تبصبص إلي وكن في ذلك حيا ولا تكن ميتا

God said to Jesus, peace be unto him, "O Jesus! Remember Me in your self, and I will remember you in My Self. Speak of Me in [your] public, and I will speak of you in [My] public, which is better than man's public. O Jesus! Soften your heart for Me, remember Me very often in private, and know that My pleasure is in your humility before Me. Become alive in that, and do not be dead."[89]

Commentary:

God says in the Quran, "Remember Me, and I will remember you." (2:152) Whoever praises God in public, God will speak about him in His company of angels.

The believer's tongue should regularly be glorifying God in the day and at night.

---

[89] Ibid, Volume 2, pp. 502.

أَوْحَى اللهُ تَعَالَى إِلَى عِيسَى عَلَيْهِ السَّلَامُ: تَزْعُمُ أَنَّكَ لَا تَسْأَلُنِي شَيْئًا

فَإِذَا قُلْتَ مَا شَاءَ اللهُ فَقَدْ سَأَلْتَنِي كُلَّ شَيْءٍ

God revealed to Jesus, peace be unto him, "You contend that you do not ask Me for anything; but when you say, "whatever be the will of God (*mashaAllah*)", you ask Me for everything."[90]

Commentary:

Once one aligns his will with the will of God, he will only want for himself what God wants for him. His prayers will be answered, and he will find peace in all that God gives him.

Zayn al-ʿAbidīn said, "The exalted ranks cannot be reached except by submitting to God, abandoning proposals contrary to His, and being content with what He plans for you. The Friends of God are patient with adversity and misfortunes in a way that others are not, so because of that, God grants them success in all their requests. However, with that, they only want from Him what He wants for them."[91]

---

[90] Abu Nuʿaym, *Hilyat al-Awliya'*, Volume 6, pp. 201.
[91] Saduq, *al-Amali*, pp. 537.

Noble Character

مر عيسى وأصحابه بجيفة فقالوا: ما أنتن ريحها فقال: ما أبيض
أسنانها

Jesus and his companions passed by a corpse. They said, "How rancid is its smell!"

So, he said, "How white are its teeth!"[92]

Commentary:

---

[92] Ibn Kathir, *al-Bidaya wa al-Nihaya*, Volume 2, pp. 106.

This is a popular story in Muslim circles that has even made its way to Jewish and Christian sources. The corpse is often identified as a carcass of a dog. Ibn Paquda (d. 1120 AD), the Jewish Andalusian scholar, mentions this account and anonymously refers to Christ as "one of the pious" (a *Hasid*).[93] Howard J. Chidley (d. 1966 AD), a clergyman from the United Church of Christ, retells this story in his *Fifty-Two Story Talks to Boys and Girls*.[94]

The story shows Jesus' ability to see the bright side of an overtly unpleasant encounter. Some Muslim commentators noted that Jesus was avoiding backbiting (*ghiba*) – instead of speaking negatively of the carcass, he may have wanted to speak positively, so as to avoid evil gossip.

كان عيسى يضع الطعام لأصحابه ويقوم عليهم ويقول: هكذا فاصنعوا بالقرى

Jesus would put food out for his companions, and he would stand among them and say, "Put food out for your guests."[95]

---

[93] Daniel Haberman, *Duties of the Heart*, pp. 577
[94] Howard J Chidley, *Fity-Two Story Talks to Boys and Girls*, Christ and the Dog, https://biblehub.com/library/chidley/fifty-two_story_talks_to_boys_and_girls/christ_and_the_dog.htm
[95] Ibn Kathir, *al-Bidaya wa al-Nihaya*, Volume 2, pp. 106.

Commentary:

Feeding others is a basis of hospitality. It is a way for brethren to share a good mood. There is little blessing in a meal that is eaten alone. Always offer to share your meal with others, and to buy that which satiates them.

بَلَغَنَا أَنَّ عِيسَى، عَلَيْهِ السَّلَامُ مَرَّ هُوَ وَرَجُلٌ مِنْ بَنِي إِسْرَائِيلَ مِنْ

حَوَارِيِّهِ بِلِصٍّ فِي قَلْعَةٍ لَهُ فَلَمَّا رَآهُمَا اللِّصُّ أَلْقَى اللهُ فِي قَلْبِهِ التَّوْبَةَ ,

قَالَ: فَقَالَ لِنَفْسِهِ: هَذَا عِيسَى ابْنُ مَرْيَمَ عَلَيْهِ السَّلَامُ رَوْحُ اللهِ

وَكَلِمَتُهُ وَهَذَا فُلَانٌ حَوَارِيُّهُ وَمَنْ أَنْتَ يَا شَقِيُّ؟ لِصُّ بَنِي إِسْرَائِيلَ ,

قَطَعْتَ الطَّرِيقَ , وَأَخَذْتَ الْأَمْوَالَ , وَسَفَكْتَ الدِّمَاءَ , ثُمَّ هَبَطَ إِلَيْهِمَا

تَائِبًا نَادِمًا عَلَى مَا كَانَ مِنْهُ فَلَمَّا لَحِقَهُمَا , قَالَ لِنَفْسِهِ: تُرِيدُ أَنْ

تَمْشِيَ مَعَهُمَا لَسْتَ لِذَلِكَ بِأَهْلٍ , امْشِ خَلْفَهُمَا كَمَا يَمْشِي الْخَطَّاءُ

الْمُذْنِبُ مِثْلُكَ , قَالَ: فَالْتَفَتَ إِلَيْهِ الْحَوَارِيُّ فَعَرَفَهُ فَقَالَ فِي نَفْسِهِ:

انْظُرْ هَذَا الْخَبِيثَ الشَّقِيَّ وَمَشْيَهُ , وَرَاءَنَا قَالَ: فَاطَّلَعَ اللهُ عَلَى مَا فِي

قُلُوبِهِمَا مِنْ نَدَامَتِهِ وَتَوْبَتِهِ , وَمِنَ ازْدِرَاءِ الْحَوَارِيِّ إِيَّاهُ وَتَفْضِيلِهِ نَفْسَهُ

عَلَيْهِ , قَالَ: فَأَوْحَى الله عَزَّ وَجَلَّ إِلَى عِيسَى ابْنِ مَرْيَمَ عَلَيْهِ السَّلَامُ:
أَنْ مُرِ الْحَوَارِيَّ وَلَصَّ بَنِي إِسْرَائِيلَ أَنْ يَأْتِنِفَا الْعَمَلَ جَمِيعًا , أَمَّا اللِّصُّ
فَقَدْ غَفَرْتُ لَهُ مَا مَضَى لِنَدَامَتِهِ وَتَوْبَتِهِ , وَأَمَّا الْحَوَارِيُّ فَقَدْ حَبِطَ عَمَلُهُ
لِعُجْبِهِ بِنَفْسِهِ , وَازْدِرَائِهِ هَذَا التَّائِبَ

Jesus, peace be unto him, walked with an Israelite apostle of
his by a bandit in his stronghold. When the bandit saw them,
God placed [the need for] repentance in his heart.

So, he said to himself, "This Jesus, the son of Mary, peace be
unto him, is the Spirit and Word of God, and this person is
his apostle. Who are you, O wretched one? You are the bandit
of the Children of Israel. You have robbed highways, stolen
wealth, and shed blood."

Then, he went down to them, repenting and regretful over
what he had done. When he followed them, he said to
himself, "You want to walk alongside them, but you are not
worthy of that. Walk behind them, as an erring sinner like
you should."

Then, the apostle turned to him and recognized him. He said
to himself, "Look at this despicable and wretched man and
how he walks behind us."

So, God looked into their hearts: from the regret and
repentance [of the bandit] to the conceit of the apostle and his
contempt for him.

Then, God revealed to Jesus the son of Mary, peace be unto him, "Order the apostle and the bandit of the Children of Israel to work together. As for the bandit, I have forgiven his past sins due to his regret and his repentance. As for the apostle, his good deeds have fallen due to his self-conceit and his contempt for this penitent."[96]

Commentary:

In this unique account, the penitent thief is considered superior to an apostle in the sight of God. One should always vie to improve, and not be conceited by his own deeds. Good deeds should never make one arrogant, and the sins of others should only serve as a warning.

The Prophet Muhammad ﷺ said, "If you did not sin, God would replace you with people who would sin, and they would seek forgiveness from God and He would forgive them."[97]

قَالَ عِيسَى عَلَيْهِ السَّلَامُ: «بِحَقٍّ أَقُولُ لَكُمْ، كَمَا تَوَاضَعُونَ فَكَذَلِكَ تُرْفَعُونَ، وَكَمَا تَرْحَمُونَ كَذَلِكَ تُرْحَمُونَ، وَكَمَا

---

[96] Abu Nuʿaym, *Hilyat al-Awliya'*, Volume 8, pp. 146.
[97] Sahih Muslim, Book 50, Hadith 13.
https://sunnah.com/muslim:2749

تَقْضُونَ مِنْ حَوَائِجِ النَّاسِ فَكَذَلِكَ اللهُ تَعَالَى يَقْضِي مِنْ حَوَائِجِكُمْ»

Jesus, peace be unto him, said, "Truly, I say to you: you will be exalted if you are humble. You will receive mercy if you are merciful to others. God will fulfill your needs if you fulfill the needs of the people."[98]

Commentary:

The Prophet Muhammad ﷺ said, "Surely, I am a slave: I eat as a slave eats and I sit as a slave sits."[99] [100] Our proximity to God is in proportion to our humility. Modesty and simplicity do not lower us – they exalt us.

Jesus said, "Blessed are the merciful, for they shall obtain mercy." (Matthew 5:7)

---

[98] Abu Nu`aym, *Hilyat al-Awliya'*, Volume 5, pp. 238.
[99] Musnad Abu Ya`la, Hadith 4920.
[100] `Abd al-Razzaq, *al-Musannaf*, Volume 1, Page 415, Hadith 19543

كَانَ الْمَسِيحُ عَلَيْهِ السَّلَامُ يَقُولُ: «إِنْ أَحْبَبْتُمْ أَنْ تَكُونُوا أَصْفِيَاءَ اللهِ

وَنُورُ بَنِي آدَمَ فَاعْفُوا عَنْ مَنْ ظَلَمَكُمْ، وَعُودُوا مَنْ لَا يَعُودُكُمْ، وَأَقْرِضُوا

مَنْ لَا يَجْزِيكُمْ، وَأَحْسِنُوا إِلَى مَنْ لَا يُحْسِنُ إِلَيْكُمْ»

Christ, peace be unto him, would say, "If you would like to
become the elect of God and the light of the Children of
Adam, then forgive those who wrong you, visit those who do
not visit you, lend to those who do not give to you, and be
good to those who are not good to you."[101]

Commentary:

This corresponds with Matthew 5:14-16, where Jesus says, "Ye
are the light of the world. A city that is set on an hill cannot
be hid. Neither do men light a candle, and put it under a
bushel, but on a candlestick; and it giveth light unto all that
are in the house. Let your light so shine before men, that they
may see your good works, and glorify your Father which is in
heaven."

---

[101] Abu Nu`aym, *Hilyat al-Awliya'*, Volume 5, pp. 238.

قال عيسى ابن مريم عليه السلام: يا معشر الحواريين لي إليكم حاجة اقضوها لي، قالوا: قضيت حاجتك يا روح الله، فقام فغسل أقدامهم فقالوا: كنا نحن أحق بهذا يا روح الله! فقال: إن أحق الناس بالخدمة العالم إنما تواضعت هكذا لكيما تتواضعوا بعدي في الناس كتواضعي لكم، ثم قال عيسى عليه السلام: بالتواضع تعمر الحكمة لا بالتكبر، وكذلك في السهل ينبت الزرع لا في الجبل

Jesus said, "O assembly of Apostles! I have a request of you. Fulfill it for me."

They said, "Your request is fulfilled, O Spirit of God!" Then he stood up and washed their feet. They said, "It would have been more proper for us to have done this, O Spirit of God!"

Jesus said, "Surely it is more fitting for a scholar to serve the people. I humbled myself only so that you may humble yourselves among the people after me, just as I humbled myself among you."

Then, Jesus said, "Wisdom is developed by humility, not by pride, just as plants grow from soft soil and not from stone."[102]

---

[102] Kulayni, *al-Kafi*, Volume 1, pp. 37.

Commentary:

This corresponds to John 13, where Jesus washes the feet of his disciples. In the Gospel account, Peter first refuses to have his feet washed by Christ, out of obsequiousness. Jesus then says, "You do not realize now what I am doing ... Unless I wash you, you have no part with me." (John 13:7-8) Then, Jesus washes his disciples' feet, and he finished by saying, "I have set you an example that you should do as I have done for you." (John 13:15)

In Near Eastern culture, when one washes your feet, they do so out of submission, love, good service, and care. The foot is often seen as the lowliest and dirtiest appendage, hence the use of shoes and slippers as a form of humiliation. Jesus, however, washed the feet of his disciples to teach them humility and grace.

A tree is judged by its fruits, but a tree cannot even grow on arid, solid stone. Softness and tenderness must be the foundation of any good thing. A baby must be treated delicately before it can grow strong. Knowledge itself must be preceded by humility because arrogance otherwise will corrupt and misuse it.

قال عيسى بن مريم عليه السلام لبعض أصحابه: مالا تحب أن يفعل

بك فلا تفعله بأحد، وإن لطم أحد خدك الأيمن فأعط الأيسر

Jesus the son of Mary, peace be unto him, said to some of his
companions, "Whatever you do not like to be done to you,
then do not do it to others, and if someone hits you on your
right cheek, then give him your left."[103]

Commentary:

Many have a hard time reconciling the instruction to "turn
the other cheek" with Islam's hawkish spirit. When one
revisits the Quran and the Sunna, they will find the correct
balance. People have a permit (*rukhṣa*) to self-defence; a
permit that was not always there. In the story of Cain and
Abel, Abel does not fight back against Cain (Quran 5:27-28).

In Muhammadan Islam, one is permitted to defend
themselves upon attack, but even then, we read the following:

Saʿd b. Abī Waqās asked the Prophet Muhammad ﷺ, "What
shall I do if [a Muslim] enters my house and extends his hand
to kill me?" The Prophet replied, "Be as the son of Adam
(Abel)."[104]

The Prophet Muhammad ﷺ said, "He who is killed defending
his property shall be at the status of a martyr. If he does not

---

103 Saduq, *al-Amali*, pp. 448.
104 Jamiʿ al-Tirmidhi, Book 33, Hadith 37.
https://sunnah.com/tirmidhi:2194

fight, then there is no problem. Were it me, I would have left it and not fought."[105]

"Turn the other cheek" means that one should not insist on exacting vengeance. In vengeance there can be transgression. Instead, it is better to suppress your ego and be a good example even to your enemy. Escalation often leads to more harm. It would be a pity to die, and cause your family trauma, over a possession, regardless of how valuable it is.

قال عيسى ابن مريم (عليه السلام): إن صاحب الشر يعدي وقرين السوء يردي فانظر من تقارن

Jesus, peace be unto him, said, "Surely, a companion of evil is harmful, and a consort of iniquity is destructive, so look to whom you accompany."[106]

Commentary:

It is said that "you are who your friends are." The Prophet Muhammad ☪, similarly, said, "A person is upon the religion

---

[105] Kulayni, *al-Kafi*, Volume 7, pp. 296.
[106] Ibid, Volume 6, pp. 24.

of his friend."[107] Most people are products of their surroundings, and it is difficult for them to transcend that influence. It is thus incumbent on a believer to surround himself with other believers. No one is perfect, but the congregation of believers will collectively reflect prophetic qualities.

مر عيسى بن مريم (عليه السلام) بقبر يعذب صاحبه، ثم مر به من
قابل فإذا هو ليس يعذب فقال: يا رب مررت بهذا القبر عام أول،
فكان صاحبه يعذب، ثم مررت به العام فإذا هو ليس يعذب! فأوحى
الله عز وجل إليه: يا روح الله، إنه أدرك له ولد صالح، فأصلح
طريقا، وآوى يتيما، فغفرت له بما عمل ابنه. قال: وقال عيسى بن
مريم (عليه السلام) ليحيى بن زكريا (عليه السلام): إذا قيل فيك ما
فيك، فاعلم أنه ذنب ذكرته فاستغفر الله منه، وإن قيل فيك ما ليس
فيك، فاعلم أنه حسنة كتبت لك لم تتعب فيها

Jesus, peace be unto him, passed by a grave whose occupant was being punished. Then, he passed by it again the following year, and he was not being punished. So, he said, "O Lord! I

107 Sunan Abi Dawud, Book 43, Hadith 61.
https://sunnah.com/abudawud:4833

passed by this grave last year, and its occupant was being punished. Then, I passed by it this year, and I found that he was not being punished."

So, God revealed to him, "O Spirit of God! He has a righteous son who rectified a path and sheltered an orphan, so he was forgiven due to what his son had done."[108]

Commentary:

The Prophet Muhammad ﷺ said, "When a man dies, all his accumulation of good deeds comes to an end, except for three types: a recurring charity, knowledge by which people benefit, or a pious child who prays for him."[109]

All believers should strive to leave behind a recurring charity, such as a water well, a mosque, a school, sponsoring a child, or teaching a skill. Likewise, believers should pass down sacred knowledge in forms of books, and they should raise righteous children to pray for them after they have died.

---

[108] Saduq, *al-Amali*, pp. 603.
[109] Sahih Muslim, hadith 1631.

كان المسيح (عليه السلام) يقول: من كثر همه سقم بدنه، ومن

ساء خلقه عذب نفسه، ومن كثر كلامه كثر سقطه ، ومن كثر

كذبه ذهب بهاؤه، ومن لاحى الرجال ذهبت مروءته.

Christ would say, "He whose worries multiply, his body
becomes ill. He who worsens his character, his soul suffers.
He whose speech multiplies, his errors multiply. He whose
lying multiplies, his splendour dissipates. Whoever disputes
men excessively, his chivalry dissipates."[110]

The physical symptoms of excessive worrying include an
increased heart rate, headaches, high blood pressure, high
cortisol levels, gastrointestinal problems, and more. One
should do their best to trust God's plan, persevere in hard
times, and have gratitude for good times.

All humans have a natural proclivity toward goodness (called
the *fiṭra*). Having good character in our social circles is part of
that *fiṭra*. The further away we move from the *fiṭra*, the more
discomfort we will feel in our soul; because the soul longs for
God.

Speaking excessively will inevitably cause one to argue, gossip,
lie, exaggerate, manipulate, insult, cause emotional injury,
and be misunderstood. Limiting speech to the remembrance

[110] Saduq, *al-Amali*, pp. 636.

of God, goodly exhortations, tender words and professional
language will only be to one's benefit.

أن عيسى روح الله مر بقوم مجلبين فقال: ما لهؤلاء؟ قيل: يا روح
الله، إن فلانة بنت فلان تهدى إلى فلان بن فلان في ليلتها هذه.
قال: يجلبون اليوم ويكون غدا. فقال قائل منهم: ولم يا رسول الله؟
قال: لان صاحبتهم ميتة في ليلتها هذه. فقال القائلون بمقالته
صدق الله وصدق رسوله. وقال أهل النفاق، ما أقرب غدا! فلما
أصبحوا جاءوا فوجدوها على حالها لم يحدث بها شئ، فقالوا: يا
روح الله، إن التي أخبرتنا أمس أنها ميتة لم تمت! فقال عيسى (عليه
السلام): يفعل الله ما يشاء: فاذهبوا بنا إليها. فذهبوا يتسابقون حتى
قرعوا الباب فخرج زوجها، فقال له عيسى (عليه السلام): استأذن لي
على صاحبتك. قال فدخل عليها فأخبرها أن روح الله وكلمته بالباب
مع عدة. قال: فتخدرت، فدخل عليها، فقال لها: ما صنعت ليلتك
هذه؟ قالت: لم أصنع شيئا إلا وقد كنت أصنعه فيما مضى، إنه كان
يعترينا سائل في كل ليلة جمعة فننيله ما يقوته إلى مثلها، وإنه جاءني
في ليلتي هذه وأنا مشغولة بأمري وأهلي في مشاغيل، فهتف فلم

يجبه أحد، ثم هتف فلم يجب حتى هتف مرارا، فلما سمعت مقالته
قمت متنكرة حتى أنلته كما كنا ننيله، فقال لها: تنحي عن
مجلسك، فإذا تحت ثيابها أفعى مثل جذعة عاض على ذنبه. فقال
عليه السلام: بما صنعت صرف الله عنك هذا

Jesus, the Spirit of God, passed by a people who were noising about. So, he said, "What is wrong with these [people]?"

It was said, "O Spirit of God! So-and-so the daughter of so-and-so is being married to so-and-so the son of so-and-so tonight."

He said, "They will noise about today, and they will weep tomorrow."

So, one of them said, "Why, O Messenger of God?"

He said, "Because your [female] friend will die on this night."

So, some said, "God has spoken the truth, and His Messenger has spoken the truth." The people of hypocrisy said, "How close is tomorrow!"

When they awoke, they went, and they found that nothing had happened to her. So, they said, "O Spirit of God! Surely, you informed us yesterday that she will die, but she did not die!"

So, Jesus, peace be unto him, said, "God does what He wishes. Take us to her."

So, they raced to her until they knocked on the door and her husband came out. Then, Jesus, peace be unto him, said to him, "Give me permission to see your wife."

So, he (the husband) went to her and informed her that the Spirit of God and His Word was at the door with a group."

He said, "She is staying in her place."

So, he entered her room [instead] and said to her, "What did you do last night?"

She said, "I did not do anything [special] except that which I have done in the past. A beggar would come to us every Friday eve, and we would give him what would suffice him till the next week. He came to me last night, but I was busy with my affairs, and my family was busy. Then, he called out, and no one greeted him. He called out again, and no one answered, so he kept repeating. When I heard his calls, I stood, I veiled myself, and I gave him what I would give him."

So, he said to her, "Move away from your sitting place."

Then, they found a serpent like a tree trunk under her clothes, with its teeth clenching its tail.

So, he, peace be unto him, said, "Because of what you did, God spared you from this."[111]

أَنَّ عِيسَى ابْنَ مَرْيَمَ، لَقِيَ خِنْزِيرًا بِالطَّرِيقِ فَقَالَ لَهُ انْفُذْ بِسَلاَمٍ .
فَقِيلَ لَهُ تَقُولُ هَذَا لِخِنْزِيرٍ فَقَالَ عِيسَى إِنِّي أَخَافُ أَنْ أُعَوِّدَ لِسَانِي
النُّطْقَ بِالسُّوءِ

Jesus the son of Mary encountered a pig on the road. He said to it, "Go in peace."

Somebody asked, "Do you say this to a pig?"

Jesus said, "I fear lest I accustom my tongue to evil speech."[112]

عيسى بن مريم عليه السلام لما مر على البحر ألقى بقرص من قوته
في الماء فقال له بعض الحواريين يا روح الله وكلمته لم فعلت هذا
هو من قوتك قال فعلت هذا لتأكله دابة من دواب الماء وثوابه ؟
عند الله العظيم.

---

[111] Ibid, pp. 589.
[112] Malik, *al-Muwatta'*, Book 56, hadith 4.

When Jesus the son of Mary, peace be unto him, sailed the sea, he threw a portion of his food into the water.

Some of his apostles said, "O Spirit and Word of God! Why did you do that? That was from your food."

Jesus replied, "I did this so that a sea creature may eat it. The reward of that is with God the Greatest."[113]

رَأَى عِيسَى ابْنُ مَرْيَمَ رَجُلاً يَسْرِقُ، فَقَالَ لَهُ أَسَرَقْتَ قَالَ كَلاَّ وَاللَّهِ الَّذِي لاَ إِلَهَ إِلاَّ هُوَ. فَقَالَ عِيسَى آمَنْتُ بِاللَّهِ وَكَذَّبْتُ عَيْنِي

Jesus, seeing a man stealing, asked him, "Did you steal?"

He said, "No, by God, besides whom there is none who is worthy of worship."

Jesus said, "I believe in God and I suspect my eyes."[114]

Commentary:

---

[113] Saduq, *Thawab al-A`mal*, pp. 144.
[114] Sahih al-Bukhari, Book 60, hadith 114.

In this report, Jesus has so much faith in those who believe in God that he'd rather suspect what his own eyes see than the word of the faithful. He assumes the best in the fellow believer, and he assumes seeing the wrong thing. This is called having *ḥusn al-thun* for others and *sū' al-thun* for himself.

Faith and Spirituality

طوبى لمن بكى من ذكر خطيئته وحفظ لسانه ووسعه بيته

Jesus said, "Blessed is he who weeps over his sins, guards his tongue, and is sufficed by the expanse of his house."[115]

Commentary:

When we sin frequently, we become numb to the evils of that sin. The heart becomes hard, and it loses its ability to flux naturally to the signs of God. Weeping is a genuine expression

---

[115] Ibn Kathir, *al-Bidaya wa al-Nihaya*, Volume 2, pp. 106.

of emotion, and it is the sign of a heart that can be moved healthily from mood to mood. Weeping is difficult to fake, and it can be a sign of a believer. It is not a weakness, but a strength, because weakness is to numb yourself to emotion. The hard heart is the root of all evil.

It is better to be a regretful and blameworthy soul (*nafs al-lawwāma*) than to be ruled by your appetites (*nafs al-ammāra*). God accepts sincere repentance and forgives sins.

The best way to guard one's tongue is to practice silence. Silence prevents one from speaking about that which they have no knowledge of, speaking poorly of others in an unjust manner, speaking falsely, using foul language, speaking over others, speaking too much about oneself, complaining about unworthy things, argumentation, failing to listen to others, and failing to remember God. In many sentences, you are the subject and others are the object. Silence rids us of this dichotomy and brings back the primordial oneness of our surroundings.

One who is "suffced by the expanse of his house" is one who is satisfied with spending time at home away from sedition and temptation. At home, one can devote more time to worship and accustom oneself to minding one's own business.

طوبى لعين نامت ولم تحدث نفسها بالمعصية وانتبهت إلى غير اثم

Jesus said, "Blessed is the eye that sleeps without tempting itself with sin and pays heed to other than sin."[116]

Commentary:

The believer is to avoid gazing at that which God has prohibited (Quran 24:30). One of the most extreme forms of temptation is pornography, which damages the dopamine reward system and leaves it unresponsive to natural forms of pleasure. One should preferably even avoid thoughts of fornication (Matthew 5:27-28), which can corrupt the mind. A temptation that excites one too much is bad for his soul. Instead, get married, be loyal to your spouse, and avoid the beauty of women or men that are not yours.

قال عيسى بن مريم عليه السلام :لا تكثروا الحديث بغير ذكر الله فتقسو قلوبكم فإن القلب القاسي بعيد من الله ولكن لا تعلمون، ولا تنظروا في ذنوب العباد كأنكم أرباب وانظروا فيها كأنكم عبيد، فإنما الناس رجلان معافى ومبتلى فارحموا أهل البلاء واحمدوا الله على العافية

---

[116] Ibid, Volume 2, pp. 106.

Jesus the son of Mary said, "Do not increase in your words without mentioning God, lest your hearts become hard. Surely, the hard heart is far from God, if you but knew. Do not look at the sins of the servants [of God] as though you are lords, but rather, look at them as though you are servants. Surely, the people are of but two types: one who is well, and one who is suffering. So, be merciful to those who are suffering, and praise God for wellness."[117]

Commentary:

It is reported that ʿAlī b. Abī Ṭālib said, "Every silence that is devoid of thought is heedlessness. Every speech that is devoid of remembrance [of God] is prattle."[118] Speech is a unique gift that humans have been endowed with, and it should be sufficiently used to remind oneself and others of God. In the Islamic tradition, this can be done through *tasbīḥ* (praising, glorifying, and exalting God), supplication, prayer, and mentioning God in everyday encounters.

Dr. Timothy Winter once wrote, "Faith may be measured by the number of verses that soften one's heart."[119] The mention of God, the creator of life and death, should harken one to their purpose in this world. Obsessing over entertainment and

---

[117] Abu Nuʿaym, *Hilyat al-Awliya'*, Volume 6, pp. 58.
[118] Saduq, *al-Amali*, pp. 80.
[119] "Contentions by Shaykh Abdal Hakim Murad", May 4th, 2020, https://www.facebook.com/Contentions/posts/2970154023041012

pleasure takes us away from the fundamental questions of life: where we come from, why we are here, and where we are going. Frivolity numbs us to our purpose in this world. Pronouncing the many names of our Sustainer should remind us of our vital responsibilities and our finite time on this planet. It should break the spell that worldliness has on us.

A regular pastime of those who claim belief is to observe and mock the sins of others. True faith, however, knows that all ordinary people are susceptible to sin. The sins of our peers are tragic, and if we cannot kindly turn them to the right direction, then we should at least be of those who take heed of their lesson.

The believer must be empathetic to those in trial and tribulation. The believer should look at his own problems as a storm in a teacup. If one is well, he should not boast of his wellness, but rather, he should retain humility and gratitude for the blessings of God.

قال الحواريون للمسيح :يا مسيح الله انظر إلى مسجد الله ما أحسنه .قال :آمين آمين بحق ما أقول لكم لا يترك الله من هذا المسجد حجرا قائما إلى أهلكه بذنوب أهله، إن الله لا يصنع بالذهب ولا بالفضة ولا بهذه الأحجار التي تعجبكم شيئا إن أحب

إلى الله منها القلوب الصالحة وبها يعمر الله الأرض، وبها يخرب

الله الأرض إذا كانت على غير ذلك.

The apostles said to Christ, "O Messiah of God! Look at the Temple of God and its beauty."

He said, "Amen, amen. In truth, I tell you that God will not leave one stone from this Temple standing except that He will destroy it due to the sins of its people. Surely, God does not do anything with the gold, the silver, or these stones that impress you. Surely, what God loves therein are the hearts of the righteous – by them, God builds up the Earth, and without them, God ruins the Earth."[120]

Commentary:

Similar passages can be found in Matthew 23:16-21 and Matthew 24:2. The Pharisees believed that one had to swear by the gold ornamentation of the Temple for his oath to be binding. This practice was condemned by Jesus in the Woes of the Pharisees because the Temple's gold was not sacred in and of itself. The real treasure of God is the heart of the believer, wherein His remembrance is enlivened. The Prophet Muhammad ﷺ said to the Kaʿba in Mecca, "The sanctity of the believer is greater to God than your sanctity."[121]

---

[120] Ibn Kathir, *al-Bidaya wa al-Nihaya*, Volume 2, pp. 107.
[121] Sunan Ibn Maja, Book 36, Hadith 7.
https://sunnah.com/ibnmajah:3932

Perhaps the most prominent prophecy of Jesus is that the Temple in Jerusalem would be torn to the ground. This occurred under the Romans in 70 AD. The Gospels were said to have been written soon after this point, perhaps in reaction to Jesus' prophecy hitting close to home.

In the time of Jesus, most Jews were eagerly awaiting a Messiah that would redress the political problems of their time. Even in the story of Barabbas, Pilate gave a crowd a choice between freeing Jesus and freeing Barabbas, an insurrectionist. The crowd chose Barabbas and condemned Jesus. Jesus' kingdom was "not of this world" (John 18:36), and he was neither a Pharisee on the side of Rome nor an insurrectionist on the side of the zealots. Barabbas, on the other hand, may have been a zealot. The normative Islamic tradition has historically been wary of rebellions and has usually opted for self-rectification as the way to amend society.

It was a Jewish insurrection in 66 AD that led to the destruction of the Temple. Then, it was the messianic insurrection of Bar Kochba in 132 AD that led to the destruction of Jerusalem altogether. These devastating events give further credence not just to Jesus' prophecy, but his political strategy as well.

Ironically, it is said that, in early manuscripts of the Gospel of Matthew, the first name of Barabbas was also "Jesus". Barabbas literally means "the son of the father". It is almost as though the Barabbas story is a literary device comparing the neglected, suffering Messiah and the doppelganger messiah that the Jews had hoped for.

وقف عيسى هو وأصحابه على قبر وصاحبه يدلى فيه، فجعلوا

يذكرون القبر وضيقه فقال: قد كنتم فيما هو أضيق منه في أرحام

أمهاتكم فإذا أحب الله أن يوسع وسع.

Jesus and his companions were standing at a grave. They began to speak about the grave and its narrowness. So, he said, "You were in something narrower than it in the wombs of your mothers, yet when God wanted to expand it, He expanded it."[122]

Commentary:

The darkness of the grave is the womb of the next world. We exit the hole of our mothers, and we enter the hole in the ground of mother Earth.

Although the grave is shallow and narrow, the next world is more expansive and everlasting. The next world is what the eye has not seen, what the ear has not heard, and what the heart has not imagined. Just as this world would be

---

[122] Ibn Kathir, *al-Bidaya wa al-Nihaya*, Volume 2, pp. 107.

inconceivable for those in the womb, the next world is
inconceivable for those who are still alive.

أَنَّ عِيسَى عَلَيْهِ السَّلَامُ قَالَ: فَكَّرْتُ فِي الْخَلْقِ فَإِذَا مَنْ لَمْ يُخْلَقْ كَانَ
عِنْدِي أَغْبَطُ مِمَّنْ خُلِقَ

Jesus, peace be unto him, said, "I thought about creation, and
I found that He who is not created is more immediate to me
than he who is created."[123]

Commentary:

God says in the Quran, "And indeed We have created man,
and We know whatever thoughts his inner self develops, and
We are closer to him than his jugular vein." (Quran 50:16)

God is all-knowing, all-hearing, and all-seeing; He is with us
everywhere we go. God is with us as a microscopic cell, He
carries us throughout this toilsome world, and He is the light
in the darkness of our grave. Everything comes in and out of
our life, but God remains.

Jesus emptied his heart of this world and filled it with the love
of God. For this, God favoured Jesus, and made him His

---

[123] Abu Nu`aym, *Hilyat al-Awliya'*, Volume 6, pp. 57.

Messiah, His messenger, His prophet, and His proof over the creation.

بَيْنَمَا عِيسَى عَلَيْهِ السَّلَامُ جَالِسٌ مَعَ الْحَوَارِيِّينَ إِذْ جَاءَ طَائِرٌ مَنْظُومُ

الْجَنَاحَيْنِ بِاللُّؤْلُؤِ وَالْيَاقُوتِ كَأَحْسَنِ مَا يَكُونُ مِنَ الطَّيْرِ فَجَعَلَ يَدْرُجَ

بَيْنَ أَيْدِيهِمْ، فَقَالَ عِيسَى عَلَيْهِ السَّلَامُ: دَعُوهُ لَا تُنَفِّرُوهُ فَإِنَّ هَذَا بُعِثَ

لَكُمْ آيَةً، فَخَلَعَ مِسْلَاخَهُ فَخَرَجَ أَقْرَعَ أَحْمَرَ كَأَقْبَحِ مَا يَكُونُ فَأَتَى بِرْكَةً

فَتَلَوَّثَ فِي حَمْأَتِهَا فَخَرَجَ أَسْوَدَ قَبِيحًا فَاسْتَقْبَلَ جِرْيَةَ الْمَاءِ فَاغْتَسَلَ ثُمَّ

عَادَ إِلَى مِسْلَاخِهِ فَلَبِسَهُ فَعَادَ إِلَيْهِ حُسْنُهُ وَجَمَالُهُ، فَقَالَ عِيسَى عَلَيْهِ

السَّلَامُ: إِنَّ هَذَا بُعِثَ لَكُمْ آيَةً إِنَّ مَثَلَ هَذَا كَمَثَلِ الْمُؤْمِنِ إِذَا تَلَوَّثَ

فِي الذُّنُوبِ وَالْخَطَايَا نُزِعَ مِنْهُ حُسْنُهُ وَجَمَالُهُ، وَإِذَا تَابَ إِلَى اللهِ عَادَ

إِلَيْهِ حُسْنُهُ وَجَمَالُهُ، هَذَا لَفْظُ حَدِيثِ حَمَّادٍ، عَنْ دَاوُدَ وَلَمْ يجَاوِزْ بِهِ

شَهْرًا وَلَفْظُ ابْنُ الْمُبَارَكِ قَرِيبٌ مِنْهُ وَجَاوَزَ بِهِ إِلَى أَبِي هُرَيْرَةَ رَضِيَ اللهُ

تَعَالَى عَنْهُ

Jesus, peace be unto him, was sitting with the apostles when a bird came. Its wings were adorned with pearls and rubies; it was the most beautiful of birds. It began to crawl before them.

Then, Jesus, peace be unto him, said, "Leave it, and do not scare it away, for surely, it has been brought to you as a sign."

It shed off its adornment, and it was red and uglier than it was. Then, it went to a basin and basked in its murky water. It came out an ugly black. Then, it went to flowing water, bathed in it, returned to its adornment, and wore it. It returned to its beauty and its splendour.

Then, Jesus, peace be unto him, said, "This has been brought to you as a sign. This example is like that of a believer – when he basks in sin and error, he sheds his beauty and his splendour. When he repents to God, he returns to his beauty and his splendour."[124]

Commentary:

God does not leave us with the scars of our previous sins and trespasses. Instead, repentance cleanses and purifies us completely. When our sins are atoned, we are like a newborn baby with a clean slate. Unlike most people, God always turns a new page with His creation. He constantly gives the penitent a second and third chance. Only the Great One can forgive great sins. The righteous will have their sins exchanged for good deeds, and they will be granted Paradise by God's grace.

---

[124] Abu Nu`aym, *Hilyat al-Awliya'*, Volume 6, pp. 59-60.

قَرَأْتُ فِي التَّوْرَاةِ أَنَّ عِيسَى عَلَيْهِ السَّلَامُ قَالَ: يَا مَعْشَرَ الْحَوَارِيِّينَ

كَلِّمُوا اللهَ كَثِيرًا وَكَلِّمُوا النَّاسَ قَلِيلًا. قَالُوا: وَكَيْفَ نُكَلِّمُ اللهَ؟ قَالَ:

اخْلُوا بِمُنَاجَاتِهِ، اخْلُوا بِدُعَائِهِ

Jesus, peace be unto him, said, "O apostles! Speak much to God and speak little to the people."

They said, "How shall we speak to God?"

He said, "Isolate yourself in supplication and prayer to Him."[125]

Commentary:

Whilst it is good to call people to righteousness through your actions, there is a special reward for one who conceals some of his good deeds. Righteous acts done anonymously purifies the intentions of a worshiper. When one prays in private, they are not seeking the satisfaction of others, but rather, they are alone with the Alone. The believer is not just concerned with having a good reputation: he wants his real, private self to be even better than his reputation.

Jesus said, "And when thou prayest, thou shalt not be as the hypocrites are: for they love to pray standing in the synagogues and in the corners of the streets, that they may be

---

[125] Ibid, Volume 6, pp. 94.

seen of men. Verily I say unto you, They have their reward. But thou, when thou prayest, enter into thy closet, and when thou hast shut thy door, pray to thy Father which is in secret; and thy Father which seeth in secret shall reward thee openly." (Matthew 6:5-8)

اجتمع الحواريون إلى عيسى (عليه السلام) فقالوا له: يا معلم الخير أرشدنا، فقال لهم: إن موسى كليم الله (عليه السلام) أمركم أن لا تحلفوا بالله تبارك وتعالى كاذبين وأنا آمركم أن لا تحلفوا بالله كاذبين ولا صادقين، قالوا: يا روح الله زدنا، فقال: إن موسى نبي الله (عليه السلام) أمركم أن لا تزنوا وأنا آمركم أن لا تحدثوا أنفسكم بالزنا فضلا عن أن تزنوا، فإن من حدث نفسه بالزنا كان كمن أوقد في بيت مزوق فأفسد التزاويق الدخان وإن لم يحترق البيت

Jesus, peace be unto him, was with his apostles, when his apostles said, "O Teacher of Goodness, guide us."

So, he said, "Surely, Moses, the one whom God spoke to, peace be unto him, commanded you to not swear to God whilst lying, whereas I command you to not swear to God whilst lying nor whilst telling the truth."

They said, "O Spirit of God! Tell us more."

So, Jesus said, "Moses, the prophet of God, commanded you to not fornicate, whereas I command you to not have thoughts of fornication in your mind, in addition to not fornicating. For one who has thoughts of fornication in his mind is like on who kindles a fire in a decorated house. The smoke ruins the decorations, even if the house does not burn."[126]

Commentary:

I have often wondered if the title "Teacher of Goodness" (*mu'allim al-khayr*) in this report is an allusion to the Dead Sea Scrolls' "Teacher of Righteousness". The Teacher of Goodness is one who would know the Torah, "reveal the hidden things in which Israel had gone astray", and "guide them in the way of [God's] heart."[127]

Moses led the Israelites out of the idolatry and slavery of Egypt. As they wandered the desert, Moses trained the Israelites to become proper law-abiding law-interpreting citizens. Simple laws like "an eye for an eye" were necessary for a simple and nomadic people. Jesus' mission, however, was quite different. He came to an established civilization with a Temple, synagogues, and scholarship. The Pharisees

---

[126] Kulayni, *al-Kafi*, Volume 5, pp. 542.
[127] Cairo Damascus Document.

and Sadducees were quite familiar with scripture, and they would even test Jesus with it.

The role of Jesus was to teach the people the spirit of the Law. It is not enough for a growing civilization to stick to "an eye for an eye" – forgiveness had to be emphasized. Rituals also often lose their meaning and become formalities. Even in the Muslim world, there are those who are more concerned about the length of their beard and the shortness of their robe than they are about the state of their heart. There are those who avoid gold and silver, yet they pursue every other type of luxury that money can buy.

In the Gospels, Jesus instructs his disciples to not just abstain from killing, but to abstain from anger. Don't just avoid adultery, but avoid lust. Don't just avoid using the Lord's name in vain, but avoid swearing upon anything, and let the chips fall as they may. Being obsessed with convincing others can be a form of egoism. (Matthew 5:21-37)

Thinking about a sin is a way to normalize the sin and tempt oneself toward it. All sins begin with an evil thought.

كان المسيح (عليه السلام) يقول: لا تكثروا الكلام في غير ذكر الله، فان الذين يكثرون الكلام في غير ذكر الله قاسية قلوبهم ولكن لا يعلمون.

Christ, peace be unto him, would say, "Do not increase your words except in your remembrance of God. Surely, those who increase their words in other than the remembrance of God are hard-hearted, but they do not know."[128]

قال عيسى بن مريم صلوات الله عليه: إذا قعد أحدكم في منزله فليرخي عليه ستره، فإن الله تبارك وتعالى قسم الحياء كما قسم الرزق

Jesus the son of Mary, the blessings of God be unto him, said, "He who is sitting in his house should close his curtain, for God apportions modesty just as He apportions sustenance."[129]

مر عيسى بن مريم (عليه السلام) على قوم يبكون، فقال: على ما يبكي هؤلاء؟ فقيل: يكون على ذنوبهم قال فليدعوها يغفر لهم

[128] Kulayni, *al-Kafi*, Volume 2, pp. 114.
[129] Al-Himyari al-Qummi, *Qurb al-Isnad*, pp. 46.

Jesus the son of Mary, peace be unto him, passed by a people who were weeping. So, he said, "What are these people weeping over?"

So, it was said, "They are weeping over their sins."

He said, "Then, they should abandon them, and they will be forgiven."[130]

وكان نقش خاتم عيسى (عليه السلام) حرفين، اشتقهما من الانجيل: طوبي لعبد ذكر الله من أجله، وويل لعبد نسى الله من أجله

The etching on the ring of Jesus, peace be unto him, was two phrases taken from the Gospel, "Blessed is the servant who remembers God for his own sake, and woe is the servant who forgets God for his own sake."[131]

---

[130] Saduq, al-Amali, pp. 585.
[131] Ibid, pp. 543.

كان عيسى بن مريم عليه السلام يقول اذا تصدق احدكم بيمينه

فليخنها عن شماله واذا صلى فليدن عليه ستر بابه فان الله عز و

جل يقسم الثناء كما سقيم الرزق

Jesus the son of Mary, peace be unto him, would say, "If one were to give charity with his right hand, he should hide it from his left hand. If one were to pray, he should close the door behind him. Surely, God apportions the commending [of the people] just as He apportions sustenance."[132]

مَرَّ عِيسَى عَلَيْهِ السَّلَامُ بِثَلَاثَةٍ مِنَ النَّاسِ قَدْ نَحِلَتْ أَبْدَانُهُمْ وَتَغَيَّرَتْ

أَلْوَانُهُمْ فَقَالَ: مَا الَّذِي بَلَّغَكُمْ مَا أَرَى؟ قَالُوا: الْخَوْفُ مِنَ النِّيرَانِ ,

قَالَ: مَخْلُوقًا خِفْتُمْ وَحَقًّا عَلَى اللَّهِ أَنْ يُؤَمِّنَ الْخَائِفَ , قَالَ: ثُمَّ

جَاوَزَهُمْ الى ثَلَاثَةٍ أُخْرَى فَإِذَا هُمْ أَشَدُّ تَغَيُّرِ أَلْوَانٍ وَأَشَدُّ نُحُولِ أَبْدَانٍ ,

فَقَالَ: مَا الَّذِي بَلَّغَكُمْ مَا أَرَى؟ قَالُوا: الشَّوْقُ إِلَى الْجِنَانِ , فَقَالَ:

مَخْلُوقًا اشْتَقْتُمْ وَحَقًّا عَلَى اللَّهِ أَنْ يُعْطِيَكُمْ مَا رَجَوْتُمْ , ثُمَّ جَاوَزَهُمْ

الى ثَلَاثَةٍ أُخْرَى فَإِذَا هُمْ أَشَدُّ نُحُولِ أَبْدَانٍ وَأَشَدُّ تَغَيُّرِ أَلْوَانٍ كَأَنَّ عَلَى

[132] Ahmad b. Hanbal, *Kitab al-Zuhd*, pp. 55.

وُجُوهِهِمُ الْمِرْآةَ مِنَ النُّورِ , فَقَالَ: مَا الَّذِي بَلَّغَكُمْ مَا أَرَى؟ قَالُوا:
الْحُبُّ لِلَّهِ , قَالَ: أَنْتُمُ الْمُقَرَّبُونَ أَنْتُمُ الْمُقَرَّبُونَ

Jesus, peace be unto him, passed by three people whose colour had changed and whose bodies had become undone.

So, he said, "What has caused this that I see in you?"

They said, "Fear of Hellfire."

He said, "You have feared a creation, and it is the duty of God to safeguard the fearful."

Then, he passed by them, and found three others whose colour and bodies had changed more severely.

So, he said, "What has caused this that I see in you?"

They said, "Desire for Paradise."

So, he said, "You long for a creation, and it is the duty of God to grant you that which you hope for."

Then, he passed by them, and found three others whose colour and bodies had changed even more severely. It was as though they had reflections of light over their faces.

So, he said, "What has caused this that I see in you?"

They said, "Love for God."

He said, "You are in His nearness; you are in His nearness."[133]

Commentary:

One of the Pharisees asked Jesus, "What is the greatest commandment?" He said, "Thou shalt love the Lord thy God with all thy heart, and with all thy soul, and with all thy mind. This is the first and greatest commandment. And the second is like unto it, thou shalt love thy neighbour as thyself. On these two commandments hang all the law and the prophets." (Matthew 22:37-40)

ʿAlī b. Abī Ṭālib said, "A group of people worshipped God out of desire for reward: surely, this is the worship of traders. Another group worshipped God out of fear: this is the worship of slaves. Still another group worshipped God out of gratitude; this is the worship of free men."[134]

The best form of worship is to worship God *for His own sake*. Having hope for Paradise and having fear of Hell is good, but these are instinctual impulses of one who has not reached full spiritual maturity. The believer knows that God is wise, merciful, and just, and thus, he puts his full trust in God's judgment. None will be wronged on the Day of Judgment.

---

[133] Abu Nuʿaym, *Hilyat al-Awliya'*, Volume 10, pp. 7.
[134] Nahj al-Balagha, Saying 237.

The believer simply worships God because He alone has the right to be worshiped – this is the best way to live.

Ja'far al-Ṣādiq said in his supplication, "O my God, even if You tie me with chains, deprive me of the stream of Your bounties in the presence of people, divulge all my scandalous acts before the eyes of all Your servants, order me to Hell, and prevent me from the pious ones, I will never stop hoping for You, and I will never stop expecting Your pardon, and Your love will never exit my heart … If You order me to Hellfire, I will tell all the inhabitants therein that I love You."[135]

---

[135] Du'a Abu Hamza al-Thumali.

Ascension and Return

لما أراد الله أن يرفع عيسى إلى السماء خرج على أصحابه وفي البيت اثنا عشر رجلا منهم من الحواريين يعني فخرج عليهم من عين في البيت ورأسه يقطر ماء فقال لهم إن منكم من يكفر بي اثني عشرة مرة بعد أن آمن بي، ثم قال: أيكم يلقى عليه شبهي فيقتل مكاني فيكون معي في درجتي؟ فقام شاب من أحدثهم سنا فقال له: اجلس ثم أعاد عليهم فقام الشاب فقال أنا: فقال عيسى اجلس ثم أعاد عليهم فقام الشاب فقال أنا. فقال: أنت هو ذاك. فألقى عليه شبه عيسى، ورفع عيسى من روزنة في البيت إلى السماء

When God wanted to raise Jesus up to heaven, he went out to his companions. In the house, there were twelve apostles – he came out to them from a basin in the house. His head was dripping with water.

He said to them, "Among you is one who will renounce me twelve times after believing in me."

Then, he said, "Which of you will take on my likeness and be killed in my place? He will be with me at my level [of Paradise]."

A young man, who was the youngest of them in age, stood up.

So, he said to him, "Sit down."

Then, he repeated [the question] to them, and the young man stood up again. He said, "Me."

So, Jesus said, "Sit down."

Then, he repeated [the question] to them, and the young man stood up again. He said, "Me."

So, he said, "You are him, then."

So, he was given the likeness of Jesus, and Jesus ascended to heaven from a niche in the house.[136]

Commentary:

---

[136] Ibn Kathir, *al-Bidaya wa al-Nihaya*, Volume 2, pp. 109.

"They said: 'We killed Christ Jesus the son of Mary, the Messenger of God' – but they did not kill him, nor did they crucify him, but so it was made to appear to them. Those who differ therein are full of doubts, with no [certain] knowledge, but only conjecture to follow, for surely, they did not kill him. Rather, God raised him up to Himself; and God is the Powerful, the Wise." (Quran 4:157-158)

Despite the documentation of the crucifixion in the Gospels, the letters of Paul, the Annals of Tacitus, and the Antiquities of Josephus, the Quran offers this cryptic account. The Quran does not deny the historicity of the crucifixion per se – as "it was made to appear" that such an event took place – but it may deny the reality of the event.

Muslims have differed in their interpretation of this verse. Dr. Ali Ataie illustrates three main theories upheld by Muslims historically: (1) Jesus was physically substituted with someone else, who was crucified in his place, (2) Jesus was nailed to the cross, but he swooned and did not physically die, and (3) Jesus did indeed die on the cross, but God is the ultimate giver of life and death; and Jesus' spirit was not killed.[137]

Among Muslims, the first model is most popular. Some, like Ibn Isḥāq, Mujāhid, Qatāda, and Ṭabarī, said that either an enemy of Jesus Christ was crucified as a punishment, or an

---

[137] Ali Ataie, "The Crucifixion and the Qur'an: An Exegetical and Historical Inquiry Into Surah 4:157-158", Zaytuna College, https://www.youtube.com/watch?v=09-JthSnyic&t=921s

apostle volunteered himself to be martyred in Jesus' place.[138] Whether the apostles knew that it was not *really* Jesus on the cross differs from authority to authority. Zamakhsharī and Rāzī argued that God did not deceive the people supernaturally, but that the alleged event was essentially a misunderstanding.[139]

Surprisingly, there may be some precedent for this idea among early Christians. Basilides (c. 117-138 AD), who claimed to be a student of Matthias (the apostle that replaced Judas in the Book of Acts) and Glaucias (an alleged disciple of Simon Peter), said that Simon of Cyrene was crucified in the place of Jesus.[140] Some Gnostics believed that the real Christ was not truly of flesh, but that he was a spirit. This is taught in the Gnostic Apocalypse of Peter (early 2nd century AD), which has the real Christ sitting on a tree, laughing, as he watched the crucifixion of the body transpire.[141] St. Ignatius of Antioch condemns this belief and the Docetists in his Epistle to the Trallians.[142]

Whether these beliefs had precedents in the first century AD is anyone's guess. Some have suggested that the Gospel of

---

[138] Ibid.
[139] Ibid.
[140] Irenaeus of Lyons, *Against Heresies*, Book 1, http://www.earlychristianwritings.com/text/irenaeus-book1.html
[141] James Brashler and Roger A. Bullard, *The Apocalypse of* Peter, http://gnosis.org/naghamm/apopet.html
[142] Lightfoot and Harmer, *Ignatius to the Trallians*, http://www.earlychristianwritings.com/text/ignatius-trallians-lightfoot.html

John's omission of Simon of Cyrene, as well as its solitary inclusion of a spear thrusted into Jesus while he was on the cross, were designed to quell doubt that existed regarding Jesus' death on the cross. Interestingly, John's Gospel is the only one to assert explicitly that Mary the mother of Jesus witnessed the crucifixion; and he puts the witnesses at the foot of the cross, while the other Gospels have the witnesses watching at a distance. In 1 Corinthians 15, Paul appears to be rebuking a community that was denying the death and/or resurrection of Jesus. Apparent contradictions between the Gospel accounts invite further doubt.

I have often thought about Judas Iscariot and Thomas the Apostle and their relationship to the crucifixion. Judas dies right after the crucifixion, but one account says that he fell headlong and burst asunder (Acts 1:18), and another says that he hanged himself (Matthew 27:5). Christians attempt to reconcile the two accounts by saying that Judas hanged himself, and then a faulty noose eventually led his body to a high fall. Whether this reconciliation between two distinct texts by different authors is satisfactory depends on one's level of skepticism. Then, there is Thomas, whose name literally means "twin", who conveniently goes off to India to proselytize. Is it possible that he was the one made in the likeness of Jesus Christ? God only knows.

The idea that Jesus was crucified but survived (the "swoon theory") is a modern view held by the Ahmadiyya and some Sunni Muslim historians and apologists. The Quranic verse says that they did not "crucify him" (*mā ṣalabūhu*), and "crucify" (*ṣalaba*) in Arabic means "to kill by crucifying."[143] Thus, one can technically say that Jesus was nailed to the cross – but did not die there – without contradicting the Quran.

Some of the anecdotes from the Gospels that are used to reinforce this position include: (1) Jesus said, "For as Jonah was three days and three nights in the whale's belly; so shall the Son of Man be three days and three nights in the heart of the earth." (Matthew 12:40) Just as Jonah was alive in the whale, it could be expected that Jesus would also be alive in his sepulchre. (2) Pilate was amazed that Jesus was already dead (Mark 15:44), as crucifixions could last several days.[144] (3) The women came to Jesus' tomb with spices and oils days after he was buried. It was not a typical Jewish custom to open a coffin after burial; so perhaps the women came to treat a wounded Jesus. (4) The "resurrected" Jesus was in disguise, as Mary Magdalene mistook him for the gardener (John 20:14-16) – this may make better sense if Jesus had survived the crucifixion and was trying to escape the detection of Jewish and Roman authorities. (5) Jesus ate food with his disciples (Luke 24:41), even though resurrected bodies would have no need for nourishment.

The final position, which affirms Jesus' crucifixion, argues that 4:157-158 of the Quran is only a refutation of the claim that the Jews had killed and crucified Jesus. The preceding verses (4:153-156) address the Jews, and at this time, the Jews

---

[143] See *Lisan al-Arab*'s section on صلب
[144] FP Retief and L Cilliers, *The history and pathology of crucifixion*, https://pubmed.ncbi.nlm.nih.gov/14750495/

may have been boasting that they were the ones that killed Jesus.[145] Since it was the Romans that allegedly crucified Jesus, to say that the Jews killed him would technically be incorrect.

The crucifixion of Jesus was probably accepted by Ghazālī[146] and scholars that affirmed the authenticity of the four Gospels. It was also the official position of the Ismailis by the 10th century AD as per Abu Ḥātim al-Rāzī.[147] The Fatimid court cleric Mu'ayyad al-Dīn al-Shīrāzī argued that martyrs do not really die but remain alive with God (Quran 3:163).[148] When he was being crucified for blasphemy, the famous Sufi mystic al-Ḥallāj reportedly recited the Quranic verse "they did not kill him, nor did they crucify him, but so it was made to appear to them" to emphasize his union with the Living God.

According to this understanding, Jesus being "raised up" is a reference to his soul being raised up after death, not his body. One reason why I am less sympathetic to this view is because all souls are raised up, yet Islamic literature tends to single out Jesus with this expression. When ʿAlī died, his son Ḥasan famously eulogized him by saying, "On this night, the Quran was revealed, and on this night, Jesus the son of Mary was raised up, and on this night, Joshua the son of Nun was killed, and on this night, my father, the Commander of the Faithful

---

[145] M. Albert, *Homilies contre les juifs* by Jacob of Serugh, 44, 1. 17.
[146] Todd Lawson, *The Crucifixion and the Qur'an: A Study in the History of Muslim Thought*, pp. 118
[147] Ibid, pp. 118-119.
[148] Ibid, pp. 119.

ʿAlī b. Abī Ṭālib died."[149] Had Jesus been a martyr like Joshua and ʿAlī, perhaps this grandson of the Prophet Muhammad ﷺ would not have used a unique way to describe Jesus' alleged death.

It is arguable that the Quranic motif is one of triumph. The prophetic stories of the Quran echo the life of the Prophet Muhammad ﷺ. Just as Noah is rescued from the flood, and just as Abraham is rescued from the inferno, and just as Moses is rescued from Pharaoh, and just as Jesus is apparently rescued from the cross, the Quran suggests that Muhammad ﷺ would be delivered from the pagans. There are no drawn-out martyrdom stories in the Quran because that is not the pattern Muhammad ﷺ is modeled on. This may give subtle credence to the idea that Jesus, too, was saved by God and made triumphant over his enemies. A similar theme is iterated in the Old Testament: "Now I know that the LORD saveth his anointed (*māšîaḥ*); he will hear him from his holy heaven with the saving strength of his right hand" (Psalm 20:7) and "There shall be no evil befall thee, neither shall any plague come nigh thy dwelling, for he shall give his angels charge over thee, to keep thee in all thy ways. They shall bear thee up in their hands, lest thou dash thy foot against a stone ... Because he hath set his love upon me, therefore will I deliver him: I will set him on high, because he hath known my name. He shall call upon me, and I will answer him: I will be with him in trouble; I will deliver him, and honour him. With

---

[149] Saduq, *al-Amali*, pp. 396.

long life will I satisfy him, and shew him my salvation."
(Psalm 91:10-16)

One of the reasons why the Jews may have wanted Jesus
crucified was to discredit his teachings. Deuteronomy 21:22-
23 says that a man put to death and hung on a tree is "cursed
by God." Simply assassinating Jesus by another means would
not undo his message. This may be why the crowd insisted on
having him crucified (Luke 23:21). Of course, Paul creatively
turns this around, saying that Jesus was indeed cursed, but on
our behalf, atoning for our sins (Galatians 3:13).

Of course, an Islamic worldview has no problem with a
martyred prophet and a miraculous resurrection. After all,
John the Baptist was martyred, and in the parable of the
hamlet in ruins, the Quran mentions the resurrection of a
man after a hundred years (Quran 2:259). Affirming or
denying the historical event of crucifixion has little bearing on
Islam. The more substantive contention that Muslims have is
with the idea of atonement. Muslims believe that they will
bear the consequences of their own sins, unless forgiven by
God. The sin of Adam is not inherited by those who did not
commit it. Presumably, those between Adam and John the
Baptist were simply expected to worship God and live an
ethical life, and Muslims see no need for this to change with
Jesus. The idea of a human sacrifice absolving the past and
future sins of humanity is simply contrary to what the Quran
teaches. Putting an innocent man to death, rather than simply
forgiving mankind out of divine grace, goes against the
sensibilities of Muslims.

God says in Hosea 6:6, "For I desire mercy, not sacrifice, and acknowledgement of God rather than burnt offerings." He says, "To what purpose is the multitude of your sacrifices unto me? saith the LORD: I am full from the burnt offerings of rams and the fat of well-fed cattle; I take no delight in the blood of bulls and lambs and goats." (Isaiah 1:11)

May we be granted the full grace of our Loving God.

استخلف عيسى شمعون وقتلت اليهود يودس الذي ألقى عليه الشبه

Jesus appointed Simon, and the Jews killed Judas, who had been given his likeness.[150]

Commentary:

St. Simon Peter was the leader after the ascension of Jesus. He was one of his apostles, and in Islamic literature he is referred to as Shamʿūn al-Ṣafā ("Simon the Rock" – sorry Dwayne Johnson). Some exegetes say that he was the third man sent to warn the people of Antioch (Quran 36:14). He is considered to be the first pope in Catholicism.

Peter, of course, was an Israelite, and was even respected in Judaism as an upholder of the Torah in a time of sedition. The

---

[150] Ibn Kathir, *al-Bidaya wa al-Nihaya*, Volume 2, pp. 110.

day of his death was established as a fast day in Jerusalem (every ninth of Tevet).

He was said to have even authored a famous *piyyut* for Yom Kippur, according to Rashi's own grandson.[151] Judah ben Samuel of Regensburg (d. 1217 AD) considered Peter a righteous man. So, the example of St. Peter is a bridge between the three Abrahamic religions.

عيسى عليه السلام قبل أن يرفع وصى الحواريين بأن يدعو الناس إلى
عبادة الله وحده لا شريك له وعين كل واحد منهم إلى طائفة من
الناس في إقليم من الأقاليم من الشام والمشرق وبلاد المغرب،
فذكروا أنه أصبح كل إنسان منهم يتكلم بلغة الذين أرسله المسيح
إليهم

Before Jesus, peace be unto him, was raised up, he instructed the apostles to call the people to the worship of God alone without partners. He appointed each of them to a group of people in the provinces of the Levant, the East, and the Western countries.

---

[151] https://www.yeshiva.co/ask/57950

Christ made each of them speak the language of those they would be sent to.[152]

Commentary:

In Matthew 28:16, Jesus commissions the apostles to make disciples of all nations. Among Muslims, there is a difference of opinion on whether Jesus' message was meant only for the Children of Israel (as hinted in Matthew 15:24) or for the whole world. For Sunnis, the prophets before Muhammad ﷺ all have a localized mission, while for the Shīʿa, the five major messengers (*ulil ʿazm*), including Jesus, had a global mission.

رفع عيسى بن مريم عليه بمدرعة صوف من غزل مريم، ومن نسج مريم ومن خياطة مريم فلما انتهى إلى السماء نودي يا عيسى ألق عنك زينة الدنيا

Jesus the son of Mary ascended whilst wearing a rabbinical garment made of wool spun from the yarn of Mary, the weaving of Mary, and the sewing of Mary. When he came to

---

[152] Ibn Kathir, *al-Bidaya wa al-Nihaya*, Volume 2, pp. 110.

the heaven, it was called, "O Jesus! Remove the frills of this world from yourself."[153]

Commentary:

Since Jesus Christ was the supreme ascetic, his most cherished possession was a simple woolen garment. Jesus is being asked to shed his attachment to this sentimental article of clothing before gaining proximity to God. Removing this rabbinical garment may be a symbol for Jesus' exit from the worldly realm in his ascent.

This expression, "rabbinical garment", has a special connotation in Jewish mysticism. There is a concrete term in Kabbalah, חלוקא דרבנן, precisely "rabbinical garment", which refers to the ethereal body of saints, somewhat similar to the body of people we see in the dream, visible and tangible yet not material in our crude sense. It is linked to the Shechinah. Removing the garment may indicate ascension to higher levels beyond. It works as a bridge between physical and spiritual.

عن أبي الحسن علي بن موسى عليه قال :إنه ما شبِّه أمر أحد من أنبياء الله وحججه للناس إلا أمر عيسى وحده، لأنه رفع من الأرض حياً، وقبض روحه بين السماء والأرض، ثم رفع إلى السماء، ورد

عليه روحه، وذلك قوله عز وجل :إِذْ قَالَ اللّهُ يَا عِيسَى إِنِّي
مُتَوَفِّيكَ وَرَافِعُكَ إِلَيَّ وَمُطَهِّرُكَ وقال الله تعالى حكاية لقول
عيسى قوم القيامة :وَكُنتُ عَلَيْهِمْ شَهِيدًا مَّا دُمْتُ فِيهِمْ فَلَمَّا
تَوَفَّيْتَنِي كُنتَ أَنتَ الرَّقِيبَ عَلَيْهِمْ وَأَنتَ عَلَى كُلِّ شَيْءٍ شَهِيدٌ

Imam ʿAlī b. Mūsa al-Riḍa said, "No case among the prophets
and the guides of God has been obscured to the people except
that of Jesus alone. This is because he was raised from the
Earth whilst alive, then his soul was taken between heaven
and Earth, then he was raised to heaven and his soul was
returned to him. This is the meaning of His words, 'When
God declared: O Jesus! Surely, I will take you and raise you to
Myself and purify you ...' (Quran 3:55), and God says, quoting
Jesus on the Day of Resurrection, 'and I was a witness over
them as long as I was with them, so when You caused me to
do, You are the Observer over them, and You are a witness
over everything.' (Quran 5:117)"[154]

---

[154] Saduq, ʿUyun Akhbar al-Rida, Volume 2, pp. 193.

عَنِ النَّبِيِّ ـ صلى الله عليه وسلم ـ قَالَ لاَ تَقُومُ السَّاعَةُ حَتَّى يَنْزِلَ عِيسَى ابْنُ مَرْيَمَ حَكَمًا مُقْسِطًا وَإِمَامًا عَدْلاً فَيَكْسِرُ الصَّلِيبَ وَيَقْتُلُ الْخِنْزِيرَ وَيَضَعُ الْجِزْيَةَ وَيَفِيضُ الْمَالُ حَتَّى لاَ يَقْبَلَهُ أَحَدٌ

The Prophet Muhammad ﷺ said, "The Hour will not come to pass until Jesus the son of Mary comes down as a just judge and a just ruler. He will break the cross, kill the swine, and abolish the poll-tax. Wealth will become so abundant that no one will accept it."[155]

سَمِعْتُ النَّبِيَّ صلى الله عليه وسلم يَقُولُ " لاَ تَزَالُ طَائِفَةٌ مِنْ أُمَّتِي يُقَاتِلُونَ عَلَى الْحَقِّ ظَاهِرِينَ إِلَى يَوْمِ الْقِيَامَةِ ـ قَالَ ـ فَيَنْزِلُ عِيسَى ابْنُ مَرْيَمَ صلى الله عليه وسلم فَيَقُولُ أَمِيرُهُمْ تَعَالَ صَلِّ لَنَا . فَيَقُولُ لاَ . إِنَّ بَعْضَكُمْ عَلَى بَعْضٍ أُمَرَاءُ . تَكْرِمَةَ اللَّهِ هَذِهِ الأُمَّةَ "

.

The Prophet Muhammad ﷺ said, "A section of my people will not cease fighting for the truth, and they will prevail till the Day of Resurrection. Jesus the son of Mary would then descend, and their leader would invite him to come and lead them in prayer, but he would say, 'No, some amongst you are

[155] Sunan Ibn Maja, Book 36, hadith 153.

leaders over others.' This is the honour that God shows this nation."[156]

سَمِعْتُ رَسُولَ اللَّهِ صلى الله عليه وسلم يَقُولُ " يَقْتُلُ ابْنُ مَرْيَمَ الدَّجَّالَ بِبَابِ لُدٍّ "

The Prophet Muhammad ﷺ said, "The son of Mary will kill the Antichrist at the gate of Ludd."[157]

---

156 Sahih Muslim, Book 1, Hadith 300.
157 Jami` al-Tirmidhi, Book 33, hadith 87.

Part 2: An Anthology of Writings on Jesus Christ

Hail Mary, Mother of Christ

Bilal Muhammad

Mary, the mother of Jesus Christ, is mentioned thirty-two times in the Quran and eighteen times in the Bible. The Prophet Muhammad ﷺ included her among the Four Liege-ladies of Paradise, alongside Āsiya the wife of Pharaoh, Khadīja the wife of Muhammad, and Fāṭima the daughter of Muhammad. Unlike the other three Liege-ladies, Mary is mentioned explicitly and in great detail in the Quran. In fact, she is the only woman mentioned by name in the book. She is even given as a role model for the other wives of the Prophet Muhammad ﷺ in 66:12 of the Quran. Mary also gets a whole chapter named after her, and it is the only Quranic chapter named after a woman.

One can argue that Mary is the real bridge between Muslims and Christians (especially Catholics). While Jesus is a more primary figure in both traditions, the divinity and atonement of Jesus is not recognized by Muslims, even though these doctrines are most central to Christians. The unconditional love and godhood of Jesus are often foundation to one's relationship with Christ, and without them, many struggle to understand what a Muslim Jesus could even be besides a mere prophet. We will discuss and possibly solve this dilemma later in the book. Mary, on the other hand, is uplifted and expounded upon in the Quran, to the point where many Christians and even secular people could draw lessons therefrom.

Mary and Jesus are considered one sign (Quran 21:91, 23:50), and they are usually mentioned together. Unlike anyone else in the Quran, Jesus is repeatedly called "Jesus the son of Mary" (*'Īsā ibn Maryam*). This also differs from his biblical titles "Son of God" and "Son of Man"; perhaps done to emphasize God's lack of a child as well as the unique status of Mary.

Jesus' family, called the "House of Amram (*Āl 'Imrān*)", represent a new sacred clan in the Quran. Yes, they are still part of the greater House of Abraham, but their dispensation would include the likes of Joachim (*'Imrān*), Anne (*Hannah*), Zechariah (*Zakariā*), Elizabeth (*Alaysābāt*) – all of whom are considered saints in the Catholic tradition – as well as John (*Yahya*) and Jesus. In no unclear terms, the Quran distinguishes the House of Amram, saying, "God chose Adam and Noah and the House of Abraham and the House of Amram above all beings." (Quran 3:33) God selects families to bear forth His mighty messengers, perhaps to give them the best nature-nurture foundation that they could possibly have.

Like in the Protoevangelium of James, the Quran speaks of the birth of Mary, with some key areas of difference. In both accounts, Anne dedicates her child to the service of God (Quran 3:35, Protoevangelium 4), but in the Quran, it is implied that Anne was expecting a boy (Quran 3:36). Women were typically allowed to serve in the rectangular structure surrounding the Temple, with some restrictions. Mary was put under the care of Zechariah in the Temple. Zechariah was an ordained priest, and it is unclear if his prophetic status allowed him to take Mary into the Holy of Holies. Otherwise, it was strictly forbidden for anyone to enter the Holy of Holies except the priest during the Yom Kippur service. If Mary was, at any time, allowed to enter, then that would be truly extraordinary.

Even if she remained in the surrounding area, the young Mary would have found herself consecrated in a predominantly male institution. One can only imagine the stares of confusion a young girl like Mary would receive, but her upbringing in the Temple would guarantee that she would not be as other kids were. The Temple played an even bigger role for Jews than the Ka'ba does for Muslims, so one can picture this girl in a sacred, solemn environment, curtained away from worldly concerns and zeroed-in on worship and study. She was an ascetic being prepared to bring forth the supreme ascetic.

Zechariah would find heavenly sustenance with Mary (Quran 3:37) – which can either be spiritual or physical provision, or both.[158] The Protoevangelium says more explicitly that Mary would receive "food from the hand of an angel" (Protoevangelium 8). Unlike any other Christian apocrypha, the Quran says that Mary would communicate with the angels even before she would conceive Jesus (Quran 3:42-43). Even in the mind of a Muslim, this is quite extraordinary, as Mary was not usually considered a prophetess, yet the angels would come to her, and she would produce miracles. She was

---

[158] Seyyed Hossein Nasr et al, *The Study Quran*, Commentary of Ibn Kathir for 3:37.

purified and chosen by God and given instructions pertaining to prayer (Quran 3:42-3). All this was so problematic, that even a Sunni scholarly giant like Ibn Ḥazm would list Mary as a prophetess.[159]

Miracles, however, don't seem to be exclusive to prophets in the Islamic tradition, as the Quran attributes marvels to the Sleepers of the Cave (and their dog), Dhul Qarnayn, and Āṣif b. Barkhīyya, and premonitions to the Egyptian king and the prisoners in the story of Joseph. Perhaps revelation (*waḥī*) and inspiration (*ilhām*) are not so straightforward in Islam. Mary is called a saint (*ṣiddīqqa*) in 5:75, which appears to be a special rank that is distinguishable from the prophets and the righteous (Quran 4:69). Her being "chosen" by God (*innallāha iṣtafākī*) and likely protected from Satan (Quran 3:36) makes her anything but an ordinary believer.

Mary is an example of a woman that did not reach God through a man. Joseph the Carpenter is entirely absent, and Mary was holy before any earthly mention of Jesus. There is no iconic manger scene with the three Magi in Islamic literature. Instead, Mary is alone on a spiritual retreat (Quran 19:16) when the angel announces her pregnancy. When Mary asks how this is possible, the Gospel of Luke gives a somewhat graphic description, saying, "the Holy Spirit will come upon you, and the power of the Most High will overshadow you. Therefore the child to be born will be called holy, the Son of

---

[159] Maribel Fierro, "Women as prophets in Islam.", *Writing the feminine: Women in Arab sources*, pp. 183- 198.

God." (Luke 1:35) The Quran, in its characteristic modesty, simply has the angel respond, "So will it be! Your Lord says, 'it is easy for Me. We will make him a sign for humanity and a mercy from Us. It is an ordained matter.'" (Quran 19:21) Immediately after this, the verses have Mary withdrawing to a remote place and delivering her child. She is overwhelmed by the pangs of childbirth (unlike the painless delivery told in the infamous "Gospel of Barnabas" that is sometimes attributed to Muslims). As she cries out in pain, God provides dates and rivulets to soothe her. Till now, Muslim women that are pregnant or in labour eat dates, which may have significant medicinal value.[160] [161] [162] All of this is, too, unlike the Christian apocrypha that the Quran is so oft compared to. Would the dates imply a spring-summer Christmas?

After Jesus is born, Mary takes a vow of silence as the people are in shock to see her with the child. They cited her lineage as a descendant of Aaron and a child of a priestly household. She simply points to the child, who speaks from his cradle, declaring, "Surely, I am the Servant of God. He has given me the scripture and He has made me a prophet. He has made me

[160] Razali N et al, "Date fruit consumption at term: Effect on length of gestation, labour and delivery", US National Library of Medicine, https://www.ncbi.nlm.nih.gov/pubmed/28286995
[161] Masoumeh Kordi et al, "The Effect of Late Pregnancy Consumption of Date Fruit on Cervical Ripening in Nulliparous Women", Journal of Midwifery and Reproductive Health, http://jmrh.mums.ac.ir/article_2772_0.html
[162] Al-Kuran et al, "The effect of late pregnancy consumption of date fruit on labour and delivery", US National Library of Medicine, https://www.ncbi.nlm.nih.gov/pubmed/21280989

blessed wherever I go. He has commissioned me to pray and give charity as long as I live and to be kind to my mother. He has not made me arrogant or defiant. Peace be unto me the day I was born, the day I die, and the day I will be raised back to life." (Quran 19:30-33) A similar account is recorded in the Syriac Infancy Gospel (also known as the Arabic Infancy Gospel); but the earliest extant manuscript of this gospel is from circa the fourteenth century AD, and it shows influence from the Quran.[163] The reference could very well have been a Christian response to the Quranic birth story, as Jesus' first words therein are "I am Jesus, the Son of God, the Logos".[164]

In the Quranic account, Mary stands as an example for every woman who has been falsely accused of sexual misconduct. Jesus' words in the cradle presumably prevented her from undergoing any form of punishment in her lifetime. Afterwards, there were accusations made against Mary and Jesus recorded in the Talmud – that Mary committed adultery with a Roman soldier named Pandeira and that Jesus brought sorcery from Egypt.[165] Such accusations may have been a reaction to Roman persecution of Jews. Nonetheless, God cursed those who pronounced these calumnies against Mary (Quran 4:156). In the Quran, if a person accuses a woman of

---

[163] *Gerd Wittka, "Die Weihnachtsverkündigung in den apokryphen Kindheitsevangelien",*
https://www.grin.com/document/107479
[164] The Arabic Infancy Gospel of the Savor,
http://gnosis.org/library/infarab.htm
[165] Talmud Shabbat 104b, Sanhedrin 67a.

fornication and does not produce four valid witnesses, the accuser is to be flogged eighty times, and the accuser's testimony will be rejected forever (Quran 24:4). For men who are falsely accused of sexual misconduct, the Quran offers the example of Joseph and Zulaykha.

The main area of difference between the Muslim Mary and the Christian Mary is her status as "the mother of God (*theotokos*)". The title was formally recognized in 431 AD at the Third Ecumenical Council in Ephesus. Nestorius, the Patriarch of Constantinople, objected to giving Mary this title, leading to the Nestorian Schism. His followers in the "Church of the East" retained that Mary was only "the mother of Christ (*Christotokos*)" and not the mother of his divine nature. The Monophysite view succeeded by the sixth century AD when Nestorian patriarch Mar Aba the Great ratified the title *theotokos*. In Catholic liturgy, the most prominent usage of *theotokos* is in the "Hail Mary" rosary. Interestingly, the lines "holy Mary, mother of God, pray for us sinners, now and at the hour of our death" were only added to the Hail Mary in the sixteenth century AD. These phrases would really be the only ones that Muslims would take issue with in the Hail Mary, and they are barely five centuries old.

The Quran cites people that took Mary as a goddess in 5:116. It is unclear if this is referring to the Collyridians – an early Christian sect in Arabia that worshiped Mary as a goddess – or if it is laying a general criticism against the Christian exaltation of Mary. A hint may be in 5:75, where it is emphasized that both Jesus and Mary ate food, thus being flesh-and-blood humans with needs. Then there is the intercession of Mary, which, like in Christianity, is a disputed practice among Muslims.

What is clear is that Mary is the most highly venerated woman in the world. Billions of Christians and Muslims look to her example as a paragon of faith, perseverance, modesty, and the status of women. Yet, she was a simple woman, from a family of humble worshipers, living under a brutal occupation. She suffered the pangs of birth as women do, and God was there to assist her and defend her honour. She birthed Jesus, and her example birthed two great world civilizations.

Sharing Jesus, Sharing Earth

21st century Muslim-Christian Solidarity Prior to End Times

by R. David Coolidge

Prophet Jesus son of Mary, peace be upon them both, has been with me my whole life. I was baptized in his name as an infant, rejected the belief that he was "[God's] Son, our Lord"[166] in middle school confirmation class, and affirmed his status as a Prophet (*nabī*) and Messenger (*rasūl*) of God when I accepted Islam as an undergraduate at Brown University in 1998. In many ways, Islam allowed me to strive to love and know Jesus without those aspects of Christian theology that made little sense to me.

I remember once when, on a camping trip in my youth, an Evangelical Christian friend encouraged me to open my heart to Jesus. The memory is clear in my mind - as I looked at the stars up above, nestled in my sleeping bag, I prayed: "Jesus, if you are out there, please come into my heart." Nothing happened the next day or any day after that an Evangelical Christian would consider to be a true conversion. But over

---

[166] "Apostles' Creed," *Loyola Press*, accessed October 8, 2021, https://www.loyolapress.com/catholic-resources/prayer/traditional-catholic-prayers/prayers-every-catholic-should-know/apostles-creed/.

time, I have embraced Jesus more fully as someone with whom I feel my destiny intertwined. When the Sunnī Muslim hadith scholar al-Bukhārī (d. 870) relates the following statement from the Prophet Muhammad, blessings and peace be upon him and his family, I feel like he is talking about the Jesus I have come to know:

The Hour will not be established until the son of Mary descends amongst you as a just ruler. He will break the cross, kill the pigs, and abolish the tax laid upon those of other worldviews who live under the rule of God. Money will be in such abundance that nobody will be able to accept charity from another![167]

لاَ تَقُومُ السَّاعَةُ حَتَّى يَنْزِلَ فِيكُمُ ابْنُ مَرْيَمَ حَكَمًا مُقْسِطًا فَيَكْسِرَ الصَّلِيبَ وَيَقْتُلَ الْخِنْزِيرَ وَيَضَعَ الْجِزْيَةَ وَيَفِيضَ الْمَالُ حَتَّى لاَ يَقْبَلَهُ أَحَدٌ

Jesus was non-violent in the 1st century, but both Christians and Muslims are united that he will return at the end of history amidst great conflict. Both Sunnī and Shī'ī Islamic theology affirm that Jesus will serve as second-in-command to Imam Mahdi, the direct descendant of the Prophet Muhammad who is foretold to establish the rule of God over the entire Earth. For Muslims, a significant part of Jesus' return is to demonstrate the truthfulness (*ṣidq*) of Muhammad's claim to be a Messenger

---

[167] "Sahih Al-Bukhari 2476 - Oppressions - كتاب المظالم - Sunnah.Com - Sayings and Teachings of Prophet Muhammad (صلى الله عليه و سلم)," accessed October 8, 2021, https://sunnah.com/bukhari:2476. Translation is my own.

from God, hence the breaking of the cross (the central symbol of Christian theology) and the killing of pigs (as eating pork is a common aspect of Christian culture, sometimes used to distinguish Christians from Muslims).[168] In no uncertain terms will Jesus demonstrate that he is not God, but rather a human being who submits to God like Moses and Muhammad, upon them all peace.

But those days are not upon us yet. In the 21st century, we live in a global world where Christians and Muslims share the Earth, and both engage in the spiritual struggle to still believe that Jesus' return is real. Approximately 1/3rd of humanity is either Muslim or Christian, and thus there is no other figure whose messianic return humanity waits for more than Jesus. 1300 years ago, this messianic expectation was confined primarily to areas around the Mediterranean Sea. Now it is global. At the same time, the Qur'an declared in the 7th century that those who are closest in spirit to Muslims are the Christians (verse 5.82). This remarkable historical convergence should not be taken lightly. The global calendar is a constant reminder of how long it has been since Jesus left this world, because it is based on the approximate time of Jesus' birth. Jesus, in many ways, has insinuated himself into world history like no other figure.

Many Hindus also acknowledge Jesus, upon him peace, as a great teacher or even an incarnation (*avatāra*). The influential 20th century guru A. C. Bhaktivedanta Swami (d. 1977) called Jesus and Muhammad "two powerful devotees of

---

[168] Matthew Carr, *Blood and Faith: The Purging of Muslims Spain 1492-1614* (London: C. Hurst & Co., 2017).

the Lord" in his massive translation and commentary on the Sanskrit text *Bhāgavata Purāṇa*.[169] But Hindus do not focus on Jesus' central role in human historical time the way that Muslims and Christians do. It is easy to dismiss this Jesus-centric conception of time as a recent result of European colonialism and Christian evangelization, but for one who sees history unfolding according to God's decree, it is difficult to reject this chain of events simply because of their provenance. Rather, it is a constant reminder of the shared eschatological expectations of both Christians and Muslims. The Hijrī calendar, a pragmatic innovation by the burgeoning caliphate, has far less relevance to a global future, despite its continued importance for cataloguing the Muslim past as well as keeping track of the yearly cycle of Ḥajj, the months of Ramaḍān and Muḥarram, and other important Muslim communal observances. Arguably, the march of history has belonged primarily to Christians and Muslims for the last 2000 years, and the future is deeply dependent on the interplay between the two largest religious traditions on the globe, both of whom are waiting for Jesus to return.

Beyond matters of the past and the future, Jesus has much to teach us about how to live in the 21st century. The Shī'ī hadith scholar al-Kulaynī (d. 941) relates that some of the followers of Jesus asked him, "with whom should we keep company?" Jesus' reply was, "[keep the company of] one who reminds you of God when you look at them, their speech increases you in knowledge, and their deeds make you desirous

---

[169] "ŚB 2.4.18," accessed October 8, 2021, https://vedabase.io/en/library/sb/2/4/18/?query=jesus#bb18504.

of the world to come (من يذكركم الله رؤيته ويزيد في علمكم منطقه ويرغبكم

في الآخرة عمله)."[170] This can be experienced, most assuredly,
amongst some Protestant-Catholic-Orthodox Christians, as
well as some Sunnī-Shīʿī-Ibāḍī Muslims. Of course, each
individual must follow the theology and law/ethics that speaks
most directly to their sense of accountability before the God of
Abraham, and leave the final outcome of one's earthly striving
up to Divine Mercy and Justice. But in each other's company
much solace can be found amidst a secular world often seeking
to banish God as far as possible from our shared life together.[171]

It is this seemingly paradoxical tension between
peaceful coexistence based on interfaith solidarity and
eschatological expectation of global conflict that must be
grappled with in the 21st century. It is not enough to espouse a
secularized sense of global religious harmony that strips our
traditions of theological specificities regarding the human
future on Earth. But it is also not helpful to presuppose we are
living in end times already. As Hatem Bazian has argued, any
political vision for Israel/Palestine that does not acknowledge
the impossibility and inhumanity of displacing millions of Jews
or millions of Palestinian Christians and Muslims is a

---

[170] Mahdī Muntazir Qāim, *Jesus (Peace Be with Him) Through the Qurʾān and Shiʿite Narrations*, trans. al-Ḥajj Muhammad Legenhausen (Elmhurt: Tahrike Tarsile Qurʾan, 2005), 290. I have modified the translation.

[171] Talal Asad, *Formations of the Secular: Christianity, Islam, Modernity* (Stanford, Calif: Stanford University Press, 2003).

fantasy.[172] Put simply, until Jesus actually returns, we have to work on sharing space as best we can. Leave the era of separating the sheep and the goats (Matthew 25:31) for a time when the rationally-accessible development of political institutions, as shown by 5000 years of recorded human history,[173] is upended by miraculous events and global upheaval on a scale never before seen. It would be a tragic folly for people to kill each other en masse for the next eight decades of the 21st century over messianic expectations, only to see the 22nd century dawn with Jesus still living in another realm and not yet ready to return.

Perhaps this perspective is too North American of me, or too academic. Perhaps if I was growing up in a society fighting tooth and nail everyday, like Israel or Iran, all I would care about are those allies who have my back and those religious discourses which strengthen my cause. But I am a student of the history of religion, and as much as I believe and hope that Jesus is coming back, I cannot determine what to do today based on what may or may not happen tomorrow. Better to heed the words of Jesus, as conveyed again by al-Kulaynī, to "not grieve over what you lose of this world, just as the people of this world do not grieve over what they lose of their religion

[172] Hatem Bazian, *Palestine: ...It Is Something Colonial* (The Hague, Netherlands: Amrit Publishers, 2016).

[173] Francis Fukuyama, *The Origins of Political Order: From Prehuman Times to the French Revolution* (New York: Farrar, Straus and Giroux, 2011).

"174.(لا تأسوا على ما فاتكم من الدنيا كما لا يأسى أهل الدنيا على ما فاتهم من دينهم).
My responsibility (taklīf) is to act on my beliefs with as much
sincerity as I can muster, knowing that even if I lose this world
in the process, I can win in the end by the mercy of the Most
Merciful. And I would expect no less from a Christian
attempting to live their tradition with as much sincerity as they
can muster. As much as I believe in Jesus, upon him peace,
there is nothing in my understanding of the Islamic tradition
that implies he is more likely to come in 10 years than 1000. If
I am an ally of Jesus in this short life of mine, then even if I die
in bed at home I will be counted amongst those willing to fight
alongside him and Imam Mahdi. I take great solace in the verse
of the Qur'an that states:

> ...Had not Allah repulsed the people from one another, ruin
> would have befallen the monasteries, churches, synagogues
> and mosques in which Allah's Name is mentioned greatly.
> Allah will surely help those who help Him. Indeed Allah is
> all-strong, all-mighty (22.40, Qarai translation)

وَلَوْلَا دَفْعُ ٱللَّهِ ٱلنَّاسَ بَعْضَهُم بِبَعْضٍ لَّهُدِّمَتْ صَوَٰمِعُ وَبِيَعٌ وَصَلَوَٰتٌ وَمَسَٰجِدُ
يُذْكَرُ فِيهَا ٱسْمُ ٱللَّهِ كَثِيرًا ۗ وَلَيَنصُرَنَّ ٱللَّهُ مَن يَنصُرُهُ ۗ إِنَّ ٱللَّهَ لَقَوِىٌّ عَزِيزٌ

The balance of power keeps us from arrogating to ourselves the
right to solve the great global religious debate, wherein people
from around the world draw on their cumulative traditions to

---

174 Qāim, *Jesus (Peace Be with Him) Through the Qur'ān and
Shi'ite Narrations*, 358.

200

express their beliefs and worship of God.[175] In Islamic theology, it is only the time of Jesus and Imam Mahdi that brings about the final historical resolution, which is a preview of the comprehensive resolution of the beginning and end of all human things that happens outside of regular time "on a Day whose measure is 50,000 years" (Qur'an 70.4). So I have no problem sharing the city of Oakland, CA (where I currently live) with Jews, Christians, Muslims of all denominations, Hindus, Sikhs, Buddhists, atheists and whoever else lives here. Of course I would love for them all to join me praying towards Makkah and fasting in the month of Ramaḍān, but that is their choice and it is my responsibility to teach them what I know of Islam.

A Christian might be repulsed by what I have written here, as a heretical deviation of what they understand of Jesus' cosmic purpose. They might feel I have taken a Divine member of the Trinity and turned him into a mere human being. They may reject the traditional eschatological role of Jesus, and find it disturbing that I am grappling with the meaning of his literal return to Earth. That is good - we have to be willing to be disturbed and upset in these conversations. We must accept that Jesus is a highly contested figure, which seems to be one of the purposes for him coming back - to set the record straight. We have to live in a world where we share Jesus, upon him peace, just as we share the Earth upon which he walked 2000 years ago. It is not always easy, but it is part of our responsibility as members of the global community of the 21st century. Most importantly, we have to be willing to not grieve of what we

[175] Wilfred Cantwell Smith, *The Meaning and End of Religion* (Minneapolis: Fortress Press, 1991).

might lose from this world if we lose it on the path of our most sincere and authentic attempt to follow Jesus the son of Mary, peace be upon them both. Whether Jesus was God or Jesus was a Prophet-Messenger, no one can deny that he taught us to give up our possessions and our lives for the sake of God to the extent we are capable.

Meeting Jesus Again: A Jewish Perspective

Yaqub ibn Israil

Two thousand years ago a young charismatic teacher taught in
the hills of the Galilean countryside. His advocates have
called him teacher, prophet, and son of God. Muslims and
Christians worldwide hold him up as an example and model.
Over four billion people alive today look to Jesus of Nazareth
as an expression of human spiritual possibilities. Among
these communities he has inspired feats of self-sacrifice and
spiritual greatness. Both communities cling to his example,
just not together. At the core of their disagreement is a
question of his nature, where for over a thousand years, they
have erected walls over whether he was a mere prophet or a
part of the divinity.

Among other communities, the evaluation is mixed. Most
secularists see Jesus as a model of revolution and as a teacher
of social justice. Those who see him as a harbinger of Marx
deliberately cast aside the fact that his "kingdom is not of this
world". A scattered few humanists paint him as an
egomaniacal madman. Even among strident atheists, most
recognize Jesus as someone who inspired the marginalized of
his day to seize their dignity, while telling them that he had
only come into to the world to "serve, not to be served."

Given the scope of the debate, let's turn to what most of us
can agree on. Sources on his life paint a picture of a teacher
who was able to communicate with both the farmer and the

most erudite scholar. His focus was comforting the poor with the message of God's closeness and through performing acts of healing mercy. Jesus spoke to people where they were, coming to find them in the fields, docks, and roadsides.

The Gospels tell us that he relied heavily on parable - a powerful method that is accessible and open to interpretation. The images in these stories appear in the finest art, literature, and oratory created by Western culture. When Martin Luther King spoke of America as a "Prodigal Son", we knew that Dr. King was telling us that America needed to come to its senses and return home to God. When Abraham Lincoln told the Illinois Republican Convention that "a house divided itself cannot stand", the audience understood that division would mean desolation and that a struggle was coming that would determine whether America would be slave or free. The Good Shepherd, the Sower, the Laborers in the Field - these images resonate throughout our culture.

Considering the power of his teachings and how far they permeate into our cultures, should we be surprised that even detractors of Christianity largely try to claim him for their own? That the primary argument centers not on whether he was a spiritual giant, but on the degree of his glory?

There is one notable exception to the chorus of praise for Jesus - the Jewish people themselves. This man, who was born of a Jewish woman, who celebrated Passover, who taught in the Temple, who was called Rabbi and Messiah of Israel and son of David, has become the litmus test for Jewish authenticity. So strongly is he rejected by his own people that Rabbis have argued that accepting his teaching automatically excommunicates any Jew from the Jewish people.

"We do not accept outside, non-Jewish teaching!" this voice thunders.

Curious - because over the years, I have shared a Passover table with yogis, Buddhists, atheists, Sufis - all united by the fact that they are Jewish. No one ever batted an eye. Most rabbis I knew welcomed them and their "non-Jewish trappings" into our midst, celebrating it as a homecoming and pointing to the enduring nature of their *yiddishe neshama* (Jewish soul). Some of these go on to blend Judaism with their non-Jewish teaching of choice, and their welcome continues. If you don't believe me, do a google search of "Judaism and mindfulness". Most synagogues and Jewish community centers offer meditation and yoga classes. Clearly, non-Jewish influence isn't the problem. There must be something else.

"But they teach ideas that are so foreign. A messiah who dies and might be resurrected. Who teaches, dies, and then becomes king? We don't have such a thing. Who believes nonsense like that?"

Chabad - the single largest Jewish movement in the world, whose rabbis are in far-flung communities around the world and give isolated Jews a place to connect with Jewish tradition - is locked in a debate centering around the question of

205

whether their last Grand Rabbi (who died in 1994) is in fact the promised Messiah. If we excommunicated everyone who had their heart set on a deceased claimant as Messiah, we would have to excise the most vital and energetic force in modern Judaism from our midst.

Most of the justifications used to validate the kneejerk rejection of all things Jesus simply don't hold water. I don't believe for a moment that the Jewish rejection of Jesus has much at all to do with doctrine or teaching. It has to do with history. Understanding the Jewish rejection of Jesus requires a fundamental shift in how Judaism is perceived.

Judaism is not a religion. It's not an ancient tradition. It's an invention.

In the second century, the nation of Israel faced a crisis. Following the defeat of the Bar Kochba revolt, the Emperor Hadrian set to work uprooting every element of Jewish distinctiveness. The Temple was already destroyed, but the Emperor took the formal step of banning the study of Torah law and ceremonially torched Torah scrolls in the pagan temple built in place of the Bayt HaMiqdash on the Temple Mount. Intent on eliminating the people of Israel from memory, he took the step of renaming Judea to Syria Palestina and began executing the rabbinic sages of the time.

When we lost the temple, we lost the living ritual heart of our people. Now Hadrian sought to erase our covenant with God and our connection to our land from our memory. The Rabbinic remnant had to create a way to keep alive Jewish identity. The religion of the people of Israel had to become something more than a tribal tradition - it had to be a means for Jewishness to survive in the face of a harsh, unwelcoming diaspora existence. It would have to overcome the lures of belonging in new lands. Being Jewish had to be more powerful than both the desire to blend in or to avoid Antisemitic violence.

As a result, the Rabbis' primary concerns weren't God and simple, faithful adherence to Torah - they were survival and maintaining Jewishness. Keeping Judaism alive wasn't about spiritual connection, it was about avoiding intermarriage and making sure that we could continue to work and survive and protect ourselves. It was about excommunicating those people who provoked the ire of the surrounding majority. The rabbis took steps like forbidding foods cooked by Gentiles - not because they were unkosher, but because Jews might grow too close to them.

After the Emperor Constantine, the name of Jesus was increasingly on the lips of the majority that we had learned to fear. Forced to take refuge in foreign lands, we were ostracized for maintaining our distinctive peoplehood. Forbidden from taking trades and owning land, we were painted as greedy and conniving because we succeeded in business. Meanwhile, our Christian neighbors invented stories about us to fuel and justify their pogroms. It didn't help that we - the people of Israel - rejected the Jewish Messiah that our neighbors believed in.

If a Jew accepted Jesus, they were shedding Jewishness and identifying with the oppressive majority. A Christian Jew became a contradiction.

In the nearly two thousand years since we were expelled from Israel, the Rabbinic focus on identity has been the cure to surviving outside of our homeland. However, its single-minded obsession on peoplehood has neglected our spirit. It has led to a jurisprudence held captive by a punctilious legalism that makes it easy to gatekeep identity but chains the spirit. Modern Jewish movements define themselves by their relationship with Jewish law, using that definition to cut ourselves off from one another.

If the children of Israel are to have a future, we desperately need a reset. We need to revisit our earliest sources, enter into the debates and discussions of the first Rabbinic sages and find a way to truly live Torah - a life infused by the service of God and the love of others. We must fearlessly dig into the words of the sages who taught when the Temple stood and when the Jewish people were unafraid of ghettos and pogroms. Unfortunately, our sources are limited. The Talmud, the record of the debates of the first rabbis, is hardly objective. It preserves the opinions of the teachers who created the rabbinic agenda and serves to exalt them as teachers over Israel.

To reignite the debate, the children of Israel need the words of all our early teachers - both the Sanhedrin approved and the ones who were rejected. We need to hear the voice of Jesus. His emphasis on humility, on how our religious observance is meaningless without integrity, echoes the clarion call of the Israelite prophets more clearly than anyone who has ever bore the name of Rabbi. But how can Israel ever be convinced to pay attention to a book used by the Church to justify the slaughter of our ancestors? How can we ever trust that the gospels are much more than a record of Jesus' transformation in the hands of the Church?

Thankfully, there is another vital and authentic source for the teachings of Jesus of Nazareth. The book you find in your hands represents a collection of the traditions of Jesus cultivated by the Muslim world. Muslim seekers and saints approached the life and words of Jesus as an inspiration and a model, not as a weapon in the war to delegitimize the children of Israel. In these traditions, the profound humanity and soaring spirit of a servant in love with God comes through.

In the mind of Torah, life is a passage from one place to another. When asked by Pharaoh about his accomplishments, the patriarch Jacob spoke not of "his life" but of the "years of his sojourn". When Jesus was asked by his disciples about the world, he told them "The world is a bridge - pass over it but do not build." If we are ever to shake off our spiritual exile, we must turn to Divine law as a means for knowing God and refining our soul, free from the obsessions of gatekeeping identity. The way of Jesus of Nazareth found in these pages represents a vital link to a Torah that is living. It is not just what Judaism was, but I believe represents what we might still become.

Reconciliation of Jew and Jesus through Islam

Malik

Jesus as the Messiah is a notion that is anathema to Judaism. Despite a few positive historical evaluations (Martin Buber, Hyam Macoby), the view of Jesus in a good light is difficult to find in a Jewish context. Messianic Judaism provides its adherents with a reconciliation of Jesus with Judaism, but not without problems; namely, its rejection by mainstream Judaism as an ideology copied from Christianity and served with matza ball soup. This author wants to offer his reconciliation of Jesus through the acceptance of Islam.

Jesus Christ is seemingly inseparable from the pogroms that Jews experienced over the years. This is obvious to anyone growing up in Jewish home. Before I found Islam, I was exposed many times to evangelism, but the belief in the alleged divinity of Jesus Christ and the atonement were never satisfactory. Indeed, I found Christianity intolerable because of the political manipulations of its adherents and their dismissal of modern science. It was only after my acceptance of Islam that I decided to read the Gospels in order to understand who Jesus was in a new light. It is only in my conviction that the Quran is a revelation from God that gives credence to Jesus as having a divine role.

Reading the Gospels as a Jewish convert to Islam showed that my pre-conceived notions about the New Testament were somewhat unfounded. There is no reference to Jesus stating anywhere that he was divine. In fact, there are passages where Jesus denies he is God, such as when he asks a student, "why do you call me good when only God is good?" In the same paragraph, Jesus answers the question of salvation, and says to follow the commandments. (Mathew 18:20) Following the commandments is a belief shared by Judaism and Islam, but abhorrent to modern Protestant Christianity. It is only in Paul's letters that one will find teachings about a sacrificial atonement.

Jews have heard every argument put forth by missionaries and have responses (mostly spot on) to their claims. Websites such as "Jews for Judaism" provide a "criteria" list of expectations that the Messiah is supposed to fulfill in order to qualify as such. This criteria is largely drawn from the Mishne Torah (which in turns draws from statements in the Talmud with biblical references). The rabbis maintain that Jesus Christ does not fulfill any of the criteria. Many Jews believe that they have a strong case that Jesus Christ fails the criteria and that the proof texts used by missionaries do not help their case.

The problem with the Jewish criteria on the messiah is that it based on rabbinical opinion, which are not necessarily true to the textual proofs from the Tanach. In fact, not a single verse used in the Mishne Torah even mentions "the Messiah". That is because the only time *moshich* is mentioned is in reference to Cyrus. A reading of the Bible does not reveal a character that fits the criteria anywhere. Maimonides said that belief in the Messiah is the 13th principal of faith, but he based it a verse in Deuteronomy that can only vaguely hint to the notion at best. If we put a handful of people on a desert island (who have never read the Bible) and have them read the Bible, would they come up with a notion of a Messiah?

An assumingly perfect criteria for the Messiah did not protect the Jews from believing in false messiahs. Jesus Christ certainly convinced many Jews that he was the chosen one, but my brethren may argue that his identity was out of ignorance of Jewish doctrines. Very well. A man as knowledgeable as Rabbi Akiva was not prevented from believing Bar Kochba was the Messiah. At one time, most of the Jewish world held Shabbata Tzevi as the Messiah. The embarrassment of his apostasy caused masses of Jews to burn books. Today there are no shortage of Jews educated in the Yeshiva system that hold the Lubavitcher rebbe as the Messiah. To argue that there is a foolproof method to identify the Messiah is not something found in Jewish history.

The assertion that Jesus violated the Torah is the most serious attack on his integrity; and the one that discredits him for Jews. Do the Gospels substantiate this claim? Matthew records Jesus denying it all together; "behold I have come not to violate one iota of the Torah but to fulfill it." A serious charge requires a serious analysis. What did Jesus mean in this statement? The question of how Rabbinic and modern scholarship understand Mosaic legislation is necessary, but too much for this brief essay here. The Gospels clearly portray a man that stressed obedience and even zealousness for the law. What seems to egg on people's emotions is the numerous disputes Jesus had with the Pharisees and other groups. Jesus' critique of the former was because they upheld "tradition of the elders" over the divine word. Admittedly, this critique may be unsettling for a religion that holds Rabbinic legislation indispensable for any Torah command and places "emmunah hakchamim (faith in the sages)" as a basis for truth. The critique of such notions makes the message of Jesus and Muhammad one and the same in their upholding of divine authority.

What about the charge of Antisemitism? Medieval Christianity blamed the death of Jesus on the Jews. The Qur'an does not see the charge of prophecide as unique to the Jews. More on this topic can be said, but for the moment, it is clear that the Qur'an holds that mankind in general is guilty for trying to fight the truth of divine messengers. Was the criticism of Jesus on the Pharisees too harsh? Didn't he refer to them as snakes? The numerous debates in the Gospels show peers having discussions that are sometimes heated and sometimes not. It is also noteworthy that biblical language uses animals to illustrate character (Ishmael and the donkey, etc.) The Talmudic rabbis even refer to their previous generations as "snakes" in their opposition to their detractors.

(Berakot 19a). The charge that Jesus was Antisemitic is not one to be taken seriously.

Can a positive case be made for Jesus as the Messiah in biblical prophecy? A successful attempt would have to make us scrutinize the way scholars and rabbis interpreted prophecy over the years. Lack of success would not sting, since my conviction is based on the Qur'an in either case. More important to my faith would be the appeal of Jesus' own message as recorded in the Gospels. Are the actions and teachings of Jesus Christ consistent with the messages of the Torah and Quran? Can the Quranic claim about the prophetic mission of Jesus be found in the Gospels? I say yes, despite some shortcomings in the text. From my view, if it acts like a prophet and smells like a prophet, then by golly, it must be a prophet! Jesus said it best, "By their fruits you shall know them."

"SPRING IS CHRIST, THE TREES ARE MARY":

A CHRISTIAN REFLECTION ON JESUS & MARY IN ISLAM

By Avellina Balestri

My first encounter with Muslims was in the midst of my very Catholic childhood, when my family was visiting Mount St. Mary's Grotto in Emmitsburg, Maryland. Pilgrims from around the world came to this replica of the Grotto of Our Lady of Lourdes in France, and not all of them are Catholic, or even Christian. Muslims and Hindus both have come to pay their respects to the Blessed Virgin Mary, and even donated the beautiful rugs that were used for the chapel. The Muslim family we met after Sunday mass had come from overseas. I don't remember exactly where they were from, but I am guessing either from the Middle East or Southeast Asia. What I do remember is them telling us that, although they did not believe Jesus was the Son of God, they did view Him as a great prophet, and honored His mother accordingly.

My next conscious memories of Islamic culture pertain to TV and movies, mainly adaptations of "Arabian Nights." It was through them I first heard about polygamy being a thing, when in one animated version, Ali Baba marries his slave girl to reward her for saving his life...and that of his first wife. In another film, I remember an old wise man encouraging the hero to persevere by describing Jannah, which, though amped up for exotic effect, did paint a fairly accurate picture taken from Muslim hadiths. But what stuck out the most to me was the emphasis on destiny in these tales, and the conviction that what goes around comes around as it was meant to from the very beginning, according to the divine will. Later, I would learn an Arabic saying associated with the famous 99 Names devotion, which encapsulates this ethos succinctly: "My Master has beautiful names, and the whole of the affair returns to Him."

More specifically pertaining to religious topics, I remember watching *The Message* starring Anthony Quinn as Hamza and giving a silver screen treatment of the early days of Islam. This was the second time I'd seen the Irish/Mexican-American actor cast as an Arab (and let's face it, he nails it), the first being in the really long and really painful *Lawrence of Arabia*. I remember that depressing desert romp with a melodramatic blonde Karen mainly because I had an awful sore throat and it was Thanksgiving Day. I still can't get over the fact that Larry managed to pull the "Nothing is written" line and not have every Muslim in ear range reply "Dream on, habibi." I was also surprised none of his Arab friends offered him a calico cat to pet or a communal bowl of comfort food to ingest when everything fell apart in the end (because we know they totally would). It could have given him just enough get up and go not to embark upon motorcycle suicide on the rolling English road. But I digress.

Getting back to my impressions of *The Message*, which thankfully did not feature any misplaced Carnarvonshire natives suffering from an identity crisis, the film gripped my imagination mainly due to the epic battle scenes, which I watched on repeat. It was the first time I heard "Allahu Akbar" in terms of an actual battle cry, and the emphasis upon God being greater going up against the odds made perfect sense. Another scene that particularly sticks with me is Muhammad's triumphal return to Mecca. The cinematic vista and plot tension was top notch, from the moment the army could be heard chanting in the distance, to the moment when he smashes the idols in the Kabbah. Per Islamic tradition, we never see Muhammad's face, but rather the camera itself stands in for him. I honestly found the production at its strongest when it was most committed to the cultural context of the story it was telling, and weakest when it tried too hard to pander to western Christian audiences. And of course, I wanted more Arabic (and yes, I know there's an alternate version entirely in Arabic, but I wanted it, like, mixed!).

There is something of a recent focus upon this very thing upon the release of a new adaptation of *Dune*, Frank Herbert's cynical sandbox Game of Galactic Thrones which is peppered with Arabesque people and place names (and is basically a Larry the Wanna-Be Arab reboot). While comparisons to real world Islam are decidedly hit and miss, the old '80's movie, which most fans find to be ham and cheese (and it mostly is) has a scene I would consider to have an Islamic flavor. Though mostly remembered for Sting's magic metal winged sexy space underwear (that burned all our corneas), the sequence that stuck with me is the grand finale when Paul Atrades takes on the very prophetic role of Muad'dib, "the Teacher", declaring that the desert planet of Arrakis had been created to "train the faithful", and that one cannot go against the word of God. A higher power is palpable, right down to the meshing of worlds, as rain is finally unleashed upon Arakkis, seeming to be mystically brought forth from Paul's oceanic home planet of Caledon. The scene cuts between Paul's glowing blue eyes from the spice of the planet to flashbacks to the rolling waves from his native land. The expression on the actor's face as the musical score builds truly conveys the awe of the moment as he embraces his destiny.

In my early 20's, my interest in Islamic culture and spirituality gained speed primarily due to the poetry of Mawlana Jalal ad-din Rumi, who first grabbed my attention while scrolling through FaceBook with the following lines: "And don't think the garden loses its ecstasy in winter. It's quiet, but the roots down there are riotous." After that, I was drawn to read as much of his work as I could get my hands on, as well as other Sufi mystics such as Hafez, Rabia, and Ibn Arabi. I deeply appreciated their ability to capture, with linguistic delicacy and depth, the longing for love, enlightenment, and union with the divine. There are many similarities between them and Christian mystics, particularly from among the Carmelites, such as Saint John of the Cross and Saint Teresa of Avila. Both Spaniards, they may have had some familiarity with Islamic literary styles due to the legacy of the Moorish invasions, demonstrating the fascinating cultural crossovers that come about as a result of the movements of peoples.

My first encounter with a hard copy Quran was equally poetic in nature, when I opened it at random in a bookstore and my eyes fell on the following words from the Surah Nur: "Allah is the Light of the heavens and the earth. The example of His light is like a niche within which is a lamp, the lamp is within glass, the glass as if it were a pearly star lit from a blessed olive tree, neither of the east nor of the west, whose oil would almost glow even if untouched by fire. Light upon light. Allah guides to His light whom He wills. And Allah presents examples for the people, and Allah is Knowing of all things (24:35)." I was told later by Muslim friends that landing on this particular verse was considered a blessing, since it is one of the most highly esoteric sections in the Quran. It certainly was clearer to me than ever that the Sufi poets who I so cherished were profoundly in sync with their scriptures.

The music of Sami Yusuf, often taking such traditional works and putting them to song in classical Eastern styles, has also enriched my spiritual life. This was true of various other nasheed artists as well, and I now have several rather extensive playlists of Islamic music in Arabic, Farsi, Turkish, Urdu, and more. I came to have a keen appreciation for the sound of these tongues, which seemed charged with a type of passion which is akin to the raw beauty of Old English and Celtic tongues. This artistic appreciation extended to Islamic calligraphy, highlighting the visual aesthetics of Arabic, seeming to weave that same dancing thread of destiny, the true outcome of which is hidden from the naked eye. This is all the more striking when combined with mesmerizing geometric designs, underscoring the symmetry of mathematics as a proof of divine order in creation.

When I decided to include a Saracen character in my Robin Hood retelling series, I brought in Muslim cultural advisors to make sure I did the job right. After all, the trope has been done multiple times in past adaptations, but I desperately wanted mine to be better crafted. I wanted to avoid the cheesy stereotypes that tend to plague Muslim characters in the media, either vilifying or romanticizing them through an orientalist lens. Most of my assistants came from Muslim sub-cultures in the West, while others lived in Muslim countries in the East. All of them helped me put on the mind of a Muslim when I wrote the dialogue and flashbacks, making the Islamic East just as real and multi-faceted as the Christian West, as opposed to some exotic distraction from the main plot. Kashif Ahmed bin Suleiman, the young aide of Salahuddin Ayubi, became a hero of his own story, with a unique personality that I cannot deny being something of a hybrid of the young Muslim men in my life. It is a testament to their quirky and caring behavior.

My favorite part of research is simply having Muslims tell me stories from their tradition, or alternately send me truck loads of links featuring other people telling stories from their tradition (because...they do that). I am a storyteller by nature and calling, and I appreciate the craft. It was through this love of hearing others out that I first came into contact with the larger-than-life character of Hussain, the grandson of Muhammad and son of the warrior, sage, and caliph, Ali ibn Abi Talib. His refusal to pledge allegiance to a tyrant and made a glorious last stand at the Battle of Karbala, makes his story take on a universal quality. It is repeated over and again through history, and emphasized in popular culture in every form imaginable. As a Catholic, he rather reminds me of Saint Thomas More, insofar as he was willing to go to his death rather than sign an oath which he could not in good conscience take. As such, these figures remain eternally victorious in their defeat.

I have a personal Hussain story to share as well. Due to an allergic reaction to what I think was strawberries (like, why? Why??), I ran a fever and slept fitfully. In my dreams, I saw a man dressed in traditional Arab garb whose face was covered. Even though I couldn't see his features, I acknowledged him, without any question or doubt, as Hussain. He reached out and handed me what looked like a kind of breakfast pastry. I had not been eating well for the previous few days, so that was exactly what I needed. I thanked him, and then I woke up, a little bit sorry I hadn't gotten around to devouring the edible offering. When I told Muslim friends about it later, they were quite enthusiastic about it, as seeing such figures in dreams, and being given food by them to boot, is considered quite a blessing. From what I've read, Hussain and his father Ali were no strangers to handing out food to the needy, and even more tellingly, at the burial places of Ali and Hussain, there is a tradition of handing out bread to pilgrims. When I ran across a video of this on YouTube, it gave me pause because it greatly reminded me of the feel of that dream. So if I did have a brush with the real deal somewhere in the realms between the Dunya and Jannah, all I can say is, I am honored. And let's just hope it wasn't a strawberry pastry.

Looking at the story of Hussain's martyrdom through a Christological lens, one can also see the passing parallels with the Passion of the Christ. Now, obviously, this should not be carried too far on a theological level, but as a Christian, I believe all people who suffer for the sake of righteousness share in a mystical unity with the redemption of the cross. Whether Hussain knew it or not, believed it or not, I see him as stitched into the same fabric, laying down his life for the honor of God and the common good as he understood it. Even in the midst of his own grief, watching his family members slain around him, he never abandoned faith in his Lord, and that carried him through to the consummation of his martyrdom. This, I believe, made him very closely connected with the spirit of Christ indeed.

And this feels like a perfect place for me to segue into the main purpose of this essay, which is a commentary on the interpretation and veneration of Jesus in Islam. While Muslims do not believe Jesus to have a divine nature, and reject the Christian doctrine of the Trinity as *shirk*, i.e polytheism, they do hold Jesus (or Isa in Arabic) in very high regard among those they deem to be prophets. He is honored as the last prophet sent to the world before the coming of Muhammad, the final messenger, causing Muhammad to refer to himself and Jesus as "brothers". Hadiths contain interesting details on Jesus' supposed physical appearance, including that he had a ruddy complexion, curly hair, and a broad chest. On a spiritual level, He is seen as the ascetic prophet who manifests a particularly pure reflection of the divine and mirror of the transcendent. Terms such as the "spirit" and "word" of God are used by Muslims to denote Him, though always in a creaturely sense. He is contrasted with Moses (i.e. Musa), who is seen as the prophet of the Law. Muhammad, as the Seal of the Prophets, is believed to provide a synthesis of both asceticism and legality.

As in the Christian Gospels, Jesus is conceived in the womb of the Virgin Mary with no earthly father, but unlike the Christian belief, God is not considered His father either. Also, the "Holy Spirit" referred to in the Gospel is often interpreted by Muslims to mean the angel Gabriel, alias Jibreel. This can be seen in another Rumi quote, though it must be said that, reading it with Christian eyes, it's hard not to read some Trinitarian mysticism into it, and one cannot help but wonder if the poet had some inspiration from Christian writings: "It was Divine Love that breathed the glow of life which made the immaculate Mary pregnant with Jesus. It was Divine Love that produced the Holy Spirit which made Mary deliver the miracle of Christ."

That having been said, according to Islamic theology, this miracle is decidedly not the Incarnation with all its associated implications for Christians, but purely a command from Allah: 'Be and it is.' This is seen as analogous to the unique creation of Adam, believed to be both the first man and the first prophet, when God put spirit into the formation of clay. This nicely ties into the imagery of Islamic and Christian apocryphal stories that have Jesus breathing clay birds into life. Interestingly, Christians also connect Jesus to the first man, calling Him "The New Adam" because we believe that He represents the entirety of the human race, sharing all things with us but our sinful condition, and yet bearing the effects of that condition to the bitter end of His death on Golgotha. This motif is highlighted in an ironic way within the Gospel of John, when Pontius Pilate presents Jesus to the crowd with the words, "Ecce Homo! Behold the Man!" Through the Passion that follows, climaxing in the flow of blood and water from His side, He becomes the whole Man and the true "Adam", which etymologically means "sap of life."

Christians and Muslims both concur that Jesus traveled as an itinerant teacher, instructing the people to serve the Lord with their hearts and not merely lips, calling for repentance and reform among the tribes of Israel, and working many miracles, including healing the sick and feeding the multitudes. To quote Ali ibn abi Talib:

"If you desire I will tell you about Jesus, the son of Mary, peace be upon him. He used a stone for his pillow, put on coarse clothes and ate rough food. His condiment was hunger. His lamp in the night was the moon. His shade during the winter was just the expanse of eastward and westward. His fruits and flowers were only what grows from the earth for the cattle. He had no wife to allure him, nor any son to give grief, nor wealth to distract him, nor greed to disgrace him. His two feet were his conveyance and his two hands his servant."

In a similar vein, Rumi wrote: "Jesus used to fast all the time, never breaking the fast, and stayed up during the night, never sleeping. Jesus not only spent the nights awake, but he also spent them in devotions. Jesus was manifested in the world with the divine name, 'Time' during the day, and with the divine name, 'Self-Subsisting', or 'He who is neither overcome by sleep nor slumber', during the night."

We also agree that His enemies among the High Priests, upset with the way He called out their hypocrisy, conspired to have Him killed. But while the source and summit of the Christian faith quite literally hangs upon the Cross, drawing all Men to himself as He takes up the role of Paschal Lamb and triumphantly rising from the tomb, Muslims believe that Jesus was spared such a fate. Typically the explanation offered is that another man was miraculously made to appear like Him, and thus was crucified in His place. This could quite accurately be called a 360 degree turn on Christian atonement theories involving substitution. Narrations differ on who this crucified man was, ranging from Judas Iscariot, being divinely punished for his betrayal, to one of the beloved disciples, sacrificing himself voluntarily to save his master.

This refutation of Christ's crucifixion, in part, corresponds with a widely held Muslim belief that, while prophets can and will endure trials, crucifixion is a cursed death, uniquely agonizing and humiliating, being stripped and slowly suffocating, which God would not allow one of his major messengers to undergo. Another reason for rejecting the Cross in its entirety may well be a rejection of the Christian belief that the innocent Christ would sacrifice Himself to atone the sins of the guilty, and that it would be accepted by God. This differs from the Islamic understanding of sin and punishment residing almost entirely with the individual.

After escaping the snares of His enemies, Muslims believe Jesus was ascended into Heaven, corresponding to the Christian belief in the Ascension that takes place forty days after the Resurrection. They also believe He will return one day in the capacity of a warrior to fight the Dajjal, or anti-Christ, who will be leading the people astray. In some narrations, Jesus will also break church bells, smash crosses, and kill pigs, symbolizing all the perfidities and infidelity that Muslims perceive among Christians (I don't even want to know what they think He'll do to the pubs, since, unlike Christians, they believe He was a teetotaler). He will then give stern talk to those who worshipped Him, asking when He ever told them to do that (ala Muslim Dawah apologists), and encourage them to abandon that weird Trinity stuff and become good Muslims.

Rather unexpectedly, Jesus is shown as having some role to play judging mankind, as he does in Christianity, although the context of this trust, and why Jesus holds it out as opposed to Muhammad, is open to interpretation and ultimately a bit of a mystery. Eventually, after living a fairly normal life and, according to have writings, having the family he was denied the first time around, it is believed Jesus too will die, as all creatures must, and He will be buried beside Muhammad in the city of Madinah. Admittedly, this sounds just a bit like the plot to "The Last Temptation of Christ", though I guess a more happy ending kind of version, sans the demon angel girl and other drug trip effects brought you by the Scorsese saga.

The question here might arise in some reader's minds as to whether Muslims are honoring the same Jesus as Christians, or rather a parallel vision of Him, co-opted from Christian heretical sects and apocryphal literature to lend credence to Islam. After all, when Christians say we love Jesus, we are talking very specifically about loving the Incarnate Son of God, sent to save the people from their sins through His dying and rising. Regardless of how highly Islam holds the prophets, and it is very high, it is still a major demotion from the orthodox Christian position, and even the heretical Arian position. The understanding of Christ's nature, mission, and even ultimate fate diverges quite decisively in Islam, relegating Him to a subplot hero instead of being the main character in the drama of salvation. Muhammad viewing Jesus as a brother is no doubt true, but that was *his* form of Jesus, decidedly declawed and defanged from Christian theology.

Meanwhile, many Muslims believe that Christians have simply become fanatical over their personal pan prophet and really just need to douse these flaming pagan tendencies. But the real question that gnaws upon the Christian faithful remains: how does God come into communion with us, and was Jesus, in fact, the ultimate source of that communion, the incarnate Emmanuel, God-made-Man who pitches His tent among us? These are the tremendous questions posed every

229

Christmas and Easter, even if they have been all but lost in secular celebrations.

Sometimes, I feel that an easier crossover point might be found in Jesus' mother, since we both agree upon her purely human nature. The Virgin Mary, or Maryam in Arabic, is held in very high regard in Islam as a woman of piety, patience, and unwavering faith when faced with accusations of unchastity. Catholics and Muslims might find some commonality in the fact that we both view her as particularly preserved from the evil one. A hadith according to Abu Hurairah says: "I heard the Messenger of Allah saying: No son of Adam shall be born unless that he should be afflicted by the Satan at the hour of birth, when he initiates his life crying out of the Satan's touch, except Maryam and her son." Indeed, in Sufi thought, there has been a tradition of seeing the dome of mosques as a reflection of the fullness of Maryam's womb. She is counted by Muslims among the four highest women of Jannah, the others being Khadijah, the first wife of Muhammad, Fatima, the daughter of Muhammad, and Asiyah, the righteous wife of the Pharoah who cared for the prophet Musa.

In Christian belief, this pristine reality instilled within and embraced by the Virgin Mary enables her to become the gateway of the mystery of the Incarnation, God's chosen means of revealing Himself to Man, through the Person of Jesus Christ. She is a guidepost on the journey of the

Christian life, traversing the one-ing of God and Man through the life, death, and resurrection of her Son. In the same way, she stands in the liminal places between our passing from one world into another, and we invoke her to "pray for us now and at the hour of our death." She carries this immense creative force within her very body, like a seed ready to burst open and bear new fruit. The Muslim image of the date tree lowering its branches and the spring bubbling to the surface of the sand while she is in labor mirrors this notion of the abundance of God in which she partakes to a unique extent. Her sanctified fertility is captured well in yet another excerpt from Rumi, who also uses trees to bring her to mind: "Spring is Christ, raising martyred plants from their shrouds. Their mouths open in gratitude, wanting to be kissed. This wind is the Holy Spirit. The trees are Mary."

There are particular connections worth noting between Mary and Fatima. For Catholics, the two names are inextricably intertwined through the apparitions of Our Lady in Fatima, Portugal to three shepherd children, culminating in a miracle where the sun was seen to "dance" in the heavens. But focusing upon the women themselves, it is interesting how both are seen in their respective traditions as feminine vessels of grace who are visited by angels and serve as conduits of wholeness and holiness for others. They share a common archetypal place in the spiritual imagination, distinct from the goddess traditions within paganism, in that they claim no divinity for themselves, but rather reflect an intimate connection with the Creator as His creations.

There are countless stories about both women's interior lives that nurture the divine presence and enable them to demonstrate spontaneous love of their neighbors. In the Gospel of Luke, she rushes off to visit her aging cousin Elizabeth, and aids her through her pregnancy. She keeps secrets deep in her heart, when shepherds, kings, and prophets tell her mysteries of her son's destiny. In Coptic tradition, she bathes her child first in a spring so that a sickly child may bathe afterwards and be cured, and the cave where she nurses becomes a source of renewed milk for the dry breasts of mothers who make pilgrimage there. In the Gospel of John, Mary famously urges Jesus to perform the miracle of the Wedding Feast at Cana, instructing the servers to do whatever He tells them. Although initially showing reluctance, Jesus changes the water into wine so that the young couple will not be embarrassed.

In Islamic tradition, Maryam receives fruit from the angels in her cell, in preparation for the coming fruit of her womb. Fatima, too, seems to reside both in the world and beyond it, and is the recipient of angelic gifts and treasures or virtues. Her father's mission to proclaim the oneness of God to a polytheistic society costs his family's worldly security. She has to clean off the camel dung thrown at him, and suffers the loss of her mother Khadijah after they are driven out of

Mecca. She bears it all with grace. Later, as a wife and mother, she teaches her children to always pray for their neighbors before their own household. She gives her clothes away to the poor, and the angels show themselves adorned in them. She offers food to any who supplicate, even if it means going hungry herself, and the angels tend to her needs.

One story tells how, after falling ill, she sends her husband Ali out to find her a pomegranate to ease her fever, even though they are out of season. When he finally finds one, he winds up splitting it between two sick beggars he meets on the way home, believing it will help to cure her fever. But when he returns to his house, feeling guilty for failing his wife (even though we might easily imagine her being pleased that his generosity matches her own), he finds her sitting with a full basket of pomegranates outside the door. Evidently the angels set about another task to show favor to those who live in daily remembrance of their Lord.

As sorrowful mothers, we find another parallel between the two women as well. In the Gospels, we find Mary standing at the foot of the Cross, a grieving witness to glory. She becomes the mother of the "Beloved Disciple", who takes her into his home upon Christ's final instruction. Through this, she surrogates not only Saint John, but also the whole Church, even as she cradles the body of her son before He is laid in the tomb. In stories taken from Shia tradition, we see a similar image of the spirit of Fatima, cradling her son Hussain as he is martyred at Karbala, and later wandering the battlefield to lament the slaughter caused by sinful men. Both women, in the depths of their emotions, capture a certain fullness of being. The divine light shines through them, like the sun through a prism, and plays upon them, like wind through a reed. They are both covered in "noor", in that angelic light that bears fruit in ways that are always surprising, and ever ripe. They make space between the notes for suffering.

Touching again upon the Christian doctrine of the Incarnation, it might be said that the act of Christ's materialization within Mary is, in and of itself, a form of sacrifice, a pouring out of the eternal essence that comes before the pouring out of blood. It might accurately be said that Christ died from the very act of becoming human, being brought down into the mess of human history, and allowing it to kill Him. He felt both faith and despair, commending His spirit to His Father not long after asking why He had been forsaken. He would be plunged into the pit spared to others; He would finish the unfinished stories, consummate the love song of death, to sleep until the dawn of resurrection, and grant us hope for all things to be made new. And so the son of Abraham, laid upon the altar, may easily find its echo in the fate of the Son of God. Yes, God gives us His mercy, by an angel's word upon the day of Annunciation, the Day of Creation, and the Day of Redemption. Yes, by the Lamb that was Slain from the foundations of the world.

I feel it is worth noting here that the Christian understanding of sin is in contrast to the Islamic vision. We see it as not simply the wrongs which we commit, but rather the lack within our natures that causes us to have a "downward spiral" towards darkness, an imbalance between flesh and spirit, which causes corrupted or inordinate desires and attachments. We shared a primal union with the divine, symbolized by the Garden of Eden, but then sought to be our own gods and decide for ourselves what was good and what was evil. We cut the chain of being and bear its internal consequences. The weight of this condition of sin which we share in common with our archetypal first parents, as well as the personal sins we commit in our own lives, separates us from the perfection that is God. We are not responsible for the sins of others on a personal level, but we all share in common a fallen nature, weakened and wounded. That is what Original or Ancestral sin is really about at its core. Adam stands for the entire human race which is caught in the grips of the devil's dysfunction and stands in need of divine restoration. It is that which, we believe, needs to be addressed on a root level, through the drama of salvation we believe unfolds in history through Jesus Christ.

This is why we see the curtain in the Temple tearing down the center at the crucifixion of Jesus. It is a symbol that the separation between God and Mankind has been abolished, through the divine grace of this death on a Friday afternoon we dare to call good. Christ lays his life down in accordance with the Father's will, just as martyrs do. It is a sacrifice, yes, but not a suicide. It is a demonstration of the "weight of sin" that we see manifesting upon the cross. He bears that weight, and it kills Him, yet this very thing is what ultimately breaks the strength of it and allows frail human beings to enter fully in the mystery of the divine life. This is what it means to be a Christian. "If any man be in Christ, He is a new creation." Our very condition of being spiritually separated from God is something that Christ underwent. He went down to the very darkest points of human God-forsakenness to draw us into the essence of the divine, and I personally would say Trinitarian, life. Because that, to me, is what the Trinity is, and ultimately what the Incarnation is. It is that quality of God which pulls us ever up into His very dynamism.

The heart of Christianity is Christ not holding equality with God as something to be grasped, as Adam and Eve sought to grasp after it, but rather emptying Himself and becoming small and despised, more like a worm than a man, so that the foundations of this original deviation would be shaken. This is the nature of Divine Kenosis at the heart of Christian hope. We all carry our own crosses, in this jagged-edged world full, and are called to plant them alongside the Cross on Calvary. In this way, even our smallest share in His suffering becomes redemptive. This may seem like foolishness to some, the icon of the dying God which Christians worship, but in the words of Saint Paul, the foolishness of God is wiser than man's

236

wisdom, and the weakness of God is stronger than man's strength. That is the mystery of the faith, which I believe is meant to expand our minds and hearts beyond their human capacity. We are meant to be broken beyond our bounds, and torn through, like the temple curtain was torn. We are meant to be pierced, as Christ was pierced and, as such, grow smaller, and greater, at the same time.

I believe God likes to throw the ice cube in the soup and watch it crack. Maybe that is what the Incarnation, contingent upon the Trinity, is: a cracking, a tearing, of curtains in the temple and seals on the tomb, and stone table split down the center, and indeed, a chasm that separates Christianity from all other faiths, making it a scandal and an absurdity to those on the outside looking in. It is like a wild hedgerow, and has a common function of holding together seeming opposites, paradoxes, contrasts, dichotomies with the belief that it actually reveals a new, often radical, truth. This spiral effect of Christianity, you might say, goes deeper and deeper down – plumbing the depths of things which cannot be dissected with tools of logic. It is like the unfolding of that great secret, the fulfillment of a promise that is like a twist ending to a plot. It is not how we would have expected it, but there you have it. And once that twist happens, it changes everything, even our own natures. I believe grace doesn't just give us what we deserve; it gives us a ridiculous overabundance. It lavishes. It is Christmas morning and sparkly packages and colored ribbons a thousand times over. That's what all these holiday trappings represent: Grace, the bloodstream of the Body of Christ. This must either prove it to be our greatest folly or our greatest prize, for it is a strange, mysterious thing to cling to unto death.

That having been said, those on the outside looking in, particularly from the Islamic sphere, still tend to just think the cheese has slipped off our collective Christian cracker. And trying to put myself in their place, and see the world through their particular set of theological and cultural goggles, I suppose I can understand that. Nevertheless, since Christians *do* believe Jesus was fully human, and Muslims do focus quite a bit on His humanity, we certainly should do our best to find common ground in that. And heck, who on this end is denying that He was a prophet? Of course He was. He prophesied all the time, including about His death on the Cross, if one is to take the Gospels seriously, though that's another bone of contention. But sometimes we just need to let the bones lie for at least a while. Unless we want to get sucked into a perpetual round of the song that doesn't end. And anyone who grew up on "Lamb Chops" knows that we don't. Unless you're like a masochist. But I digress again.

This much I believe can be a stable bridge to cross while maintaining integrity: Islam expresses mankind's desire for God as a striving for "excellence", encompassing all that is worthwhile to achieve in any human field as flowing back to and reflecting the glory of the One. Perhaps this reaches its pinnacle in reverence for the human person of Jesus and his mother Mary, testified through so many narrations, stories, and poems. As divergent as our doctrines regarding Christ may be, we cannot help but see Him as in some way reflecting the font of our origins as human beings in the personification of Adam, and know that seeking to mirror His characteristics is the ultimate sign of humanity striving after unadulterated excellence. We want to be close to Him, and it is my sincere belief that He will read our innermost hearts, and enter therein. To conclude with a final quote from Rumi:

"Why should I suffer from heartache? Jesus, the Physician of Souls, is with me. Why should I be afraid of the dogs? Christ, the Master of the Hunt, is with me."

The Call of the Christ

by El-Hajj Hisham Mahmoud

In his book *Rawḍat al-Muḥibbīn wa Nuzhat al-Mushtāqīn* (The Meadow of Lovers and the Outing of Yearners), Ibn Qayyim al-Jawziyyah interprets sixty terms in the Arabic language connoting "love." Among the closest of God's ninety names to "love" is *al-Wadūd* (the Affectionate toward the faithful), and the one condition of *wudd* (affection), according to one of many definitions, is that it be without condition. Rumi once said, "What a love the sun gives the earth! It never says, 'Look at all I have done for you! That is a love that can brighten the world!'" Perhaps this is the kind of love that Randy Travis was feeling in his song, "Forever and Ever, Amen," when he wrote:

> They say that time takes its toll on a body,
> makes a young girl's brown hair turn grey.
> But honey, I don't care.
> I ain't in love with your hair,
> and if it all fell out, well I'd love you anyway.

Love ever surpasses the poet's every attempt. To speak of it is a betrayal, for the sweetness of honey is nowhere in a dictionary to be found. But it is known by its traces, some of which are discussed in *Ṭawq al-Ḥamāmah* (The Necklace of the Dove) by Ibn Ḥazm, e.g., insomnia, sickness, even death. In Arabic, the word for "platonic love" is *al-ḥubb al-ʿudhrī*, which is the love of the tribe of Banū ʿUdhrah in Yemen, which was so intense that many of their men would fall dead from prolonged estrangement from their beloved, or from the plight of unconsummated love. All Majnūn's poems about Laylā trace back to a single, fleeting moment wherein he beheld her, never to hold her.

Love has its proofs as well, as detailed by Ibn Ḥazm, one of which is submission to the will of the beloved. God says with reference to the Prophet Muhammad ﷺ, "Say, 'If you love God, then follow me, and God will love you" (Āl ʿImrān 3:31). This was the behest of every Prophet of God, but it had a particular and tenacious urgency in the voice of our Messiah, the Word of God, Jesus, the Son of Mary, the Spirit of God, who once said to a hopeful disciple, "Follow me." He answered, "Master, allow me first to bury my father," to which Jesus replied, "Let the dead bury the dead. But as for you, go and proclaim the Kingdom of God" (Luke 9:59–60). And another said, "I will follow you, master, but first let me bid my family farewell." Jesus said, "No one who sets a hand to the plow then looks to what was left behind is fit for the Kingdom of God" (Luke 9:61–62). Ultimately, the imperative of Messianic love is the urgent renunciation of the world and everything and everyone therein. "And behold, one came and said unto him, 'Good master, what good thing shall I do, that I may have eternal life?' Jesus answered, 'Why do you call me good? There is none good but one, that is God! But if you will enter into life, then keep the commandments . . . and if you will be perfect, go and sell all that you possess, and give their value to the poor, and you shall have treasure in heaven; then come and follow me.' But when the young man heard that, he went away crestfallen, for he had amassed great wealth. Then said Jesus unto his disciples, 'Verily I say unto you: a rich man shall hardly enter into the kingdom of heaven.' And again I say unto you, 'It is easier for a camel to pass through the eye of a needle than for a rich man to enter into the Kingdom of God.' When his disciples heard that, they were exceedingly amazed, saying, 'Who then shall be saved?' But Jesus beheld them, and said unto them, 'With men this is impossible; but with God, all things are possible'" (Matthew 19:16–26).

For Jesus, especially, the Creator has no place in a heart even slightly given to the creation. This is evident in hundreds of his teachings archived in the Muslim tradition,[176] such as:

> "Make hungry your livers and make bare your limbs; perhaps then your hearts might perceive God."

> "Blessed is he who abandons a present pleasure for the sake of a promise in what is absent and unseen."

> "The heart, so long as it is not torn by passion, nor befouled by desire, nor hardened by comfort, shall become a vessel for wisdom."

---

[176] All statements ascribed to Jesus herein from the Muslim tradition can be found in Tarif Khalidi's compilation, *The Muslim Jesus*.

Jesus possessed only a comb and a cup, until on one occasion, he saw someone grooming his beard with his fingers and another drinking from a stream with his hands, so he gave both to them in charity.

We must consider here that the Messiah was raised by a single mother, and that he learned the important lessons of life under the tutelage of poverty. This circumstance undoubtedly left its mark on him, for Jesus was a constant traveler in the land, never abiding in one house or village. His clothing consisted of a cloak made of coarse hair or camel stub. In his hand he carried a staff. Whenever night fell, his lamp was the moonlight, his shade the blackness of night, his bed the earth, his pillow a stone, his food the plants of the fields. At times, he spent whole days and nights without food. In times of distress, he was happy, and in times of ease, he was sad. He was called *rūḥ Allāh* (the spirit of God) because he had completely renounced the world. His presence was that of a pure spirit whose flesh was accidental. In his own words, the Messiah said, "I toppled the world on its face and sat upon its back. I have no child who might die, no house that might fall into ruin." The disciples once asked him, "Will you not build a house for yourself?" He replied, "Build me a house in the path of a flood." Jesus used to eat the leaves of the trees, dress in wool shirts, and sleep wherever night fell upon him. He saved not his lunch for dinner, nor his dinner for lunch, but would say, "Each day brings its sustenance." The Spirit of God once said, "The world is a bridge: cross it, and build nothing upon it." He once lay his head down on a stone. Satan, passing by, said, "How fond you are of this world!" So he hurled the stone at him and cried, "Take that, and the world with it!" The Messiah used to say, "Let whoever deems God slow with His bounty beware, for out of His wrath, God may just grant him his every desire!" The Word of God once said, "Hunger is my seasoning, fear of God is my garment, wool is my raiment, the light of the dawn is my heat in winter, the moon is my lantern, my legs are my beast of burden, and the produce of the earth is my food and fruit. I retire for the night with nothing to my name, I awake in the morning with nothing to my name; yet there is no one on earth richer than I!" His disciples once asked him, "How is it that you can walk on water while we cannot?" He answered, "Through certainty of faith." They said, "We also have certainty of faith." He asked them, "How do you deem gold, stones, and mud?" They said, "Gold is superior to stones while stones are superior to mud." He said, "Nay, they are all equal."

"The worth of this world and everything in it," in the words of the Prophet Muhammad ﷺ, "is less than the wing of a mosquito." So let us understand together: imagine yourself uninsured and suffering from a bout of urinary retention that was so excruciatingly painful that it would not allow you to walk, stand, or sit still without squirming in agony, and the only way to restore your health was through a medical procedure in the urinary tract. But the cost of the procedure amounts to one-third of your wealth. Would you get the procedure done? Suppose the cost amounted to one half of everything you possess. Would you get the procedure done at that point? Suppose it cost all your life's savings. Who would pass on the procedure? Then know that the true value of all your possessions is just as the Prophet Muhammad ﷺ described; rather, it is not even worth a cup of urine. So let us now imagine ourselves as that young man who sought to follow Jesus, yearning so fervently to take him as our teacher, to dedicate ourselves to him, that he would raise us to be worthy of the highest degree of God's love.

Jesus would have us all live as wandering ascetics to be perfect in the eyes of God, but this proposition may strike us as an outright forgery given how he has been branded to us. There are socio-historical reasons for this, and perhaps the most devastating blow to the urgent and unwavering demand of Jesus to denounce and renounce the world was the "Protestant work ethic," a phrase coined in 1904 by Max Weber in his book *The Protestant Ethic and the Spirit of Capitalism*. This phrase traces back to the Reformation of the late Middle Ages, when it was taken as doctrine that no one could be entirely certain he was saved and that all people were either destined for salvation or damnation, formalized as "double predestination." One's fate was contingent upon God's good pleasure, which was indicated by signs, the first of which was worldly success. So while Jesus insisted that all of our wealth go to the poor and that we ourselves live impoverished, the Calvinists discouraged charity to the poor lest it beget beggary. The Protestant work ethic evolved over time and the simple deeds of righteousness became activity; activity became industry; industry became industrialized; industrialization became manufactured; manufacturing became technologized; technology became militarized; militarization became nuclearized.

The Protestant work ethic mutated into raw capitalism over time, and the Calvinists essentially christened Christianity with the caste system of Hinduism, rendering the wealthy whom Jesus forsook as the Brahmins and the lepers whom Jesus healed with his own two hands as the untouchables. Jesus turned into a white man, and the "Santa-Clausification," as Rev. Cornel West put it, of Jesus in our age is a blatant disregard for what Jesus demanded of his disciples and followers. In December 2013, Megan Kelly (a Fox News anchor) asserted that it was a historical fact that both Santa Claus and Jesus were white men. This assertion went unchallenged by the all-white panel of three she was addressing mainly because they had all internalized the Brahmin presumption of the Protestant work ethic. Of course Santa Claus is white—is he not the CEO of the largest toy distribution multinational the world over? And Jesus was necessarily white—are not the saved made in the image of God? The depiction of God the Father in the Sistine Chapel alone instils the cognitive frame for the Protestant work ethic to thrive uncontested as a theory of white economy vested for the inheritance of heaven and for its stockholders to become its socio-economic gatekeepers.

Yet any honest study of the teachings of the Messiah reveals the hypocrisy of such a doctrine, and the nailing of his timeless legacy to a cross is a convenient façade to sufficiently blur the focus of his indictment against the world in the three years leading to his trial. Jesus was a firebrand, an agitator, a bona fide menace to society, and Judea was essentially a Roman temple-state. "And making a whip of cords, he drove them all out of the temple, along with the sheep and oxen. And he poured out the coins of the money-changers and overturned their tables" (John 2:13). Another biographer writes: "And Jesus went into the temple of God, and cast out all them that sold and bought in the temple, and overthrew the tables of the moneychangers, and the seats of them that sold doves, and said unto them, 'It is written, "My house shall be called the house of prayer"; but you have made it a den of thieves'" (Matthew 21:12–13). But since Jesus has been so thoroughly "theologized" in our minds, we have brushed aside the parting wish of a man so weary of our love of the world that he sought to whip it out of us! Paul wrote that Mosaic law was nailed to the cross (Collosians 2:14), but along with it was what Jesus himself taught to fulfill that law, for his own law found men in contempt who could not reclaim their hearts from the world.

Jesus once declared: "Think not that I am come to send peace on earth. I came not to send peace, but a sword. For I am come to set a man at variance against his father, and a daughter against her mother, and a daughter-in-law against her mother-in-law. And a man's foes shall be they of his own household" (Matthew 10:34–36). And just as he waged war against the temple-state in Judea, he shall wage war in his Second Coming against the anti-Christ, who teaches salvation through the Prosperity Gospel, not through the poverty that Jesus demanded, who teaches worship of himself, not of God as Jesus commanded. He stands in opposition to Christ, and the reality of a thing is known through its opposite.

After the crucifixion, it is the miracles of Jesus that tend to crowd the thoughts of many. Even here the point is sadly missed, however, for we have limited his miracles to questions concerning his alleged divinity, and hardly ever consider the implications of his miracles beyond this allegation. We tend to reduce his life's work to a list of miraculous feats and are oblivious to our own agency in the miracle. We fail to see his turning water into wine as our purification of polluted water; his healing the sick as our reform of a broken health care system; his calling the deaf to hear, the dumb to speak, and the blind to see as our struggle to reform education; his empowering the paralyzed to walk as our enriching the indigent to stand up on their feet; his feeding the multitudes as our reallocation of resources; or his resurrecting the dead as our granting the hopeless a new lease on life. The essence of his miracles was that they abide and can be witnessed when we take up his mantle, and this was the imperative of his call to "follow me."

What separates us from our Messiah is his willingness to actually do the work. In the Old Testament, the laws concerning leprosy and lepers are prescribed thus: "As for the leper who has the infection, his clothes shall be torn, and the hair of his head shall be uncovered, and he shall cover his mustache and cry, 'Unclean! Unclean!' He shall remain unclean all the days during which he has the infection; he is unclean. He shall live alone; his dwelling shall be outside the camp" (Leviticus 13:45–46). Thus were lepers quarantined even until the days that Jesus inhabited Judea. And anyone who touches a man who is unclean becomes himself unclean (Leviticus 5:3). However, "When Jesus came down from the mountainside, large crowds followed him. A man with leprosy came and knelt before him and said, 'Master, if you are *willing*, you can make me clean.' Jesus reached out his hand and touched the man. 'I am *willing*,' he said. 'Be clean!' and immediately he was cleansed of his leprosy" (Matthew 8:1–3).

The question for us is, are we *willing* to perform the miraculous feats required of us by faith? If so, then purifying the unclean means that we must first be willing to become unclean and take up that Prophetic mantle and work, and only after becoming unclean will we ourselves be purified. In this light let us understand his words, "I came not to destroy the law or the Prophets, but to fulfill" (Matthew 5:17).

To conclude, Jesus once said, "I have come to bring fire on the earth, and how I wish it were already kindled" (Luke 12:49). Yes, God brought him into the world out of love, but it was an imposing, zealous love, enforced with a whip in his right hand, and the earth glows not only because of the light he brought to it, but because he lit it up with fire! May our hearts be lit with the passionate heat of his fire, to burn every attachment we have to a world worth less than the wing of a mosquito, that we may tread the earth as true disciples of the Christ. And may Allah bless and sanctify our Prophet and Messenger Muhammad ﷺ, who once declared, as related by Muslim from Abū Hurayrah, "I am the most entitled of all people to Jesus, the Son of Mary. The Prophets are all brothers, with different mothers, and their religion is one."

Zuhd and Jesus in the Qur'an
Julia Kassem

The anxieties felt in the COVID-19 pandemic were characterized by the confrontation with the reality of death, undistracted from the daily deluge of life and inundation with the distractions of the material world.

Few easily accepted the conditions and embraced the retreat from the pacing and difficulty of the modern world. While the pandemic brought about a lot of trials and exasperation, it also exposed the superficial attachments to the material world. This was evident in a number of Covid-related tropes and trends in the US. Toilet paper hoarding represented the most comical of them, yet these underlying societal afflictions were more deeply evident in an aggravation of pandemic-related isolation that manifested in increased substance abuse, alcoholism, and domestic violence. The faulty lack of protection and support to small businesses, families, and those considered "essential" laborers revealed the nature of a political milieu built around consumption rather than social welfare. But the inability for the Western, and more broadly, modern world, to deal with crisis at a personal and social level also revealed the faulty state of the *nafs*, conditioned and numbed by distractions in the pre-Covid environment that oscillated between drudgery, alienation and hedonism.

In the West, there is a constant topic of discussion and debate over what has been 'lost' in the pandemic and of its aftermath; with these losses mainly oriented around the loss of perceived individual liberties. On the contrary, a more constructive approach to identifying what can be *gained* in the context of these challenges is missing such as perhaps more concern for human and social welfare. But all too often, we mistake material losses for personal losses and vice versa, and fail to consider the lessons and opportunities for growth in our challenges: "But perhaps you hate a thing and it is good for you; and perhaps you love a thing and it is bad for you. And Allah knows while you know not." (Al-Baqarah, 2:216).

The path to accepting the circumstances of our existence and the inevitability of our death is recognized in the Christian and Islamic traditions as a strive to detach from the material world and its affect on us; as Jesus said, "for what does it benefit a man to gain the whole world and lose his soul?" (Mark 8:36) The material world and the human attachment to the material world –in its fleeting and temporary nature – is a distraction from our observance and devotion to God and our service to one another.

In Islam, this concept is known as "zuhd," roughly translated as "asceticism." With its complexity and philosophical depth, zuhd finds itself at odds with both asceticism and monasticism, with asceticism a set of philosophical principles that may accompany certain practices and monasticism a widely known practice that seeks to emulate ascetic philosophical principles. Yet monasticism, ironically, in its emphasis on material deprivation rather than spiritual ascension, bases its conceptualization relative to the dunya rather than apart from it. Zuhd doesn't mean the deprivation and complete rejection of the material world, but the emotional and personal detachment from it. It is articulated as the "gratitude of one's blessings" along with the "shortening of desires" and marked by the abstinence of "what's prohibited" (Nahj al Balagha, Sermon 81).

While there is an emphasis on gratitude for blessings, there is a careful distinction and fine line between this and the prideful exultation over worldly rewards.

Corruption and sin have their roots in ego, which is the source of sin in Islam. This anti-tawhidic inclination causes one to delve into their individual desires rather than to collectively maintain their service to Allah.

Jesus said, "Love of the world is the root of all sin. Worldly wealth is a great sickness.[177]" He establishes this link by identifying this sickness as the afflicted person unable to "avoid pride and self esteem," reiterating that "The cultivation of wealth distracts man from the mention of God."

In the Calvinistic canon, asceticism has a self-punishing dimension that reflects the necessary punishment of man as an "original sinner". To the contrary, Islam, which emphasizes man's free will that, through conscious effort, can raise man to the highest of beings or to lower than beasts with zuhd as a spiritual path. Of course, the Christian interpretation of wealth in relation to the soul varies across denominations, with the Orthodox emphasis on ascetic rituals and philosophy and shunning materialistic greed contrasting from the Protestant "prosperity gospel;" which represents a more transactional relationship with good deeds and material rewards. To the contrary, the Calvinist creed, believing in predestination, rejects the concepts of struggle, like that of

---

[177] Ibn Hanbal; al-Zuhd; al-Salam Shahin, Beirut; also referenced in Khalidi ,T. 2003. The Muslim Jesus p. 87 no 62.

which we see in the concept of jihad al-akbar, in attaining personal mastery over the self. Rather, the inclinations of Calvinism towards material works ensure material rewards as a worldly and externally focused existential motivation.

But it's not to say that this mischaracterization of Zuhd is an inherent feature of Christianity or of the teachings of Jesus. But more importantly, Jesus is, in Islam, just like Christianity, seen as the restorer and reformer of Abrahamic laws from its deviation. The Abrahamic tradition essentially came to lay down the law in a society subsumed by ignorance through prophet Moses, and continued by Jesus, as the reformer of divine law in the context of an established nation years later.

The Qur'an ascribes great importance to Jesus as providing a clarification of Christ and his social impact. Jesus is mentioned more times in the Qur'an than the Prophet Muhammad ﷺ the final messenger of God. His purpose in both the Christian and Islamic traditions was in restoring and reforming the spirit of the law in an established political society and governance. This was exemplified by both the reformation and rectification of a just society and righteous political leadership in the context of worldly decadence and lavishness. For Jesus, the extent of this was taken in the relatively extreme level of asceticism he displayed, where owning nothing was the necessary response to the extreme level of corruption and unlawful wealth accumulation or political tyranny represented by both the Roman order and the Pharisees.

As it stands in the Qur'an, both the Christian and Muslim depiction of Jesus exemplify zuhd on a personal and spiritual level as well as in a political dimension. The famous saying by Jesus is that it is "easier for a camel to go in the eye of a needle than a rich man to enter the kingdom of heaven" (Matthews 19:24). Multiple times in the Book of Matthew, Jesus admonishes the Pharisees, the corrupt pseudo-religious elite at the time, for their corrupt hold on power and worldly ambitions under the guise of religion. There is a lot of similarity between the characteristics of the corrupt political order that the prophet Muhammad and his family confronted as well as Jesus; and thus, the extent that zuhd can be considered every bit as a political message as it is a personal and spiritual one.

Let's examine the historical basis of zuhd and the political context of this verse. This verse came down before the Treaty of Hudaibiyyah. Following the Muslims' victories at the Battle of Badr, the Quraishite polytheists aimed at launching an offensive to kill the Prophet Muhammad. While the following battle, the Battle of Uhud, failed at destroying the Prophet, the Muslims had witnessed their impending victory at Uhud turned into a loss when, out of overconfidence following the initial Muslim successes in the battle, the marksmen placed at the slope descended from their posts, exposing the Muslim army and inviting the Qurayshites to attack the Musims from behind. Ultimately, the Muslims were able to redeem themselves politically following the Battle of the Trench and the establishment of the treaty, establishing and furthering Islam politicially against the Qurayshites and other enemies of the prophet. At the same time, the lessons against prideful arrogance, and acting on whims of temporary material situations and outcomes, are enshrined in the lessons of Surah al-Hadeed. This chapter was established at the time where, as the Islamic State was coming into fruition, the ethical, moral, and communal lessons and obligations of Muslims were outlined; both as lessons from the past but as guidelines for the Muslim community in the formation of its political entity. In Islam, the development and expansion of the Islamic nation brought along with them great success and material wealth - but also the stress of the attacks by nonbelievers seen in the Battle of Uhud. Sura al-Hadid 57:23 reminds us to detach from external circumstances as well as external objects, that derail us from faith and contentment; "So you may not grieve at the things that you fail to get, nor rejoice over that which has been given to you. And Allah likes not prideful boasters." Zuhd commands believers to not only be unphased by material possessions, but also by material circumstances that also potentially misguide the spirit and our conduct. As Imam Ja'far al-Sadiq said, "When the true believer becomes angry, his anger should not take him out of the truth; and when he becomes satisfied, his satisfaction should not bring him into falsehood.[178]"

It is a significant trope in both Christianity and Islam that among the enemies of the main prophets (Muhammad and Jesus) were not always disbelievers, but sometimes those in positions of power that claimed to be believers and authorities on faith. For Muhammad, while his battles against unbelievers showed that his main opposition usually consisted of unbelievers, he warned extensively about the dangers of hypocrisy within the faith. Ultimately, the source of political corruption is understood as a moral and ethical one rather than a systemic one, and challenging political corruption lies

---

[178] Al-Kafi, vol 2. P 183

in challenging the innate attachment people in a society have on the material world and of matters of the dunya. Love of worldliness is a factor that is understood in Christianity and Islam both to lead to unjust rule and of inclination towards unjust rule amongst people in a society. As Allah says in Surah al-Raad (13:11): "Verily a society can't change until people change within themselves." This is both understood to refer to the necessity for people themselves to make political change, but also for the necessity for the hearts and minds of society to be inclined towards justice before there can be a just society. The level of spiritual discipline exemplified by zuhd ensures that the ethical standing both of the masses and of leadership retains tempered against opportunist or corrupt inclinations, and zuhd serves as a litmus test of a people's loyalty and devotion to God over worldly incentives.

By inviting his followers to embrace asceticism, Jesus encourages transgression against unjust rule by rejecting the existing practices of worldliness of the corrupt society. He emphasizes that political justice can only be built on foundations of values and ethics: "The stone in the structure which is there unlawfully is an assurance of its destruction.[179]" Likewise, the Qur'an reminds people to not incline towards the rule of oppressors [11:113]. For any corrective measure to truly make lasting change in society, efforts must be made at reforming spirits before systems, lest tyranny and corruption would endlessly govern society regardless of the temporary figure in power. As the Qur'an says, even as the evidence on the righteousness of the Believers was clear, the "hardened

---

[179] Khalidi, 2003. "The Muslim Jesus," no. 187. Cited from a translation from Abu Nuayam al-Isbahani, Hilyat al-Awliya, 6:95 (Mansur, no. 77).

hearts" of those too arrogant and fixated on their earthly standing, namely the Bani Israel in this case, would ensure that enemies of Islam from within the People of the Book as well as unbelievers would always be resistant to Allah's message and Islam's political as well as spiritual leadership in society:

"Then your hearts hardened after that, so that they were like rocks, rather worse in hardness; and surely there are some rocks from which streams burst forth, and there are some of them which split asunder so water issues out of them, and there are some of them which fall down for fear of Allah, and Allah is not at all heedless of what you do." (Sura al-Baqarah, 2:74)

Monasticism, as a lifestyle choice, ironically becomes materially-oriented in its focus on shunning luxuries and things. There still is an idealization of materialism, ironically, as it is the idolization of the lack of things whereas in the concept of zuhd the idea is to hone one's devotion to God of one's level of wealth or material state. In retaining the same discursive practice the same regardless of one's material state, zuhd realigns focus on the spiritual rather than the external (material) factors as a litmus test to one's devotion to God. Zuhd doesn't mean owning nothing, it means nothing owns you.

Zuhd, therefore, is not defined by a static set of characteristics; in the Islamic tradition, following in its example and practice is dependent on the factors of its historical context. As such, the ways by which it has been practiced has varied between exemplary religious figures in time. The zuhd displayed by Prophet Jesus looks different than the zuhd of the Prophet Muhammad. In the latter's example, wealth wasn't intentionally shunned, and it was clear that the continued example of *zuhd* as the state by which a believer's motivations operate independent of material incentives was a consistency regardless of the personal wealth of the figure. In fact, a number of wealthy figures in the Islamic and Biblical traditions - from Khadija, the first Muslim, to Imam Ja'afar, prophets Abraham and Muhammad demonstrate this possibility, especially in instances where the resources and wealth- Allah's rizq- come with added responsibility:

"We raised some above others in ranks, so that some may employ others in their work. But the Mercy of your Lord (O Muhammad SAW) is better than the (wealth of this world) which they amass." [43:31]

There is a strong directive to leaders to govern with a sense of humility that can be derived from one's sense of zuhd. Christ said to his followers: "If people appoint you as their heads, be like tails." Thus, leaders, who also assume a lofty material and social position are tested over their responsibility in how they use the ranks and position Allah has given to them. Those that assume themselves as in service to people have annihilated the ego, which, in its association with worldly aspirations, is fleeting, temporary, and distracts people from their tawhidic duties both in society and in worship.

While Islamic political history was unveiled centuries after Christianity, both the Islamic and Christian traditions warn against the pitfalls of arrogance and submitting to rule that is oriented around worldliness. The Jewish revolt against the Romans, the Bar Kochba revolt, in 132 AD is an illustration of this point. In 135, the Jews put their faith in

Simeon Bar Kochba, regarding him as a potential Messianic figure due to his prospects of promising them earthly rewards and rule. The prospect of Bar Kochba's rule would have been an alternative to Jesus for the Jews, as in the days of Jesus a hundred years prior they feared that his leadership would "take away both our temple and our nation." (John 11:48) As a result, their rebellion was crushed in a 135 AD and Jerusalem completely overtaken by the Roman pagans. The lessons of this unsuccessful revolt, as well as the ego and material-driven mistakes that had cost the Muslim's greatly, serves as a lesson to Muslims today amidst our decisive political struggles and developments in West and Central Asia today. While economic hardship may not have been the choice of millions currently suffering under sanctions and siege in Yemen, Syria, Palestine, Iraq, Iran and Lebanon, the principles of zuhd in the political context in the verse of Surat al-Hadeed serve as a reminder for those struggling to remain steadfast in their preservation of their political dignity and morale amidst their challenges. In a region that has historically developed as the cradle of the Abrahamic faith in the past to the volatile turning point sending US imperialism toward the trajectory of its decline today, zuhd as a philosophy and as a practice exemplifies its necessity in the face of challenges, and possibilities of triumph and victory against arrogance and aggression - that are every bit as personal as they are political. It also provides the baseline values upon which our sovereign leadership will be built up on new and just foundations. Zuhd, commanding mastery over the self as a prerequisite to assuming any political role in society, ensures that any struggle against unjust rule revolt will result in liberation of soul and society alike rather than just a transfer of power.

Digital Zuhd: What Would Jesus Do in the Digital Age?
Tricia Pethic

"He who seeks after the world is like one who drinks sea-water; the more he drinks the more his thirst increases, until it kills him." - Jesus

"It isn't until you begin to become self-aware and explore the programs that you're living out; you stand apart from them. That is one of the unique human endowments that animals do not possess. They do not have the power to stand apart from their programming and examine it." -Stephen R. Covey

In a world of plenty, how do we decide what is important? This is the question of minimalism, and of the spiritual path in general. We learn in the Islamic tradition, that each prophet was given a choice. They could be a king-prophet, exemplified by David or Solomon, or a servant-prophet, as exemplified by Jesus and later by Muhammad who said that he had been offered either path early in his prophetic career but had selected servanthood when he chose milk over wine.

Often translated as "asceticism," Islamic studies researcher Justin Parrot translates zuhd as temperance: "Ali ibn al-Madini reported: It was said to Sufyan ibn 'Uyaynah, may Allah have mercy on him, "What is the definition of temperance?" Sufyan said, "It is that you are grateful in prosperity and patient in adversity. If one is like that, he is temperate."

عن عَلِيِّ بْنِ الْمَدِينِيّ قَالَ قِيلَ لِسُفْيَانَ بْنِ عُيَيْنَةَ رحمه الله مَا حَدُّ الزُّهْدِ قَالَ أَنْ تَكُونَ شَاكِرًا فِي الرَّخَاءِ صَابِرًا فِي الْبَلَاءِ فَإِذَا كَانَ كَذَلِكَ فَهُوَ زَاهِدٌ قِيلَ مَا الشُّكْرُ قَالَ أَنْ تَجْتَنِبَ مَا نَهَى الله عَنْهُ

180 "شعب الإيمان 4214

Since asceticism is often glossed as a class of spiritual practitioners who neglect the physical self, "temperance" carries the connotation of restraint rather than pure monasticism.

These two poles: that of zuhd or abstemiousness on the one hand and of splendor and bounty on the other, are both valid options. We know, for example, that the Prophet did not only chase the poor and the meek; he also sought and preached to those who were privileged in status and/or wealth. Focusing on the latter only became a problem if preoccupation with calling the privileged occurs at the expense of the underprivileged as Allah points out to His Prophet in Qur'an 80: 1-4.

Thus, it is said, a man could have the world in his palm, but it should not occupy his heart. Minimalism may be the practice of removing material things from one's life, but it may also be the ability to enjoy the things of this life without becoming too attached to them. In either case, the things that do remain ought to be important enough to warrant our attention.

The Prophet had few items and he bestowed names on those items he did own. To name something is to attach and endear oneself to the thing in question. It is hard to endear

---

[180]https://www.abuaminaelias.com/dailyhadithonline/2021/01/21/sufyan-definition-zuhd/

oneself to a disposable cup which finds as the apex of its existence the mere 30 seconds in which someone sips out of it before it is thrown away. The tree the paper cup was formed from, and the energy that went into its molding in a factory, not to mention its transport from factory to store and store to home----all of this energy culminates in a few sips. If the energy expenditure seems imbalanced it is because it is; even the kings of old could not imagine a cup that would only exist mere moments for one's pleasure.

Here we encounter a bit of a paradox: do we pay more or less attention to the items we own? The one who can easily detach from his disposable cup is not practicing zuhd; his separation is not an indication of his detachment from the world. It is actually an indication that the world exists for him, and once it is no longer useful, he tosses it. This is in contrast to the one who appreciates the cup, the potter who made it, the craftsmanship and durability of the cup, and so he retains the item, washing and storing it numerous times until it is broken. His relationship with the cup is one of appreciation for the one who made it; and this is like the relationship of the one who appreciates the world as the vessel that it is, a means towards God but not a means in and of itself. The world is the cup but it points towards the Potter. The paradox is that when one truly contemplates the world, they transcend it. But the one who does not spend time contemplating what is before him, but merely consumes and defecates it, is said to be entirely a cog in its machinery.

Much in the same way that the disposability culture renders impermanence to things that were once forged to last, so too has another form of wealth been fractured and sacrificed for profit: that of our attention. Our gaze is the most sought-after currency today. Tech giants and advertisers hire psychologists to study human behavior and great sums are spent in deploying strategies to achieve maximum views and engagement in this "attention economy." It is therefore important that we value not only our material wealth, but the wealth that resides within our gaze. Today we have the kingly ability to bestow wealth with simply a glance. If we began to see our time and our attention as something with limited supply, we might learn to apply a kind of digital zuhd, or what some have called "digital minimalism."

In digital minimalism, one engages with the attention economy insofar as it serves a predetermined set of goals. Intentionality must be present, and one must approach the tools of the internet with the same sense of purpose that one would use when grocery shopping: what do I need here and how can I get it most efficiently without lingering too long? The likeness of the attention economy to a grocery store trip would be like scouring every aisle for something that catches your eyes, but after you pass each aisle, unbeknownst to you the displays are changed ever so slightly, new items are flagged as "on sale," and new discounts are slapped on the shelf. You thought you'd been down that aisle before, but it seems new again. How did you miss this item? The aisles around you are, unbeknownst to you, constantly being redesigned after you go down them. A 10 minute trip becomes a 10 hour trip down the rabbit hole. Oh yes, where was the milk?

A small part of digital zuhd is recognizing the "built-in" nature of these platforms and disabling things like notifications which we assume we need but do not. If I download twenty apps to my phone, and each of them gives me a notification twice daily (to be conservative) then that is

40 notifications a day. Forty interruptions. Forty moments where our children notice our eyes wander, moments where a very subtle idea that was almost in our mental grasp suddenly became foggy, moments where our attention spans were fractured again and again, each time rewiring our brain to expect interruption. And then, we cannot concentrate. If I am capturing it well, it is because I know this myself, all too well.

Practicing digital zuhd is also about not constantly needing to upgrade, even if we are aware that the latest and best version has come out. Certainly a security patch is understandable, but if the graphics are only slightly better, or the phone only slightly better....is it worth the attention paid?

Our experiences online should not be great, they should be good enough. Good enough to give us valuable information, good enough to make our lives easier, but not so great that in the process of making life more instantaneous and our experiences "seamless" we begin the unseaming of our minds. A mind created for tadabbur---contemplation---must be trained. Training means becoming aware of the "programming" of digital platforms and the way in which they are skewed towards fractured, pithy communication and shocking subject matter. It means recognizing that the built-in algorithms are the very definition of sea water that Prophet Jesus alludes to at the start of this essay. Sea water appears for all intents and purposes, like thirst-quenching water. Similarly for the one who engages in serial scrolling, there is always plenty to see and yet somehow never enough.

Khalidi, Tarif. "The Muslim Jesus: Stories and Sayings in Islamic Literature." Harvard University Press Cambridge, 2001.

Newport, Cal. "Digital Minimalism: Choosing a Focused Life in a Noisy World." Portfolio: New York: 2019.

Parrott, Justin. "Sufyan on zuhd: Definition of asceticism is being thankful, patient." https://www.abuaminaelias.com/dailyhadithonline/2021/01/21/sufyan-definition-zuhd/
Accessed December 2, 2021.

Quadri, Mir Habeebullah. "A Comparative Study of Minimalist Lifestyle and the Islamic Practice of Simple Living." https://cifiaglobal.com/issue/2/article/cgj-2-6.pdf   Accessed December 2, 2021.

Jesus as the Messiah in Islam

Bilal Muhammad

Messiah comes from the Hebrew word Moshiach (מָשִׁיחַ) and
the Arabic word *Masīḥ*, and it means "anointed one". In the
way that kings and consecrated objects were anointed with
oils, the scriptures speak of those whom God has anointed for
sanctity and authority. In the Old Testament, the word
"messiah" has been used to describe King David (2 Samuel
23:1), the Persian King Cyrus (Isaiah 24:38), and even
inanimate objects (like the Temple's altar).

The possible meanings and the implications of this title in
Islam have been discussed by various scholars. Ibn Kathīr
notes that Jesus may have been called *Masīḥ* because he
traversed the land (*li masḥahul arḍ*), fleeing with his religion
from the slander hurled against him and his mother. He offers
another possibility – that his feet were anointed (*mamsūḥ al-
qadmayn*),[181] which may be a reference to John's saying that he
was not worthy to untie the strap of his sandal (John 1:27).
Ṭabarī wrote that Jesus was called *Masīḥ* because he was
purified from sin.[182] Qurṭubī said that it means "saint"
(*ṣiddīq*), and he reports that he may have been anointed
(*mamsūḥ*) with a blessed ointment.[183] Jesus sometimes appears

---

181 Ibn Kathir, Bidaya wa Nihaya, Volume 2, Page 114.
https://bit.ly/3n6HEzi
182

https://islamweb.net/ar/library/index.php?page=bookcontents&ID=1
455&bk_no=50&idfrom=1448&idto=1448
183 Tafsir al-Qurtubi, Volume 2, Page 69.

with wet hair in reports, which may be an allusion to his head being divinely anointed.

Jewish scriptures speak of the messiahs to come in the End Times. Polymessianism is the idea that God will send multiple deliverers; this was arguably the dominant belief in Judaism before the medieval period. The Dead Sea Scrolls represent a snapshot of Essene Jews between the third century BC and the first century AD. The Essenes were an ascetic sect that devoted their lives to mysticism, voluntary poverty, and writing and preserving sacred texts. Some of these texts, including "The Testimonia" (4Q175) and "The Community Rule" (1QS), indicate the coming of three deliverers: (1) the Prophet, (2) the kingly messiah, and (3) the priestly messiah. In more canonical collections, like the Talmud, there are the Four Craftsmen, who are four deliverers identified as: (1) the Davidic messiah, (2) the Josephine messiah, (3) Elijah the prophet, and (4) the Righteous Priest. The Zohar, which is the foundational work in Kabbalah, speaks of the Davidic messiah, the Josephine messiah, and even the return of Moses at the End Times.[184]

The Prophet mentioned in the Dead Sea Scrolls is a reference to Deuteronomy 18:18-20 – that God would send a "prophet like unto Moses" and put His words in his mouth. John the Baptist was asked if he was this Prophet, and he denied it. (John 1:21) Peter said that heaven would continue to hold Jesus until Deuteronomy 18:18-20 is fulfilled (Acts 3:18-22). It is the belief of Muslims that Muhammad ﷺ was this prophet

---

[184] Zohar, Bereshit A, Chapter 21.
https://www.zohar.com/zohar/Bereshit%20A/chapters/21

like Moses, as they both attained prophethood at the age of 40, they were both lawgivers, they both led exoduses, they were both accepted by their people, and they were both statesmen. Even the Scottish orientalist William Montgomery Watt affirmed the sincerity of Muhammad ﷺ [185] and the connection between Moses and Muhammad ﷺ, as they both represent a reset of the divine law.[186]

All of these deliverers are part of a redemptive process that brings God into the immediate focus of mankind. The prophets and the Josephine messiahs are all preparatory for the final kingdom. They represent a line of righteous, meek, and suffering figures that carry the torch of God's light and illumine others. The Davidic messiah is the kingly ruler that will bring justice and peace to a world fraught with injustice and oppression. The co-leadership of a king and a priest has its precedents in the scriptures: Samuel was a prophet while Saul was king. Moses was a lawgiver and political head while Aaron was his vizier and minister.

In the Quran, Jesus is called a descendant of Aaron (19:28). Whilst this is not the position of the Gospels according to Matthew and Luke, it is said in Luke 1:5 and Luke 1:36 that Mary was the cousin of Elizabeth, a descendant of Aaron. Since Joseph was not the biological father of Jesus, and since Mary was a virgin when Jesus was conceived, we would hold that Jesus was a Cohen. A Cohen is a male descendant of

---

[185] William Montgomery Watt, Muhammad at Mecca, Page 223.
[186] William Montgomery Watt, Religious Truth for Our Time, Page 80.

Aaron, the first male priest. The Quran also refers to Jesus as the *Masīḥ*.

The Aaronic lineage of Jesus accords with his priestly messianic role. Jesus' kingdom is "not of this world" – otherwise, his disciples would have fought the Jewish leaders and the Romans (John 18:36). His role in Islamic eschatology is paired with that of the Mahdi. The Mahdi will be the caliph destined to bring justice, while Jesus will return as a "just minister" (*ḥakaman muqsiṭan*) to rectify Christian dogma ("he will break the cross, kill the swine, and abolish the poll-tax").[187] Jesus will pray behind the Mahdi out of respect for those whom God has appointed over the Umma of the Prophet Muhammad ﷺ.[188] The Mahdi, in this arrangement, is the Davidic messiah, who will "judge by the judgment of David and Solomon".[189] [190] It is unclear if the Mahdi has a genealogical connection to King David, but he is a descendant of ʿAlī b. Abī Ṭālib, who may have had Jewish lineage on his mother's side.[191] ʿAlī's cordiality with the exilarchs is documented in Jewish sources.[192] [193]

As the priestly Messiah, Jesus' role in Islam is that of a spiritual wayfarer that highlights the inner meanings of the Law. His goal is to take the world beyond the letter and into

---

[187] Sahih Muslim, Book 1, Hadith 294.
https://sunnah.com/muslim:155a
[188] Ibid, Book 1, Hadith 300. https://sunnah.com/muslim:156
[189] Al-Kafi, Volume 1, Page 397. https://bit.ly/3Hc1W22
[190] Kamal al-Din, Volume 1, Page 699. https://bit.ly/3ogYsCT
[191] Kitab al-Munammaq fii Akhbar Quraysh, Page 402-403.
[192] History of the Jewish People: From Yavneh to Pumbedisa, Page 266.
[193] Masterpieces of Hebrew Literature, Page 350.

its spirit. He is an ascetic that has chosen to rely on as few worldly possessions as he can. Perhaps this is why he is called the "Spirit of God" (*ruḥullah*), because as a word that became flesh, he was able to even transcend the flesh, rely fully on God, purify the intentions of his disciples, and emphasize the inner values of God's religion.

Jesus Christ, merely a prophet?

Bilal Muhammad

Islam is the only major non-Christian religion that obliges its followers to believe in Jesus Christ. For all Muslims, Jesus is the Messiah, born of the virgin Mary, who healed the deaf, the blind and the lepers and resurrected the dead. For the vast majority of Muslims, Jesus is expected to return in the End Times to minister God's kingdom on Earth. The Quran mentions the name of Jesus more than it mentions the name of Muhammad. So, what's the deal?

The main substantive disagreement between most Christians and Muslims is on the divinity of Jesus. I say *most* Christians because some ancient Christian groups did not see Jesus as the eternal God, including the Ebionites, the Elchasaites, the Arians, and some Gnostics. Some more modern Protestant denominations and offshoots also reject the Trinity, like the Unitarians, Christian Scientists, Jehovah's Witnesses, Mormons, and Hebrew Israelites. There is also no shortage of renowned Christians who rejected Jesus' co-equality with God the Father, including Sir Isaac Newton, John Adams, Leo Tolstoy, and Martin Luther King. But the main body of Christians see Jesus as an eternal member of the Trinity, fully-God and fully-human. He was the Word of God, with no beginning and no end, and he became flesh-and-blood in the person of Jesus of Nazareth.

It is a curious fact, therefore, that this Prophet Muhammad ﷺ would be speaking so much of Christ in the predominantly pagan Mecca and the predominantly Jewish Medina. Yet, instead of creating a Christian denomination of his own, and instead of appeasing the Jews by keeping silent on Jesus, Muhammad ﷺ taught what Muslims believe is the true story of Christ. This chapter will explore the Quranic Jesus and the question of his divinity.

The Quran affirms much of what the Gospels say of Christ: (1) He was born miraculously of the virgin Mary (Quran 19:20, Luke 1:34-35), (2) he was supported by the Holy Spirit (Quran 2:87, Matthew 12:28), (3) he was the Word (or "a" Word) of God (Quran 3:45, John 1:1), (4) he preached the Gospel (Quran 3:48, Matthew 9:35), (5) he had righteous apostles (Quran 61:14, Matthew 10:1), (6) he healed the blind and the lepers, and he resurrected the dead (Quran 5:110, Matthew 12:22, Mark 1:40-42, John 11:43), and (7) he will return (possibly Quran 43:61, John 14:1-3).

There are even stories of Jesus in the Quran that are not mentioned in the Bible: (1) He spoke as a baby in his cradle (Quran 19:30), (2) he created a bird out of clay (Quran 3:49, 5:110), (3) he brought a banquet of food down from heaven (Quran 5:114), (4) and he is aware of what the people eat and store away in their houses (Quran 3:49). Further accounts are mentioned in the *ḥadīth* literature, some of which could also be found in the Gospels or apocrypha, and some of which cannot.

But the Quran also takes issue with some of Christianity's central doctrines: (1) It has a different telling of the crucifixion and atonement, (2) it rejects the Trinity and incarnation outright (Quran 4:171, 5:17, 5:72), and (3) it rejects Jesus' status as the Son of God (Quran 9:30, 19:88-92).

Since Jesus is not God according to this arrangement, how then is he to be understood? It is often said in polemics that Muslims see Jesus as "merely a prophet". This is half true, in that the Muslim Jesus came with the same essential message as all the prophets: to worship none but God and to behave ethically. But firstly, one must understand that prophetology in Islam differs from prophetology in Judaism and Christianity. A prophet is not just a man chosen by God to tell the future or reveal a scripture. Most Muslims are shocked to read about a Noah that got drunk and naked (Genesis 9:21), a Lot that slept with his daughters (Genesis 19:33), and an Aaron that built the golden calf (Exodus 32:4). For most Muslims, the prophets are sinless, because God cannot be expected to speak through an unclean vessel. If one claims to speak and act on God's behalf, then we would expect him to walk the walk. If a prophet fails to practice what he preaches, then the people would have little excuse to behave righteously. So, even if a Muslim were to hold that Jesus was "merely a prophet", he would still consider Jesus perfect in his own right. In Islam, a prophet's words are God's words, his likes are God's likes, his dislikes are God's dislikes, his justice is God's justice, and his obedience is God's obedience. He is the best, most knowledgeable, most pious, and most perfectly formed person in his community. The prophets and the Friends of God are the primary signs of God.

But that's just part of the picture. Jesus is put on par with the lawgiving messenger-prophets of determination (*ulil 'azm*), which only include Noah, Abraham, Moses, Jesus, and Muhammad ﷺ. This would automatically exalt Jesus above the likes of Adam (who lacked his determination, Quran 20:115), Isaac, Ishmael, Jacob, Joseph, and even the kings David and Solomon. He is given the unique title of "Messiah". Jesus may be the only prophet to return in the End Times. The *ḥadīth* literature even calls him the Spirit of God (*rūḥullāh*); which is not to be understood as the soul that imbibes God, but a special, created spirit in God's possession.

The Muslim does not deny Jesus' divinity to denigrate, dilute, or demote him in any way. On the contrary, the most beloved and revered Muslim personalities are humble servants of God. As the Creator of all things, God is unlike all things. He created male and female, and thus He cannot be a "male".

An immediate question that may come to mind is, "Well, if Jesus' father was not God, then who was he?" The Quran's response: Jesus did not have a father, just as Adam did not have a father nor mother (Quran 3:59). Here, Jesus is a "Word" of God – God simply uttered "be!" and he was able to come into being without a father. In this sense, Jesus is not entirely like the Hellenic Logos, but rather a quickened word manifesting God's will. The Logos (*kalima*) here is the presentation of God's active will to demonstrate His power. A miracle birth does not make Jesus a god, just as Isaac's miracle birth did not make him a god (Genesis 21:1-6).

But didn't "God so love the world that He gave His only begotten son" (John 3:16)? There are many reasons why the Quran may have taken issue with this statement. God does not beget (Quran 112:3) because begetting is a bestial act of one that requires helpers, inheritors, or a family. It usually requires sex – and even if it does not, it is immoral for a Father to produce a child with Mary out of wedlock. Keep in mind that the Bible frequently calls people children of God: David was called the first-born son of God (Psalm 89:27), Israel was called the first-born son of God (Exodus 4:22), and the Israelites are even "gods, children of the Most High" (Psalm 82:6). These are to be understood metaphorically, as the "children of God" can even be peacemakers (Matthew 5:9).

It should also be noted that the words "only begotten" are not an exact translation of the original Greek. Many translations, including the New International Version, New Living Translation, English Standard Version, International Standard Version, and others drop the word "begotten" altogether.

Would Jesus' relationship to the Holy Spirit make him God? The Holy Spirit is the third person in the Trinity, and it is described in the Bible as eternal (Hebrews 9:14) and omniscient (1 Corinthians 2:10). The Holy Spirit certainly had a role in Mary's conception, but the Bible says that John the Baptist was filled with the Holy Spirit in his mother's womb

(Luke 1:15). The Holy Spirit is described in the Psalms as omnipresent (Psalm 139:7-10), and it fills soldiers (Judges 3:10) and prophets (2 Chronicles 15:1), so its presence in one place or another does not give something divinity. Even if one filled with the Spirit speaks God's words, that does not mean that the person *is* God Himself. Muslims believe that the Spirit is a creation of God – it is usually identified with the Angel Gabriel, but some consider it a distinct being. The matter that makes up a spirit that operates in the universe must be created, because God is beyond all matter and makeup.

Does Jesus claim to be God? The closest the words of Jesus in the Gospels get to this is his statement "I and the Father are one." (John 10:30) But when read in context, a different image is painted. He says that none can snatch his followers out of his grasp (John 10:28), and none can snatch them out of the grasp of the God that gave them to him (John 10:29) – and in this sense, Jesus and God are one, together, in the same divine hierarchy. The Jews began pelting Jesus for blasphemy, but Jesus clarifies further: he says that those who receive the scripture are all gods, sons of the Most High (John 10:31-37). So, Jesus does not set himself apart in these verses, and conditions his bond with God on righteous works. This is consistent with the prophetology of the Quran.

God is all-knowing, but Jesus is not privy to all of God's knowledge. Speaking of the Day of Judgment, Jesus says, "but about that day or hour no one knows, not even the angels in heaven, nor the Son, but only the Father." (Matthew 24:36)

Even Paul puts the Son in a subordinate position to the Father in 1 Corinthians 15:25-28. Jesus' will is not always the same as God's will (Luke 22:42). Jesus prayed to God. One can try to attribute all of this to Jesus' "human nature", but for a man who is simultaneously described as "fully divine", he cannot only *sometimes* be all-knowing, *sometimes* be aligned with God's will, and *sometimes* inferior to his co-equal Father. Instead of forcing the Trinity onto the scripture, it is more natural to come to the same conclusion as nontrinitarian Christians.

The basis of Islamic monotheism is simple: we do not worship any created thing. No creature or object can be God, because they have a beginning, they have an ending, they have limits, and they have needs. We do not make for ourselves "an image in the form of anything in heaven above or on the earth beneath or in the waters below." (Exodus 20:4) A person born on an island, with no access to a Bible or a Christian, can never come to know a Trinitarian God that consists of a Father, Son, and Holy Spirit. On the other hand, such a person could come to know a singular Creator. He may even develop a basic form of morality; but he would not be able to reproduce the doctrines of original sin or atonement. Whether it is Xenophanes in the fifth century BC, or the Great Spirit of aboriginal peoples, the One God is universal. A Quran and a prophet are not needed for one to come to monotheism. On the contrary, logic and intuition can only affirm a scripture and a prophet once they have already affirmed the everlasting God.

Was Jesus *merely a prophet?* Jesus is the face by which God is recognized and come to. He is the proof (*ḥujja*) of God and His conclusive argument. He is the perfect man (*insān al-kāmil*). He is infallible (*ma'ṣūm*). He is the one anointed (*masīḥ*) by God. But like the meaning of his name, God is our Saviour and God is the Saviour of Jesus.

The Apostles, the Early Church, and Islam

Bilal Muhammad

The Quran uses a peculiar word to describe the apostles of Jesus Christ: together, they are called *al-ḥawāriyyīn*. Literally, this translates to "the whiteners" or "the bleachers" of clothing. However, in this context, *ḥawāriyyīn* means "those who were purified, refined, and cleansed from every defect."[194] ʿAlī b. Mūsa al-Riḍa, an Imam and a great-grandson of the Prophet Muhammad ﷺ, is reported to have said, "They were called the *ḥawāriyyīn* by the people because they would wash clothes. They cleansed the filth and dirt from the clothes. Also, the word '*ḥawāriyyīn*' is derived from the word *ḥawar* (bread from sieved flour). We call them this because they cleansed themselves and others through the advice that they gave."[195] This is different from the Greek Gospels' usage of *apostolos*, which translates to "a delegate … messenger, he that is sent."[196] This may be why the warners mentioned in Sūrat Yāsīn are called "messengers" – or, more accurately, "those who were sent" (*mursalīn*) in 36:13-36:20 of the Quran.

---

[194] https://www.almaany.com/ar/dict/ar-ar/%D8%AD%D9%88%D8%A7%D8%B1%D9%8A/

[195] Saduq, ʿUyun Akhbar al-Rida, Volume 2, Chapter 2, Hadith 10. https://thaqalayn.net/hadith/12/1/2/10

[196] Strong's Definitions. https://www.blueletterbible.org/lexicon/g652/kjv/tr/0-1/

According to most exegetes, these were apostles of Christ sent to Antioch.[197]

A legitimate question one may ask is on Islam's view of these apostles. After all, much of the New Testament is attributed to the apostles, and Catholic and Orthodox Christians claim to be apostolic in their genealogy. If the New Testament and the Early Church taught original sin, crucifixion, atonement, and perhaps even the divinity of Christ, how then could Muslims claim to be faithful to Jesus' original message?

The apostles are mentioned three times as a group in the Quran, and they are mentioned in more detail in the *ḥadīth* and *tafsīr* literature. Their presence in the latter is always positive. Unlike the Quran, the *ḥadīth* and *tafsīr* literature note that there were twelve apostles in total, and they offer various names that correspond to persons in the New Testament. In Sunni *ḥadīth*, it is reported that the Prophet Muhammad ﷺ said, "For every prophet is an apostle, and my apostle is Zubayr b. al-'Awwām."[198] In Shī'ī books, the apostles are sometimes compared to the twelve Imams and sometimes compared to the Imams' supporters – who are even "more obedient".[199]

In 3:52-53 of the Quran, the apostles call themselves "Muslims", because they say that they are supporters of and

---

[197] Bilal Muhammad, *Muslim Perspectives on St. Paul*, https://bliis.org/research/saint-paul-islam/
[198] Jami' al-Tirmidhi, Book 49, Hadith 4109. https://sunnah.com/tirmidhi/49/141
[199] Kulaynī, *al-Kāfī*, Vol. 8, 268.

submitters to God, and that they have believed in and borne witness to Jesus.

In 5:111-115, a more nuanced account appears, where the apostles bid Jesus to descend a banquet of food from heaven. Their request suggests a "certain doubt in God's omnipotence" or even a "disrespect or lack of appreciation for God's Power" and Jesus' other miracles.[200] It is unclear if this story fits with the Quranic genre that recounts the Jews' lack of gratitude for God's blessings, but the apostles say that they only want such a miracle to reassure their own hearts; not dissimilar to Abraham's request in 2:260. This story has no direct parallel in the Gospels, but it might correspond to Jesus' multiplication of loaves and fish (Matthew 14:13-21) or the Last Supper.

Jesus then brings the banquet down "as a holiday (ʿīd) for the first of us and the last of us." (Quran 5:114) Zamakhsharī said that this was a reference to the Sunday Eucharist.[201] However, the miracle came down with a warning: "God said: I shall surely send it down unto you. But whosoever among you disbelieves thereafter, I shall surely punish him with a punishment wherewith I have not punished any other in all the worlds." (Quran 5:115) I have always thought that this may be a reference to Judas because he was the apostle that was said to have betrayed Jesus. Alternatively, this may be a reference to Christians that stray from the path.

---

[200] Seyyed Hossein Nasr et al, *The Study Quran*, 5:112-113.
[201] Ibid, 5:114-115.

Lastly, in the Quran, Jesus asks the apostles, "Who are my supporters (*anṣār*) for God?", to which they reply, 'We are the supporters of God.'" (Quran 61:14) The word for "supporters" comes from the same root as the Quranic term for Christians, *Naṣāra*. This may also parallel the *Anṣār* in the life of Muhammad 鵹, who were his recipients in Medina. The verse continues: "So, a faction of the Children of Israel believed and a faction disbelieved. So, We supported those who believed against their enemy, and they became dominant." This is a somewhat cryptic verse, because it is referring specifically to the Israelites that believed and those that disbelieved. According to some exegetes including Rāzī, the disbelievers here include those who rejected Jesus and those who worshiped him.[202] Most Christians are, of course, gentiles, and the empires that would rule in Jesus' name were gentiles. The verse is also connected to the apostles; therefore, it is probably a reference to the Jerusalem Church and the early Jewish Christians. But in what way did they become "dominant"?

According to Catholic and Orthodox tradition, Simon Peter became Jesus' vicar. Upon this rock, he built his Church (Matthew 16:18). The Islamic tradition, especially the Shī'ī tradition, echoes the deputyship (*waṣāya*) of Simon Peter (*Sham'ūn al-Ṣafā*). Quranic exegetes say that Peter was the third messenger sent to Antioch; and Origen and Eusebius even say that Peter built the first church in Antioch.[203] Peter is

---

[202] Ibid, 61:14.
[203] Origen's homilies on Luke VI, 4. Patrologia Graeca 13:1814, Eusebius, *Church History*, Book III, Chapter 36.

attributed with miracles akin to Jesus' in both Islamic exegeses and Acts 3 and Acts 9. The Shīʿī *ḥadīth* literature is full of parallels between Peter and ʿAlī b. Abī Ṭālib, because they are both considered the successor and deputy of their respective messenger-prophets, Jesus and Muhammad ﷺ. Some Shīʿī reports even say that Peter was the cousin of Mary(!),[204] [205] perhaps to make the parallel more analogous, since ʿAlī was the cousin of Muhammad ﷺ. This would make Peter a member of the sacred House of Amram, a reflection of the Prophet Muhammad's Ahl al-Bayt.

Peter has a prominent presence in the Gospels and in Acts. According to Galatians 2:9, Peter, James the Just, and John the Apostle were considered the three pillars of the Church. Some early Jewish Christian denominations and Christian chroniclers claimed that James the Just was the successor of Jesus. James was called "the brother" of Jesus by Paul (Galatians 1:19), Josephus,[206] and Hegesippus.[207] Jude was also called the brother of Jesus. It is unclear if they were Jesus' blood brothers, relatives, or companions – Islamic literature does not take a formal position on the doctrine of Mary's perpetual virginity after Jesus' birth. In the Gospel of Thomas, Jesus appoints James the Just as the leader after him, and he says "heaven and earth came into being" for James' sake

---

204 Al-Saffar, *Basa'ir al-Darajat*, Page 119-122. https://bit.ly/3IAwLOF
205 Al-Rawindi, *al-Khara'ij wal Jara'ih*, Volume 2, Page 858.
206 Josephus, *Jewish Antiquities*, 20.9.1.
207 Hegesippus (d. 180 AD), in the fifth book of his Commentaries, writing of James, says 'After the apostles, James the brother of the Lord surnamed the Just was made head of the Church at Jerusalem.'"

(Thomas 12). The argument for James' succession is delineated in Robert Eisenman's magnum opus *James the brother of Jesus*.

The New Testament's Epistle of James makes a case for faith *and* works being necessary for salvation. This became the hallmark of Jamesian sects, such as the Ebionites and the Nazarenes. Their adherence to the Law would mean that they did not share the same crucifixion and atonement theology that Pauline Christianity preached. The root of this schism can be seen in the Early Church. Paul was at the centre of this schism. Of course, Paul did not meet the historical Jesus, but he claimed to have seen Jesus in a revelation on the road to Damascus. In his letter to the Galatians, which is almost undisputedly the authentic voice of Paul,[208] he rebukes the Galatians for accepting another Gospel (Galatians 1:6-9), and then berates Peter and the Jewish Christians for their emphasis on the Law (Galatians 2:11-18).

Acts 15 recounts a meeting between Paul and the Jerusalem Church, which is often depicted as a reconciliation of the two factions. However, while the Jerusalem Council agrees that the gentiles did not need to submit to the full Law, they still insisted that they were to abstain from foods polluted by idols (Acts 15:20). This would, therefore, leave the disagreement between Paul and the Church unresolved. Peter would have been justified in Galatians. One should also keep in mind that the Book of Acts was, at least in part, written by Luke, a

---

[208] David Aune, *The Blackwell Companion to the New Testament*, pp. 9

student of Paul; so, if it is subject to any bias, it would be in favour of Paul. The epistles attributed to Peter in the New Testament are almost universally considered pseudepigrapha.

To understand the historical Jesus and his teachings, one must examine the historical Peter and James, who were his main executors. Eusebius calls James the Just the first bishop of Jerusalem. James does not have a prominent role in Islamic literature, but since he was a brother, cousin, or relative of Christ, then he can be included in the greater motif of the sanctity of the House of Amram, Jesus' Ahl al-Bayt. He may have been mentioned in Saduq's *Kamāl al-Dīn* under the name "Yaʿqūb b. Shamʿūn" – James the Just's name in Hebrew is Yaʿkov ha-Ṣadik. The report says, "The knowledge of God, His light, and His wisdom was in the progeny of Yaʿqūb b. Shamʿūn, and with him were the apostles from the companions of Jesus."[209] The report says that this Yaʿqūb was the son of Simon Peter. Since Simon Peter was supposedly a relative of Jesus, James' familial relation to Jesus would make sense in light of this. This may also solve the dilemma between historians on who succeeded Jesus – Peter or James – by saying that they both respectively succeeded him. It is unclear who died first (Peter died between 64 and 68 AD, and James died between 62 and 69 AD), but if Shīʿī sources are any guide, they would potentially favour the succession of Peter followed by James.

---

[209] Saduq, *Kamal al-Din*, Volume 1, pp. 253.

Eusebius lists fifteen bishops of Jerusalem, all of whom were "of the circumcision."[210] This is critical, because it means that Jesus' apostles and main Church still followed religious laws. The bishops included Simeon bar Cleophas, who was also called Jesus' brother in the Bible (Matthew 13:55, Mark 6:3) and in Eusebius and Hegesippus;[211] Justus of Jerusalem, who was reportedly the son of James the Just;[212] and Judah Kyriakos, who was reportedly the great-grandson of Jude, "the brother" of Jesus. Not much is known about the other bishops, but it is remarkably understated that the family of Jesus played such a historic role in the Jerusalem Church and preached a very different Christianity. The Bar Kochba revolt, a Jewish messianic movement and rebellion against Rome, put an end to the Jerusalem Church in 135 AD. Jerusalem was destroyed by the Romans, and the gentile Christians established a new church and a new line of Pauline bishops in Aelia Capitolina, the Roman city built just outside of Jerusalem. Jews were not allowed in the city, except on Tisha B'Av, the Jewish fast day commemorating the destruction of the Temple.

The Epistle of Jude is another text that requires decoding. The short letter was included in the New Testament, and it speaks of a threat within the early Christian community. It mentions misguided "people who pervert the grace of our Lord into a

---

[210] Eusebius, *History of the Church*, Book IV, chapter V, verses 3–4
[211] Ibid, Book 3, Chapter 11.
[212] Simon Claude Mimouni, La tradition des évêques chrétiens d'origine juive de Jérusalem, pp. 455.

license for immorality" (Jude 4), who "pollute their own bodies" and "reject authority" (Jude 8). Jude calls on the believers to persevere and take heed of the apostles' warnings (Jude 17-18). Since this epistle was a warning against hypocrites within the community, one has to wonder if he is referring to the Pauline Christians that were challenging apostolic authority. After all, Jude would have been on the side of James. Interestingly, he quotes the Book of Enoch, saying that "the Lord is coming with ten thousand of his holy ones to judge everyone" (Jude 14-15). Is this a reference to the Mahdi, whose army will reportedly consist of ten thousand?[213]

The apostles and the bishops of Jerusalem are persecuted throughout the first and early second century AD. Peter is said to have been crucified in Rome, James is said to have been stoned to death in Jerusalem, Jude is said to have been killed with an axe in Beirut, and Simeon is said to have been executed by Roman authorities in or around Jerusalem. Is this what the Quran meant when it said, speaking of the righteous apostles, "they became dominant" (Quran 61:14)? If martyrdom is victory in Islam, then their tragic end in this world may be triumphant in the grand scheme. To the Shi'a Muslim, the idea of a line of martyred leaders should sound very familiar. Allegedly, Josephus links the destruction of the Temple to the unjust killing of James.[214] This is similar to the Quranic stories of the prophets Hūd, Ṣāliḥ, Shu'ayb, Lot, and

---

[213] Saduq, *Kamal al-Din*, Volume 1, pp. 682.
[214] Eusebius, *History of the Church*, Book 2, Chapter 23.

others, whose rebellious communities are destroyed once those prophets are forced to leave.

What happened to the Jerusalem bishops after 135 AD? Their apostolic movement vanishes from history thereafter. The Ebionites, Nazarenes, Elchasaites, and Manichaeans would claim their legacy. The Quran speaks of a cessation of messengers after Jesus (Quran 5:17), which the Sunnis refer to as the interregnum (*al-fatra*). In Sunni theology, the people of the interregnum (*ahl al-fatra*), who lived and died in the years between Jesus and Muhammad ﷺ, would not be judged as others are judged. In Shīʿa theology, there is always either a prophet or an Imam in every age. Two reports attributed to Jaʿfar al-Ṣādiq suggest that there was a two-hundred-and-fifty-year occultation, or a period of seclusion, sometime between Jesus and Muhammad ﷺ.[215]

What about Pauline Christianity's claims of apostolic succession? Irenaeus, writing in circa 180 AD, claimed that Linus was the pope after Peter.[216] Linus is mentioned once in the New Testament as a companion of Paul (2 Timothy 21). Tertullian (d. 220 AD), however, claimed that Clement I was the successor of Peter,[217] and this was the position of most Roman Christians according to Jerome (d. 420 AD).[218] He, too, may have been a companion of Paul (Philippians 4:3). It goes without saying that neither of these men were disciples

---

[215] Saduq, *Kamal al-Din*, Volume 1, Page 189.
[216] Irenaeus, *Against Heresies*, 3: 3.3
[217] Tertullian, *Prescription Against Heretics*, Chapter 32.
[218] Jerome, *De Viris Illustribus*, Chapter 15.

or relatives of Jesus. Some scholars have suggested that these were presbyters and not popes coming one after the other.

One of the championed connections between the apostles and the Church Fathers is Polycarp (d. 155 AD). Irenaeus claimed to have heard Polycarp preach in his youth, and according to him, Polycarp was a student of John the Apostle. Polycarp's extant Epistle to the Philippians contains four references to Paul, but no references to John. Unless John lived a very long life and taught a young Polycarp (born in 69 AD), the John-Polycarp connection is highly dubious. It is more likely that he met John the Evangelist, who was probably writing between 90 and 110 AD.[219] Most scholars would agree that John the Evangelist was not John the Apostle, who was a pillar of the Jerusalem Church. Irenaeus writes that this John presided over "the Church in Ephesus, founded by Paul" and remained "among them permanently until the times of Trajan (98-117 AD)."[220] This period closely corresponds to the time John the Evangelist was active; and it ties him to Paul, not the apostles of Christ.

In the web of schisms, conflicting succession claims, and heresies, the soil was fertile for a new prophet to clarify the nature of God and our relationship to the divine law. The Islamic tradition claims the historical Jesus and his apostles; and from what we read of the Epistles of James and Jude, the Didache, and the Jerusalem Church, we see a community that

---

[219] Andrew Lincoln, *Gospel According to St John: Black's New Testament Commentaries*, pp. 18
[220] Irenaeus, *Against Heresies*, 3: 3.4

was committed to both Jesus' messiahship and the Law. They had their sights set on preaching the Gospel to the world, but without any emphasis on the divinity of Jesus or the atonement. A globalized Judaism, with a special emphasis on the *spirit* of the law, is Islam in a nutshell.

As the New Jerome Bible Commentary suggests, "Jewish Christianity ... a separate movement, was eventually defeated by Paulinism and died out (perhaps to be reborn in a different form as Islam)."[221]

---

[221] The New Jerome Bible Commentary, Edited by Raymond E. Brown, Page 641, Published in 1990.

Muslim Perspectives on St. Paul

Bilal Muhammad

Many modern Muslim polemicists involved in interfaith dialogue with Christians have made St. Paul of Tarsus the focus of their criticism. The late Muslim polemicist Ahmed Deedat described Paul as "the real founder of Christianity" and the cause of division between Christian and Islamic theology.[222] Bilal Philips, a prominent preacher and apologist, said that Paul opposed the way of the prophets and cancelled their laws.[223] Paul is credited with the antinomianism and Christology that many modern Muslims decry.

St. Paul, also known as Paul the Apostle, is the author of thirteen of the twenty-seven books in the New Testament. He claimed to have been a former Pharisee from a family of Pharisees in Philippians 3:5-6. Robert Eisenman speculates that Paul was from the Herodian family.[224] Paul was actively involved in persecuting early Christians (Acts 8:1) until he experienced a vision of Jesus on the road to Damascus (Acts 9:4-5). Thereafter, he joined the early Church and exported Christianity to Hellenic peoples. Modern scholars have drawn

---

[222] Ahmed Deedat, *Crucifixion or Cruci-fiction?*, 1-2.
[223] Bilal Philips, *The True Message of Jesus*, 73-74.
[224] Robert Eisenman, "Paul as Herodian", https://depts.drew.edu/jhc/eisenman.html (accessed January 24th 2020).

parallels between the mystical content of Paul's writings, Jewish mysticism,[225] and the theosophy of Philo.[226]

With the spread of Islam into the Levant, Egypt, and Asia Minor, Muslim scholars interacted with many of the doctrines and revered figures of Christianity. While the trend today is to dismiss St. Paul outright, this was not necessarily the case among Muslims historically. This paper will document pre-modern Muslim perspectives on Paul.

Perhaps the earliest Muslim reference to St. Paul is in the *Sīra* of Ibn Isḥāq (d. 767 CE), which identifies him as one sent by Jesus to carry his message. "Among those who Jesus the son of Mary sent from the apostles and the disciplines after them are Peter the Apostle and Paul with him. Paul was from among the disciples, and he was not from among the apostles. They were sent to Rome."[227] This section also documents the locations that the other apostles were sent to. Ibn Isḥāq relied on reports from Judeo-Christian sources (*Isrā'īlīyāt*) for his biography,[228] and he studied in Alexandria;[229] these may account for a perspective rooted in Pauline Christianity. Ṭabarī (d. 923 CE) records this same reference of Ibn Isḥāq in

---

[225] Timo Eskola, *Messiah and the Throne: Jewish Markabah Mysticism and Early Exaltation Discourse*.

[226] Samuel Zinner, *The Gospel of Thomas in the Light of Early Jewish, Christian, and Islamic Esoteric Trajectories*.

[227] Ibn Hisham, *al-Sira al-Nabawiyya*, https://bit.ly/2GisfWn (accessed January 24th, 2020)

[228] Aaron Hughes, *Muslim and Jew: Origin, Growth, Resentment*, 15-40

[229] "Ibn Ishaq", *Encyclopedia Britannica*, https://www.britannica.com/biography/Ibn-Ishaq (accessed January 24th 2020).

his *Tarīkh*;[230] as does Qurṭubī (d. 1273) in his *Tafsir*.[231] The status and reception of the *Sīra* may represent a toleration for this collated view.

A detailed reference to St. Paul can be found in *Tarīkh al-Ya'qūbī*, one of the earliest Islamic sources on the history of the world. It was written by Aḥmad al-Ya'qūbī (d. 898 CE), an Abbasid-era historian and geographer with Shī'ī sympathies. He writes,

"They began describing the order of the Messiah and calling the people to their religion. Paul was the harshest of the people against them, and he did them the most harm. He would kill them and look everywhere for them. So, he set out seeking a group [of Christians] in Damascus, when he heard a voice calling to him, saying, 'O Paul! How long will you persecute me for?' So, he panicked until he went blind. Then, he came to Ananias, who prayed over him until his eye healed. Afterward, he would stand in the churches, mention the Messiah and glorify him; until the Jews wanted to kill him, so he fled from them and joined the disciples in calling the people [to Christianity]. He spoke as they spoke and became ascetic in worldly matters, until all the apostles chose him as their leader. He would stand and speak about the matters of the Children of Israel and the prophets, and he would mention the state of the Messiah (or Christology, ḥāl al-messīḥ). He would say, 'Come with us to [preach to] the nations, just as God said to the

---

[230] Moshe Perlmann, The History of al-Tabari, Vol. 4, 123
[231] Qurtubi, *Tafsir al-Qurtubi*,
http://quran.ksu.edu.sa/tafseer/qortobi/sura61-aya14.html (accessed January 24th 2020).

Messiah: I have made you a light unto the nations.' So, they would go to the ends of the Earth with sincerity, and every man would speak their view. So, they said, 'We must maintain a law (nāmūs), and send one who professes this religion to every nation, and prohibit them from eating meat sacrificed to idols, committing adultery, and eating blood.' Paul set out to Antioch with two men to begin baptizing. Then, Paul returned, and set forth to the emperor of Rome and spoke. He mentioned the state of the Messiah, causing the community to want to kill him for desecrating their religion."[232]

This positive account of Paul appears to use the Book of Acts as a reference, as it recounts Paul's conversion, gives him a unique station above the apostles, and maintains a set of laws. These laws seem to correspond to Acts 15:20, where Peter and James advise Paul and the apostles to teach the gentiles to abstain from meat sacrificed to idols, sexual immorality, meat of strangled animals, and blood. Ya'qūbī does not mention Paul's antinomianism, but hints at his mystical asceticism and Christology.

Wahb b. Munabbih (d. ~725 CE) is an early authority in *ḥadīth* who is known for his transmission of *Isrā'īliyāt*. In the *Tafsīr* of al-Baghawī (d. 1122), in the exegesis of Surat Yāsīn, a tradition from Wahb b. Munabbih states that Paul was one of the messengers sent to a community of disbelievers: "'We sent two to them' (36:14). Wahb said: John and Paul ... 'so We strengthened them with a third' (36:14) the third messenger

---

[232] Ahmad al-Ya'qubi, *Tarikh al-Ya'qubi*, 89.

was Simon [Peter]."[233] Al-Baghawī identifies these "apostles" as messengers sent by Jesus to the city of Antioch.[234] After the first to were sent, calling the city and its king to abandon their idols, they were imprisoned and flogged. So, Jesus sent Peter to assist them, whereupon he cured a child of his blindness in the company of the king.

One of the earliest exegeses is that of Muqātil b. Sulaymān (d. 767 CE), a Sunni or Zaydi storyteller, who reported that the two messengers were Thomas and Paul.[235] The same account is reported by Ibn al-Jawzī (d. 1201 CE) in his *Tafsir*.[236] Ibn Kathīr (d. 1373 CE) reports from a different chain that the first two messengers were Peter and John, and the third messenger was Paul.[237] Shawkānī repeats this in his *Tafsir*.[238] Of course, historically, Paul had never physically met Jesus during the latter's ministry; and although this story is common in Muslim exegeses, it is not found in Christian literature.

In the chronicle *Tarīkh Dimishq* by Ibn ʿAsākir (d. 1175 CE), another report by Wahb details the story of Paul.

---

[233] Al-Baghawi, *Maʿalim al-Tanzil*, Vol. 7, 12.
[234] Ibid, 12-14.
[235] Ibn al-Jawzi, *Zad al-Masir fi ʿIlm al-Tafsir*, 1169.
[236] Ibid, 1169.
[237] Ibn Kathir, *Tafsir Ibn Kathir*, https://quran.ksu.edu.sa/tafseer/katheer/sura36-aya14.html#katheer (accessed January 24th 2020).
[238] Shawkani, *Tafsir Fath al-Qadir*, Vol. 2, 480.

"Paul was from the leaders of the Jews. He was the harshest among them and the most spiteful among them in rejecting what the Messiah brought ... he gathered soldiers and went to the Messiah to kill him and prevent him from entering Damascus. So, he (Jesus) sent a meteor to him, and an angel struck him with its wing and blinded him. Thus, he saw a proof for what he had brought ... resulting in his belief and confirmation of it. So, he met the Messiah upon that, and he asked him to heal his eye. The Messiah said, 'How long will you harm me and harm those with me?'"[239]

The text continues to say that Jesus directed him to Ananias. This tradition implies that Paul was working against Jesus during his ministry and was even involved in gathering troops to fight against him. It seems to muddle the post-resurrection period by implying that Jesus was heading to Damascus at the same time that Paul was.

Perhaps the classical references that are most critical of St. Paul are those in the Twelver Shī ī *ḥadīth* literature. In the *Tafsir* of ʿAlī b. Ibrāhīm al-Qummī (d. 919 CE), a narration attributed to Jaʿfar al-Ṣādiq says, "God did not send a prophet except that his nation had two devils that harmed him and misguided the people after him ... as for the two of Jesus, they are Paul and Marītūn."[240] It is unclear who Marītūn refers to – perhaps Matthew or Mark, the authors of two of the four gospels. The narration however is correct in saying that Paul's

---

239 Ibn Asakir, *Tarikh Medinat Dimishq*, Vol. 15, 333.
240 Ali b. Ibrahim al-Qummi, *Tafsir al-Qummi*, https://bit.ly/2RMHR9S (accessed January 24th, 2020).

ministry came after Jesus', unlike some of the previous accounts.

In Thawāb al-Aʿmāl, a book of reports compiled by Shaykh al-Ṣadūq (d. 991 CE), the following quote from Muḥammad al-Bāqir can be found:

"[In the pit of hell] there are seven chests, five containing persons from the previous nations, and two containing persons from this nation. As for the five, they are (1) Cain, who killed Abel, (2) Nimrod, who challenged Abraham regarding his Lord, saying 'I give life and I give death,' (3) Pharaoh, who said 'I am your Highest Lord,' (4) a Jew who Judaized the Jews, (5) Paul, who Christianized the Christians, (6-7) and from this nation, two Bedouins."[241]

There are other sources to one who "Christianized the Christians", an expression referring to one who took the people from Christ's teachings to a deviated practice.

A similar ḥadīth about the pit of hell can be found in Kāmil al-Ziyārāt by Ibn Qulawayh (d. 977 CE), where Jaʿfar al-Ṣādiq says, "Therein is all those who taught disbelief (kufr) to the servants … Paul, who taught the Jews that God's hand is tied, Nestorius, who taught the Christians that the Messiah is the son of God, and said to them 'they are a trinity'."[242] This narration seems to mix up its historical personalities: Paul is not known

---

[241] Saduq, Thawab al-Aʿmal, https://bit.ly/2TUsVJz (accessed January 24th, 2020).

[242] Ibn Qulawayh, Kamil al-Ziyarat, https://bit.ly/2O0OW5C (accessed January 24th, 2020).

to be influential among Jews (regardless of his claim of being a former Pharisee), and Nestorius (d. 450 CE) was known for opposing the use of the title "Mother of God" (*theotokos*) for Mary. It is of course plausible that this is a reference to a different Paul, although the Arabization of the Latin name would suggest that it is referring to St. Paul. Furthermore, while Nestorius did not produce the concept of the Trinity, he was indeed a promoter of it.

An early cryptic Sunni reference that may indirectly refer to Paul can be found in the *Musnad* of Aḥmad b. Ḥanbal (d. 855 CE). Also on the theme of hell, the Prophet Muḥammad reportedly says, "The arrogant ones will be resurrected on the Day of Resurrection and made into particles in the image of people. They will be stepped on by belittled ones until they enter a prison in hell called 'Būlus.'"[243] Whether the use of the same Arabic word for "Paul" is just a coincidence cannot be ascertained, but in light of other narrations that associated Paul with hell, it is possible that the use of this name was deliberate.

Lastly, Rajab al-Bursī (d. 1411), a Shī ī mystic quoted a saying, attributing it to God in the *Injīl*: "Know yourself, O people, and you will know your Lord. Your outer self will be annihilated, and your inner self will remain."[244] This saying is used in mystical Shī ī circles today, often with a slightly different wording; "... and your inner self is Me (*wa thāhiruka*

---

[243] Ahmad b. Hanbal, *Musnad Ahmad b. Hanbal*, Vol. 6, 232.
[244] Hurr al-Amili, *al-Jawahir al-Sanniyya*, https://bit.ly/3aMbzVh (accessed January 24th, 2020).

ana)." A similar passage can be found in 2 Corinthians 4:16, in which St. Paul says, "Though outwardly we are wasting away, yet inwardly we are being renewed day-by-day." Al-Bursī probably considered the epistles to be an extension of the *Injīl*, and thus considered its words to be sacred and divinely inspired.

There are several lessons that can be extracted from this review of relevant literature. It seems that many of the pro-Pauline references represent a consolidation of Christian history into the Islamic paradigm. The Quran emphasizes a belief in forerunning books and messengers, making "no distinction between any of His messengers." (2:285) This principle perhaps created an attitude that was accepting of revered Christian figures. The use of Judeo-Christian lore in early exegeses demonstrates a permissive universalism. Likewise, the effort to clamp down on *Isrāʾīlīyāt* demonstrates a need for Islam to be distinct and purified from earlier traditions. The copying of stories from one century to another may represent an uncritical attitude that many prominent scholars had toward pre-Islamic lore. Historical discrepancies between the Islamic accounts of Paul and the Christian accounts may be the result of hearsay or lost sources. Paul's appearance in exegeses of Surat Yāsīn can be attributed to prominence of Paul's relationship with Antioch, which is the burial place of Ḥabīb al-Najjār, the Islamic saint mentioned in the same Surah. The anti-Paulinism of some Shīʿī sources may be a more informed response to St. Paul's ideas; or it may be inherited from Jamesian Jewish Christians. More research needs to be done on whether the epistles of Paul were considered part of the *Injīl* in the seventh century, as that may bring about new questions. Research into the development of the Muslim position that the Bible has been distorted would be welcomed.

The Antichrist

Bilal Muhammad

The name of the Antichrist in Islamic literature is *Masīḥ al-Dajjāl* (or just simply *Dajjāl*). A *dajjāl* in Arabic is an imposter or a conman, coming from the root *d-j-l*, which means "to deceive, to con, to trick." The origin of the word was apparently the act of smearing a camel's defects with tar, so that it could be sold at a higher price.[245] Literally, *Masīḥ al-Dajjāl* does not mean "against Christ", but it means "opposite Christ" or "instead of Christ" or "in the place of Christ", with the connotation of him being the fake, fraud, imposter Messiah. This may be closer to the original Greek *antichristos*.[246] According to Rāzī, the Antichrist is called *masīḥ* for one of two reasons: (1) his right eye is "wiped" or erased, or (2) he will traverse the Earth in a short period of time.[247]

There is a vast genre of *ḥadīth* that deals with the Antichrist – his identity, his magic, the signs accompanying him, and his fateful end. Skeptics assume that Muslims only adopted a belief in the Antichrist after their conquest of Christian lands. After all, there is no direct reference to the Antichrist in the Quran. However, he is mentioned hundreds of times in Sunni and Shī'ī *ḥadīth* literature. Bukhārī records a tradition where

---

[245] Hamza Yusuf, "The Dajjal (Antichrist)", Islam on Demand, https://youtu.be/HmmtX8nt_VU

[246] Ibid.

[247] وأمّا المسيح الدجّال فإنّما سُمّي مسيحاً لأحد وجهين أولهما: لأنّه ممسوح العين اليمنى وثانيهما: لأنّه يمسح الأرض أي يقطعها في زمن قصير

303

the Prophet Muhammad ﷺ says, "Every prophet sent by God has warned his people about him. Noah and every prophet thereafter warned about him."[248] It is reported that the Prophet ﷺ would speak about the Antichrist so much, till his companions began to think that he was hiding among date palms in the suburbs of Medina.[249]

Then there is the curious example of Ibn Ṣayyād, a Jewish boy in Medina whom ʿUmar b. al-Khattāb, his son ʿAbdullāh and his daughter Hafṣa believed was the Antichrist.[250] ʿUmar wanted to strike his neck, and ʿAbdullāh b. ʿUmar would rouse him in Medina. The Prophet ﷺ told ʿUmar, "If he is the one (the Antichrist), you will not be given power over him, and if he is not, then there is no good in killing him."[251] Ibn Ṣayyād reportedly embraced Islam, but it is unclear what happened to him thereafter. Ṭabarī relates a tradition in which Ibn Ṣayyād was at the siege of Sūs, where monks taunted the Muslims, saying that they would not be able to conquer the town unless the Antichrist were with them. Thereupon, Ibn Ṣayyād called upon the town gates to open,

---

248 Riyad al-Salihin, Introduction, Hadith 205.
https://sunnah.com/riyadussalihin:205
249 Zeki Saritopak, "The Legend of al-Dajjal (Antichrist): The Personification of Evil in the Islamic Tradition", *The Muslim World*, Volume 93, April 2003, pp. 292.
250 Sahih al-Bukhari, Book 96, Hadith 82,
https://sunnah.com/bukhari/96/82
251 Sunan Abi Dawud, Book 39, Hadith 39.

and they did.[252] Abu Dawūd records that Ibn Ṣayyād was "lost" when Yazīd waged war on Medina in 63 AH.[253] Both of these accounts fit into the theme that presents Ibn Ṣayyād as an enigmatic and problematic figure. Cook argues that the disappearance of Ibn Ṣayyād at seventy years of age may have apocalyptic implications, with seventy being a ripe age to enter occultation.[254] In one report, the Jews of Isfahan celebrated Ibn Ṣayyād as their king; implying that the Antichrist would be the king of the Jews.[255] In another narration, Ibn Ṣayyād denied being the Antichrist whilst claiming to know the Antichrist's true location.[256]

To me, these episodes with Ibn Ṣayyād give more credence to the idea that Muhammad ﷺ spoke about the Antichrist. Had the belief been adopted post-hoc, then fabricating the existence of Ibn Ṣayyād would have been an arduous task. On the contrary, if Muhammad ﷺ did speak about the Antichrist, then it is natural for people to suspect their contemporaries and come up with theories – especially if Ibn Ṣayyād was styling himself as a Jewish prophet.

[252] Gerald Hawting, "Were there prophets in Jahiliyya?", *Islam and its Past: Jahiliyya, Late Antiquity, and the Qur'an*, Oxford University Press, pp. 206.
[253] Sunan Abu Dawud, Book 39, Hadith 42, https://sunnah.com/abudawud/39/42
[254] David Cook, Studies in Muslim Apocalyptic, Darwin Press, pp. 115.
[255] Ibid, pp. 115.
[256] Sahih Muslim, Book 54, Hadith 114, https://sunnah.com/muslim/54/123

The Antichrist was described with a number of characteristics. He has a deformed eye.[257] He is pigeon-toed and woolly haired.[258] He is unable to enter the cities of Mecca and Medina due to their guardian angels.[259] [260] [261] It is said that he will be so persuasive that it will be better to avoid him altogether than to confront him.[262] One tradition has a Christian man, who accepted Islam, describe a journey on the high seas. The crew disembarked on an island, where they found a hairy beast and a bound Antichrist who "will be soon given permission to emerge."[263] This more fantastical account is not prominently narrated, but Sunni *hadīth* critics deemed it reliable.

The nature of time will also be altered with the Antichrist. It is reported that he would be on the Earth for forty days; the first day will feel like a year, the second day will feel like a month, the third day will feel like a week, and the rest of the days will be ordinary in length.[264] It is unclear if this is due to a shift in the rotation of the Earth, or a change in the space-

---

[257] Sahih al-Bukhari, Book 92, Hadith 70. https://sunnah.com/bukhari:7123
[258] Sunan Abi Dawud, Book 39, Hadith 30. https://sunnah.com/abudawud:4320
[259] Ibid, Book 92, Hadith 81. https://sunnah.com/bukhari:7134
[260] Sahih Muslim, Book 54, Hadith 151. https://sunnah.com/muslim:2943a
[261] Tusi, *Tahdheeb al-Ahkam*, Volume 6, Chapter: The Sanctity of Medina, Hadith #1.
[262] Sunan Abi Dawud, Book 39, Hadith 28. https://sunnah.com/abudawud:4319
[263] Ibid, Book 39, Hadith 36. https://sunnah.com/abudawud:4326
[264] Ibid, Book 39, Hadith 31. https://sunnah.com/abudawud:4321

time continuum, or mass hysteria. There are prayers and verses to be recited by believers to prepare themselves for the Antichrist's coming.

One *ḥadīth* says that the Antichrist will reveal himself in stages: first claiming to be a prophet, then claiming to be God.[265] He would come with a garden and a fire[266] – or water and fire[267] – but his garden would actually be fire, and his fire would actually be a garden. In other words, as a conman, the Antichrist will offer reward and punishment, but their reality would be the opposite of their appearance. This is part of a much greater theme in Islamic eschatology: the complete reversal of morals and ethics. Evil would seem good, and good would seem evil. In the words of Muhammad ﷺ, "The liar shall be called truthful, and the truthful shall be called a liar. The traitor shall be trusted and the trusted shall be betrayed … mosques shall be decorated, but hearts shall be ruined. Men shall find satisfaction in men, and women shall find satisfaction in women … the destruction of the world shall be promoted, and its civilization shall be ruined."[268] Signs of the End Times often fit this pattern in the *ḥadīth* literature. The Antichrist himself offers a worldly paradise to tempt believers away from heaven, and his short kingdom on Earth is the

---

[265] Sunan Ibn Maja, Book 36, Hadith 152.
https://sunnah.com/ibnmajah:4077
[266] Ibid, Book 36, Hadith 146. https://sunnah.com/ibnmajah:4071
[267] Sahih al-Bukhari, Book 82, Hadith 77.
https://sunnah.com/bukhari:7130
[268] Tabarani, *Mu'jam al-Kabir*, Volume 10, Page 228.

culmination of a civilizational fall from grace. Satan cannot create, he can only corrupt.

Many contemporary preachers speak about a "Dajjālic system", merging New World Order conspiracies (with the prominent All-Seeing Eye) with Islamic eschatology. What is clear from the literature is that the Antichrist will be a *person*, and not just a system. However, his coming will be preceded by an overall decline in morals. There is a similar pattern in many traditions. The Shīʿī tradition, whilst recognizing the return of Jesus and the coming of the Antichrist, focuses more on the epic battle between the Mahdi and the Sufyānī. The Jewish tradition speaks of Armilus, a Roman quasi-antichrist, who has a deformed right *ear*.[269] The Hindu tradition speaks of Kali Yuga, an age of sin and conflict. The Prophet ﷺ spoke of thirty *dajjāls* who would all claim to be messengers of God.[270]

The Bible, too, speaks of the Antichrist, especially in the Book of Revelation. The beast would be given authority over the world (Revelation 13:5-7), he would control the world economy (Revelation 13:16-17), he would claim to be God (2 Thessalonians 2:3-4), and he would "cause fire to come down from heaven" (Revelation 13:13).

---

[269] Nistarot R. Shimon ben Yohai, https://pages.charlotte.edu/john-reeves/research-projects/trajectories-in-near-eastern-apocalyptic/nistarot-secrets-of-r-shimon-b-yohai-2/
[270] Jamiʿ al-Tirmidhi, Book 33, Hadith 61. https://sunnah.com/tirmidhi:2218

What is our time now, relative to the doomsday clock? No one can know for certain (Matthew 24:36). But in this age, it has become more and more taboo to espouse traditional morals. Nietzsche declared that "God is dead", and the world is run by the free market, mass media, nationalism, and moral relativism. Believers are experiencing a Dark Night of the Soul as they see their peers fall into atheism, agnosticism, and outright foolishness. Some are calling for a "Benedict Option" – flee into the Ark as the Flood destroys society. Modernism became postmodernism, which denies objectivity and promotes seeing the world as a series of power exchanges. We may not know the time, but we know that the clock is ticking.

The poles of society are not simply Order and Chaos, but Intellect and Ignorance. Chaos may exist as an intermediary between the two, but evil itself is its own meticulous anti-order. It is a reversal and a perversion of good, and not just its absence. Deconstructionism takes concepts and institutions apart, which yes, causes momentary chaos. However, that chaos is then replaced with a new system that has new rules, new taboos, new assumptions, new norms, new terminology, and a new power structure. The goal of Satan is not just to take apart the religion, but to institutionalize the reversal of ethics.

Jāhiliyya had a Kaʿba, but instead of it being a paragon of monotheism, it became a paragon of paganism. God's Throne is above the waters of creation, while Satan's throne is on the ocean of this world.[271] His minions recite the revelation backwards. Satan flips the divine hierarchy on its head. Good practices are not just ceased, but evil practices are introduced in their place; good is seen as evil and evil as good.

The armies of Intellect and the armies of Ignorance are in constant battle over your heart, your household, your institutions, your society, and your world. We see microcosms of this battle in our own lives. But this battle is temporary. On Judgment Day, death itself will be killed,[272] and the veil will be lifted from us all.

When Jesus Christ returns, he will breathe the fragrance of heaven onto the Antichrist, and he will perish. He will then restore justice and peace in the final messianic kingdom. God's will will be done on Earth as it is in heaven. In the meantime, may we be granted the peace of God in an age of pestilence, earthquakes, wars, and rumours of wars. With God's peace, we will have the patience to persevere through tough times, and the humility to appreciate good times. Amen.

---

[271] Sahih Muslim, Book 52, Hadith 60.
https://sunnah.com/muslim:2813b
[272] Sahih al-Bukhari, Book 65, Hadith 252.
https://sunnah.com/bukhari:4730

Made in United States
North Haven, CT
20 November 2022

26997315R00170